**Del Otro Lado** /

# Del Otro Lado / Literacy and Migration across the U.S.-Mexico Border

SUSAN V. MEYERS

Southern Illinois University Press / Carbondale

17  16  15  14    4  3  2  1

**Library of Congress Cataloging-in-Publication Data**
Meyers, Susan V.
Del otro lado : literacy and migration across the U.S.-Mexico border /
Susan V. Meyers.
   pages   cm.
Includes bibliographical references and index.
ISBN 978-0-8093-3342-4 (pbk.) — ISBN 0-8093-3342-2 (paperback) —
ISBN 978-0-8093-3343-1 (ebook)
1. Mexican Americans—Education—United States—Case studies.
2. Education—Mexico—Villachuato—Case studies. 3. Literacy—Social
aspects—United States—Case studies. 4. Villachuato (Mexico)—Emi-
gration and immigration—Case studies. I. Title.
LC2683.3.M49 2014
371.829'68073—dc23                                        2013050193

Printed on recycled paper. ♻

The paper used in this publication meets the minimum requirements of
American National Standard for Information Sciences—Permanence of
Paper for Printed Library Materials, ANSI Z39.48-1992. ∞

For my parents, who taught / And in deep gratitude to the
me the value of both literacy / community—present and displaced—
and the world / of Villachuato, Mexico

# Contents /

## Acknowledgments /

My deep thanks first and foremost go to Anne-Marie Hall, who believed in this project from the beginning, as well as to several other friends and mentors at the University of Arizona: Amy Kimme Hea, Rachel Lewis Ketai, Adela Licona, Stephanie Merz, Laurie Morrison, and Star Medzarian Vanguri.

Others readers and colleagues have been crucial along the way, including several friends and colleagues at Oregon State University: Anita Helle, Peter Betjemann, Rubén Casas, Lisa Ede, Rebecca Olsen, Vicki Tolar Burton, Tara Williams, and the entire staff at the Center for the Humanities. I also wish to thank the infamous ladies of Oregon State's LSPC. Where would I ever have been without our weekly dinners?

To my earliest mentors in the field of composition and rhetoric—John Bean, Lillian Bridwell-Bowles, June Johnson, and Larry Nichols—my deep thanks for introducing me to a way of seeing and acting in the world that has sustained me for many years since.

Several organizations funded portions of my work at key points throughout the research and writing of this book: the American Association of University Women, the College Composition and Communication Chairs Memorial Fellowship, the National Endowment for the Humanities, Oregon State University's Center for the Humanities, Oregon State University's Library, and the University of Arizona's David L. Patrick Dissertation Fellowship. My thanks, too, go to Roger Waldinger at UCLA who taught me so much about migration. I'm grateful to him, as well as to all of the participants of the 2011 National Endowment for the Humanities' Summer Seminar on "Rethinking International Migration," whose rich ideas and conversation helped me arrive at the final structure for this book.

I will forever be grateful to the Lopez family and to the entire binational community of Villachuato, Mexico, which opened its doors and hearts to me in ways that have shaped me far beyond the expanses of this book. I hope that I have represented the complexities, beauties, and challenges of their lives in ways that resound with them. Most importantly, I hope that the work we did together begins to reshape the ways in which educators and politicians consider the experiences of those many thousands of young people who migrate each year between communities in Mexico and the United States.

Earlier versions of some parts of this book originally appeared in other publications: Chapter 3 was adapted from S. V. Meyers (2012), "They make a lot of sacrifices": Religious rhetorics in the formation of the Mexican rural education system, in K. Donehower, C. Hogg, and E. E. Schell (Eds.), *Reclaiming the rural* (pp. 143–157), Carbondale: Southern Illinois University Press. Chapter 4, from S. V. Meyers (2011), "They didn't tell me anything": Women's literacies and resistance in rural Mexico, *Gender and Education*, 23 (7), 857–871, published by Taylor & Francis (www.tandfonline.com). And chapter 5, from S. V. Meyers (2009), "So you don't get tricked": Counter-narratives of literacy in a rural Mexican community, *Community Literacy Journal*, 3(2), 19–35, published jointly by DePaul University and the University of Arizona. I thank the editors of all of these publications for their support.

**Del Otro Lado /**

Introduction / "So You Can Buy a Taco over the Internet"

Jacqueline is the hope of her family. A bright, driven young woman who aspires to be the first in her family to attend college, she represents two prior generations' investments in education: her grandmother's strain to scrounge together enough money for basic school supplies, and her mother's truncated career, cut short by an unplanned pregnancy during her sophomore year of high school. These challenges aside, Jacqueline's family, which hails from a small agricultural town in rural Mexico, believes in the importance of education and the possibility of personal improvement.

But Jacqueline's mother is worried. After spending the last two years of elementary school in Los Angeles with her aunt and uncle, twelve-year-old Jacqueline has come back to Mexico to complete middle school and to spend time with her immediate family. While Jacqueline plans to return to the United States for high school and college, her mother is concerned that her motivation is slackening as she settles into a rural secondary school where the classrooms are packed tightly with forty children per room, and by the third month of school, there still aren't any books. What's worse, she now feels out of place in the Mexican schools: "'Cause, like, I don't really understand some words," Jacqueline told me in English. "Well, it's hard for me. . . . But over there, I understand everything. I could understand what they're saying. But here I can't, really." Having made the transition to English-language curriculum and U.S. school structures, Jacqueline must now pass through just such a transition again—only this time, in the opposite direction.

In contrast, Jacqueline enjoys the social elements of her renewed life in Mexico. Given the small size of the town, she has been able to reconnect with the same sets of friends as before—girls who, at ages twelve and thirteen, are beginning to wear more provocative clothing and to attend the weekly dances held in the town plaza. Toward the end of September, she came home from school one day to report that she had been engaged in a fight with another girl who said that her boyfriend had broken up with her because of Jacqueline. Two months later, during a town festival, Jacqueline won a sultry dance competition in the town plaza—an accomplishment of which she is quite proud. Given these influences, it seems that Jacqueline's mother's concerns are reasonable. Feeling alienated and overwhelmed at school, Jacqueline turns increasingly to her social circles and speaks less and less of returning to the United States or of fulfilling her plans to attend college.

Jacqueline comes from Michoacán: a state with one of the highest migration rates and lowest literacy levels in Mexico (Villagomez, 2008). Evidence of the difficulties of education in this region includes high drop-out rates, oversized classes, insufficient teaching materials, and increasing political conflict (Bracho et al., 2006). For instance, after a recent national curricular reform, the state teachers' union refused to adopt the changes; therefore, no books were issued for several months (M. E. Rojas Solis, personal communication, 15 September 2007). Jacqueline's experiences in the United States, however, had been more positive. Discussing her experience entering a U.S. school, she reported:

> At the beginning, I felt really nervous, because I didn't know anything and I didn't understand anyone and I didn't know how to ask questions. Until I went to the [English language] classes, and that's where they taught me. After four months, I spoke English. . . . When I started [speaking] English, nobody could believe it. They asked me how I had learned it so quickly, and how did I do it. That happened after New Year's, and the next day, I was speaking English. Can you believe it? I can't.

Like many students who make the transition from Mexican to U.S. schools, Jacqueline speaks highly of her experience, favoring the U.S. schools with their abundance of resources and their attention to individual needs (Valenzuela, 1999; Monroy, 1999). In the United States, Jacqueline felt that her mind had been opened. She met people from several different countries and learned about topics like diversity in education and other social issues. She also learned to speak English and was able to determine concrete goals for herself through college planning and beyond. In these ways, she began to reflect on what her mother wants for her: to *salir adelante* (get ahead in life). Indeed, at various moments during my interactions with her over a period of several months, Jacqueline spoke glowingly of her time in the United States and continued to talk about returning there.

Throughout our time together, I realized that there are essentially *two* Jacquelines: the popular, highly social girl living in her Mexican hometown; and the quiet but academically focused and successful ESL student in the United States. In this way, Jacqueline is part of a cyclical, transnational migration culture that moves children back and forth—both geographically and metaphorically—across the U.S.-Mexican border in *both* directions. Jacqueline's story—with its transitions, advances, and shifting priorities—encapsulates two important and related phenomena: both the bidirectional movement across the U.S.-Mexican border, and the resulting tensions in value systems. In this way, Jacqueline and her bicultural peers have become a facet of the shifting migration patterns between Mexico and the United States. Just as labor is moving back and forth across the border, so too is literacy—with all of its cultural patterns, assumptions, products, and promises. Cycling back and forth across the border every two or three years, Jackie exemplifies the dualism that many young Mexican and Mexican American children face, particularly as she experiences schisms in her identity, social loyalties, and sense of life desires and goals. In Jackie's life, it is unclear to what extent formal education—and, for that matter, migration—promises economic liberation and to what extent it threatens social harmony. As such, her life is connected to several layers of theoretical questions, not the least of which is, "*What is literacy?*"—particularly in a transnational world.

### MEXICAN STUDENTS AND THE PROBLEM OF NOT CARING

In an increasingly transnational world (Waldinger, 2011), these experiences merit attention, but little scholarship to date has considered the lives of transnational students who migrate from Mexico to the United States (Hamann, Zúñiga, and Sánchez García, 2008). Although recent studies (Farr, 2006; Pugach, 1998) have deepened our understanding of linguistic elements in these students' lives, mine is the first study to examine Mexico-U.S. transnational migrant students' literacy backgrounds and transitional experiences. This gap in the literature is significant because, while U.S. educators are aware of problems, they have lacked sufficient information to fully address those problems. That is, although the specific details of cases like Jacqueline's are not always visible to U.S. educators, such students' struggles—or at least their relative educational gains or lack thereof—are noticed. In particular, educators and policy makers express concern about the 1.5 Achievement Gap: the propensity for the educational gains of Mexican-origin students (among other groups) to lag behind those of their domestic peers (Salas, Portes, D'Amico, and Rios-Aguilar, 2011). Scholars and politicians debate reasons why students originally from Mexico who are educated in the United States tend to experience less school success than their domestic counterparts: Are they lazy? Are they underprepared? Are they just not interested (Gándara and Contreras, 2009)? Recent research has emphasized the importance of contextual analysis to address these questions, as Mexican immigrants' educational levels are consistently tied to the demands of the U.S. labor market (Portes and Rumbaut, 2006) and their economic success following arrival is contingent upon a diverse set of variables that extend far beyond immigrant status or language acquisition (Rong and Preissle, 2009). However, while new causal insights are being offered, the questions themselves are far from new. In fact, debates about Mexican literacy are as old as the formal political relationship between Mexico and the United States. For instance, in 1825, Joel Poinsett, the first U.S. ambassador to Mexico, bemoaned the state of Mexican schools, noting that the "evils" existing in Mexico "would be greatly mitigated by education" (Poinsett, 2002, p. 12). More than a century and a half later, this perception of immigrants from Mexico continues to surface in strikingly similar ways. In 1981, for instance, economist Thomas Sowell complained, "The goals and values of Mexican Americans have never centered on education" (Sowell, cited in Valencia and Black, 2002, p. 84). Indeed, recent scholarly work reveals that strong negative perceptions still exist—particularly with respect to a belief that Mexican American students don't *care* sufficiently about education: "The predominantly non-Latino teaching staff sees students as not sufficiently *caring about* school, while students see teachers as not sufficiently *caring for* them" (Valenzuela, 1999, p. 61).

Ironically, teachers in Mexico seem to be saying the same thing: Students don't care sufficiently about school. In particular, the majority of the teachers and administrators whom I interviewed in rural Mexico voiced concern that their students would choose migration over education. Students often make the wrong choices, their teachers contend; they hold the wrong priorities. But how is a fifteen-year-old in rural Mexico going to pursue a high school education if bus fare is two dollars a day, and her father only earns ten dollars a day to feed a family of six?[1] Despite these teachers' critiques, more students in rural Mexico access post-middle school education by virtue of remittances sent down by family members in the United States than through the transportation and supplies scholarships that some Mexican states offer.

Therefore, in absolute economic terms, international migration facilitates formal education—at least for certain family members. Even so, rhetoric on both sides of the border continues to downplay migration, positing it as a life choice that is antithetical to education.

Contrary to these assumptions, my own experiences living and working in a rural, migrant-sending area of Mexico suggested both that community members in the area approach education thoughtfully and pragmatically and that migration often positively impacts educational gains, especially for women (Farr, 2006). In stark contrast to critiques from both U.S. and Mexican educators, I found community members in rural Mexico to be deeply invested in choices related to their children's future; and, in many ways, these parents and children were more aware of educational ideologies than the majority of students with whom I have worked in more than a decade of college teaching in the United States What, then, is causing these patterned misconceptions on both sides of the border? Moreover, given the negative influences that rural Mexican students encounter in the school context, what components of their lives most strongly impact their options and decisions with regard to formal education? This book sets out to address these questions. In so doing, it considers both the status of literacy as a concept in a transnational world, as well as foundational information that could inform our work with immigrant students. In this way, my project expands scholarship on Latinos in education, as well as literacy theory.

This particular nexus of issues—literacy experiences in the transnational U.S.-Mexico context—represents a significant gap in the existing scholarship (Hamann, Zúñiga, and Sánchez García, 2008). While some recent studies have considered education in a transnational context, these projects have tended to focus on language rather than educational experiences (Farr, 2006), or have focused explicitly on border communities, rather than broad transnational migration contexts (Pugach, 1998). In neither case have scholars yet considered the educational experiences of Mexican students *in Mexico* and the ways in which these experiences affect their relative success when they migrate to U.S. schools. Moreover, while new scholarship in literacy studies has begun to unpack the role of written literacy in the transnational migration context, studies to date have focused on communities with relative privilege, including access to the internet and related technologies (Vieira, 2013). Therefore, despite the fact that most migration from Mexico to the United States originates from rural communities (Consejo Nacional de Población, 2010), and despite the fact that such communities have their own particular history and ongoing tenuous relationship with education, we do not have a clear sense of the educational experiences of students from Mexico *before* they migrate to the United States. And, while research produced by some Mexican scholars highlights issues of inequity in education in historical contexts (Gonzalbo Aizpuru, 2000; Greaves Laine, 2001; Hernandez-Zamora, 2010) and by others looking at contemporary contexts (Jiménez and Smith, 2008; Peredo Merlo, 2005), this study maintains a focus on the Mexican context. Therefore, given the profound social and economic ties between Mexico and the United States, scholars in both nations could benefit from a more comprehensive examination of educational experiences and adaptations in the lives of students who migrate from Mexico to the United States (and sometimes back again).

In support of this work, my approach assumes that it has become insufficient to discuss literacy in a single cultural context because literacy has become quite literally transnational: constantly moving, constantly changing (Waldinger, 2011). As a phenomenon that is tied to material contexts, literacy not only crosses borders but *is*, in its most essential sense, binational: of two places, of two persuasions. Therefore, one of the most important implications of this study is not just how literacy is changing in Mexico, but how these changes—truly part of ongoing cyclical patterns of international migration—are impacting literacy within the United States, as well. As literacy becomes a more broadly international phenomenon, our most central belief systems are being thrown into question as people of different resource bases and cultural backgrounds are being merged into a single, transnational economy. Further, while U.S. scholars have taken up studies of the conditions of immigrant and generation 1.5 students (students born in the United States of immigrant parents), much less work has been conducted to examine and reflect the experiences of students in Mexico. In order to better understand these students, we need to consider not only their behaviors (e.g., whether they remain in school or not), but also the material conditions—including school systems, living conditions, and migration patterns in the home country—that influence these students' decisions. Specifically, I wish to debunk two related stereotypes about Mexican immigrant students: (1) a negative perception of such students as lazy or disengaged, and (2) a patronizing belief that such students suffer as silent victims in an unsympathetic school system. Rather, I believe that students who live in and migrate from rural Mexico find themselves in complex rhetorical situations, and they are therefore compelled to make important decisions about how best to position themselves with respect to school, work, and nationality. Finally, while this book neither purports to take a stand on immigration policy, nor to suggest the best means of managing that policy, it does seek to inform such decisions by virtue of laying open the complexities that are experienced at the local level, within the broader context of transnational economics and migration. Perhaps most significantly,

I will argue that migration and literacy are intimately connected, such that migration serves as both a catalyst and a complication for literacy acquisition. Moreover, youth from Mexico—or born of Mexican parents who have recently immigrated to the United States—exhibit signs of both savvy and distress as they attempt to negotiate alliances within both educational institutions and social support networks.

## NEW INTERSECTIONS IN A TRANSNATIONAL WORLD

With respect to analytic approaches in a transnational world, context is crucial—not only context, but likewise movement and synthesis. From fields as far flung as migration studies (Waldinger, 2011) to economics (Robertson, 1995) to development studies (Grey and Woodrick, 2002) to education (Alexander, 2000), theories of contemporary world dynamics have increasingly emphasized the connections between global and local events. As described in the opening of this introduction, for instance, Jackie is one example of many individuals whose lives are affected by—and indeed transpire in—a variety of related contexts. Therefore, a foundational assumption of this book is the importance of comparative perspectives. Such work can both help to identify changes in large social phenomena like literacy and provide useful insights into differences in material conditions across two or more related contexts. Early on, during the period following World War II, a general interest in comparative studies of education emerged. Much of this early work, however, functioned at the policy level, such that it examined the structural elements of education rather than qualitative issues of pedagogy and human interaction. More recently, scholars like Robin Alexander (2000) have taken on more qualitative agendas, surveying local classroom interactions as well as broad, programmatic contrasts.

While I agree with both the value of comparative work, as well as the importance of local perspectives and pedagogical analysis, I believe that it has become crucial not only to compare sites but to explore the spaces between them (Farr, 2006; Pugach, 1998). We need to do more than compare variables. In addition, we need consider how they cross over, combine, intersect, impact, and influence each other. As labor, goods, and currency move with increasing fluidity across international borders, formal education is becoming less a sovereign entity and more a shared, transnational phenomenon. For instance, as I began this research project, I naively assumed that, in the tradition of scholars like Robin Alexander, I would be able to document Mexican school curricula in order to inform U.S. educators about the training that students receive before they migrate to the United States. What I discovered instead is a tremendously complex history of education in Mexico, one that consistently features sites of both oppression and resistance. This is, indeed, a history that continues to develop, and its most recent front is the U.S. border itself. Quite simply, Mexican education is impacted by broader patterns in U.S.-Mexico economic and political relationships, such that, in order to report on literacy conditions in Mexico, I found it necessary to report on transnationalism itself. Most significantly, migration rates from Mexico have risen over time (Consejo Nacional de Población, 2010) and those patterns have become increasingly complex from 2008 onward due to the global recession (Alarcón et al., 2009; Cohen, 2010) and to new, more conservative legislative measures on immigration in several U.S. states, with the result that the ties between migration and literacy experiences have become even more worthy of investigation.

For instance, Marta, a neighbor and friend of mine during the year that I conducted the research for this book, was one of the few people in town who commuted to a larger, neighboring town where high school classes and other forms of adult education were available. Marta made the trip several times a week to take computer classes. I was intrigued, given that almost none of the homes in the area had computers and the internet was completely unavailable. Moreover, in the town where Marta and I were living, there is no form of external employment; residents either farm or open small commercial offerings from their home. In Marta's case, she worked with two of her female relatives selling tacos in front of their house every evening and vending corn and other goods at seasonal religious events in town (figure 0.1). These sales constituted their entire income, which was modest but sufficient. Marta told me that she had no intention of seeking work elsewhere. Why, then, I asked, did she invest in computer classes? After a few moments explaining her general understanding that computer literacy is (at least theoretically) valuable, she stopped and chuckled. "I don't know," she said. "I guess, well, someday I might have to sell a taco over the internet." We both laughed. Her comment was lighthearted and somewhat off-the-cuff. Still, it stayed with me, as I continued to mull over the irony of the fact that technological advances like computers were making their mark even in places and on people who had neither access to them nor explicit use for them (Johnson and Kress, 2003). Three years later, when I moved to Portland, Oregon, to take a new job, I discovered a local newspaper article about a Turkish immigrant who was selling kebab dinners over his Twitter account.[2] While there are certainly differences in income potential between Portland, Oregon, and rural Michoacán, Mexico, this brief news clip was startling: Marta's comment, though tongue-in-cheek at the time, had not been so very far off base.

These related examples are evidence of the *glocal* environment in which we now live—and which, scholars are beginning to argue, now demands our

Figure 0.1. Selling corn after the Día de Guadalupe mass

attention as researchers (Hernandez-Zamora, 2010). *Glocalization* frameworks assume that economic patterns and effects develop simultaneously at both global and local levels (Sarroub, 2008). These theoretical foundations are markedly different from earlier development theories that served as the basis for the first decades of comparative education research. Those earlier orientations assumed that levels of change function separately: specifically, that major change occurs in powerful contexts and trickles down to smaller contexts (Grey and Woodrick, 2002). At that point, it was possible to focus almost exclusively on structures and systems, with an assumption that stronger models could be employed in weaker contexts. Development theory has debated these assumptions for decades, moving increasingly toward models that view development as an interdependent process. As such, glocalization insists that change is simultaneous: If an event is felt on the global level, then it's felt at the local level. In the example above, for instance, technology impacts individuals in rural communities even though they don't have access to computers (Johnson and Kress, 2003). As a result, individuals like Marta are convinced of the utility of computer literacy, even if it will likely be another five to ten years before internet service reaches her town.

The significant lesson here—one that will resonate throughout this book— is that local community members in underprivileged and under-resourced areas like rural Mexico are indeed aware of the multiple levels of contexts that affect them; they know that they live in an intimately networked glocalized world. Therefore, I wish to argue against assumptions that less privileged persons are uninformed victims (Deutsch, 1965, cited in Labov, 1972). Rather, members of the community where I worked in Mexico demonstrated both awareness and agency—even if their material conditions limit the relative levels of both. Still, they make use of what they have. Part of my argument in this book is that communities like the one I studied in are profoundly aware of the impact of transnational dynamics on their lives, not simply via explicit migration but likewise through a huge range of value and assumptive qualities and changes. As Mexican scholar Gregorio Hernandez-Zamora (2010) reminds us, "The global is always present when locally situated individuals tell their stories" (p. 15). Further, I argue that just as individuals demonstrate their awareness of glocal dynamics, they are likewise self-aware of the related choices that they are making, within the frame of the resources available to them at any given moment. While these resources are not endless, and choice is not free rein, I do believe that it is significant to recognize the awareness and decision-making processes that are active in these communities because doing so reveals community members' real agency and the full range of influences that come into play in these decisions. In this respect, local actors function rhetorically, as they both consider context and make strategic decisions based on their available means (Gross, 1994). Finally, glocal patterns and local communities' responses to them do, I believe, ultimately impact the ways in which students who do migrate to the United States experience schools there and either explicitly manifest success in school or do not. In short, the answer to the question, "What makes Mexican immigrant students succeed?" is about much more than either access or caring. It has to do with contexts and dynamics in both the United States and Mexico, and more profoundly, the dynamics in the spaces between: the transnational world that is the United States-Mexico today.

A focus on intersectionality is, therefore, likewise a central characteristic of this book. While my analysis draws heavily on interdisciplinary theories of literacy, including the New Literacy Studies, I move beyond these frameworks toward more multifaceted considerations of transnational literacy experiences. For instance, the interdisciplinary grouping of theories now known as the New Literacy Studies argues that *literacy* is not simply a process of learning to read and write that functions uniformly across all languages and socioeconomic conditions (Street, 2003). The danger of this view is that it allows those in power to *blame the victim* when people in less privileged positions are not able to acquire the literacy skills that are prized in their particular context (Villenas and Deyhle, 1999). In response to these issues, NLS characterizes literacy as a dynamic array of localized activities that vary across contexts.[3]

However, while this relativistic perspective is an important advancement, the danger of focusing too heavily on local literacies is that NLS has largely ignored the broader economic and political frameworks within which such practices exist. As such, some critics believe that the "call to the local" has gone too far (Brandt and Clinton, 2002). Rather, other critics argue, literacy scholarship should consider a blend of global and local influences:

> [These] scholars have called for more ethnographies of literacy that not only describe cultural forms and situated literacy practices but also illuminate how these situated local practices are connected to larger sociohistorical influences, political processes, ideological questions, and power dimensions.... Specifically, there has been a call for more empirical research that investigates the various ways that "distant" (global) literacies are embedded in the local. (Fulton, 2007, p. 201)

In concert with this critique, I agree that the current limitations of local ethnographies of literacy are not simply the "piling up," but also a problematic neglect of the ways in which individual lives are tied up in broad, interactive global trends. Moreover, I believe that it is equally dangerous either to romanticize or naively champion rural communities, because they are indeed aware of their condition and its complexities. Further, in that awareness, they have agency—even if their material conditions are limited and their range of choices is not as broad as it might be in other contexts. What interests me, then, are not simply structures and curricular modules, as previous comparative work has emphasized (Alexander, 2000), but rather the ways in which students interface with these influences. That is, what are their reactions, and what decisions do they enact because of those reactions and reflections?

Therefore, in this book I focus on the ways in which local communities cope with and respond to officially endorsed forms of literacy (e.g., professional, technological, etc.). Because these official models of literacy are themselves constructions, most often of the dominant culture, I argue that they *exist* as cultural artifacts. So, while I accept NLS's critique of prior constructions of literacy—as well as its general theory of the socially embedded nature of literacy—I am myself interested not simply in describing new manifestations of literacy at the local level, as much NLS work has done, but rather *local reactions to dominant forms of literacy*. Specifically, I am interested in examining how communities—usually with less power—react to, incorporate, resist, and/or adapt to the dominant forms of literacy that are delivered to their home communities in the form of, for instance, public schools and curriculum. It is at this nexus of global/local literacy values that I find an important space for the analysis of the relationship between migration and education. In particular, a focus on local responses to dominant institutions can help us to identify and unpack the ideologies that drive those institutions. Therefore, this book's methodology focuses heavily on this kind of intersectional analysis: how does a local community interface with dominant institutions and ideologies? This is the particular comparative perspective that interests me and that characterizes the nature of analysis in this book. Moreover, because this driving question— *how do local communities determine how to position themselves with respect to powerful institutions?*—suggests the need for both contextual awareness and careful choices, I argue that these responses are largely rhetorical in nature. Specifically, the research participants highlighted in this book (1) demonstrate an awareness and consideration of context; (2) draw from various forms of capital, or available means; and (3) make strategic choices about how to situate themselves with respect to these contexts and resources.

## METHODOLOGY: REFLEXIVE CRITICAL ETHNOGRAPHY

Given my interest in the way that a rhetorical perspective of literacy identifies individual agency—even for those with relatively limited material means—it was important to me to adopt a field methodology that would allow me to highlight this agency and activity as much as possible. Therefore, I adopted an ethnographic approach in large part because this methodology has long been cited for its ability to provide a platform for individual experiences, particularly for underprivileged groups whose stories do not often get heard (Naples, 2003). With respect to literacy studies, this attentiveness is particularly important because disempowered or "illiterate" people are often treated as worthless information sources, even about their own lives (Hernandez-Zamora, 2010). A central aim of this book, then, is to provide space for my research participants—many of whom did not complete school or are currently struggling with the decision of how much school to pursue—to speak about their perceptions of literacy, many of which fly in the face of official beliefs and expectations about literacy. At the same time, I believe that it is likewise important for me to position myself within the contexts of these conversations, both with respect to my motivations and to the patterns of my reactions once I became involved in the recording and analysis of literacy histories in rural, migrant-sending Mexico.

To begin with, my interest in themes of literacy and transnationalism emerged during the several years that I spent working as a writing tutor, during which time I worked with dozens of international and immigrant students. Working with these students on their college writing projects, I noticed that, in many cases, language was the easy part. Rather, it was the unstated communicative features—the rhetorical patterns expected in Standard Academic English—that were so difficult to master. Years later, I wanted to experience firsthand the process of acclimating to life in another country, and I moved abroad—first to Chile and then to Costa Rica. During the two years that I spent living in Latin America, I recognized that trying to navigate another system, replete with its own cultural expectations and bureaucratic structures, was more difficult than I had imagined. By and large, it wasn't my language skills that mattered. Language is explicit; culture is not. So, just like my students from years before, the aspects of living abroad that challenged me the most were unspoken institutional expectations, as well as my own fluctuating affect as I struggled with and sometimes succeeded—and sometimes failed—to navigate a system that was not my own (Meyers, 2009).

Both my experience of living abroad and the relationships that formed during my writing center work have informed the current study. In particular, my link to the town of Villachuato, a small community in central western Mexico where I conducted my research, is a woman whom I originally met in the writing center at Seattle University, where we had both attended college in the late 1990s. Nicole Ramírez is the last of ten children and the only member of her family to pursue a college education. After being told in high school not to bother with higher education, Nicole gained access to university training and, finding herself successful, continued pursuing higher education through law school. She is now a public defense attorney who works with Latino/a youth. For the past decade, Nicole and I have been in touch on a friendly basis, and it wasn't until I mentioned to Nicole in passing that I was planning a field project in Mexico that she suggested that I utilize her ties to Villachuato, where her family owned a second home and many of her relatives still lived. That invitation was priceless. Villachuato, which turned out to be a quintessential site of Mexico-U.S. migration, is not readily accessible. Home to some four thousand people, it does not have an external commercial presence. There are no police, no hospital, and no hotel. A foreign researcher who wishes to access such a site—a site that truly harbors the most authentic information about the realities of migration—must have a personal tie, and a place to live. I cannot thank Nicole and her family enough for their gift. Without them, this book quite simply would not exist.

Given the importance of this connection, I did have a sense of wanting to give back to the Villachuato community, which I did most explicitly through offering free English classes. More unofficially, as people in the town came to know me, I became a linguistic resource, translating the English content of everything from INS application forms to hemorrhoid medicine instructions. In this way, my methodological orientation is most closely aligned with ethnographers like Ellen Cushman, who advocates an "activist methodology" in which the researcher and the participating community work together and learn from each other. I appreciate this perspective both because I believe in the ethical responsibility of adding to or giving back to the community that I am studying and because I likewise believe that such interactions strengthen the research itself. As Cushman explains, although researchers often find themselves "studying down," many research participants, far from being oppressed and silenced, are quite capable of drawing conclusions about their own lives. Moreover, these insights can lend significance and detail to a study that a lone researcher would not be able to identify (1998). In my own work, I have employed what I call a "reflexive critical ethnography": a methodology that asks the researcher to repeatedly reconsider his or her own assumptions and actions. So, while I did conduct formal observations in classrooms, distribute questionnaires to teachers, and consult archival materials, it was really my direct contact with the Villachuato community—and the ways in which this contact made me question my own presuppositions as an educator—that has become my most significant data.

I likewise believe that the human side of ethnography—the ethnographer's life experience during the study—is an important part of any study. In my case, the personal ties that I developed with members of the Villachuato community were hugely significant. Early on, I did wonder how I would make a sustainable life for myself living alone in rural Mexico. Fortunately, the community accepted and adopted me relatively quickly, and two young women in their midtwenties particularly took me under their wing. In their company, I took part in nearly all traditional activities, including weddings and funerals, annual religious celebrations, Sunday evening dances, and neighborhood games of *lotería* (Mexican bingo). This participation was in no way fabricated. Living as the only foreigner in a town of four thousand inhabitants, I had no other options for social interaction, so I participated in any and all available modes of entertainment, from evenings on my friend's couch watching *telenovelas* (soap operas) to riding idly on the backs of motor scooters through the streets of town. In this way, my friends and neighbors became my cultural tour guides: they enjoyed being the ones to show me how to light hand-held fireworks, or peel the skins off boiled garbanzo beans. In these capacities, I was treated as a novice; I was constantly protected and shown the ropes. Moreover, because they were showing me things, my friends became more thoughtful and self-aware about the reasons and histories of their own routines and traditions; so, they were able to offer me that level of self-analysis, as well. Finally, it is important to note that these interactions were almost exclusively with females. Because Villachuato's social fabric is fairly conservative, and because there were few men of working age who lived in the town, I didn't have access to observing or interviewing men. I lived in a women's world, and I was essentially forced to give up on the male portion of the research equation, choosing instead to focus my energies on the women and their dynamic. (For a parallel process and outcome in another study, see Cintron, 1995.)

Even as I was accepted by and integrated into the Villachuato community, I also realized that I needed to construct a persona for myself. First, I recognized that a full explanation of my project would not have translated to the community in which I worked. Second, for reasons that I explain further in chapter 2, I felt a need to downplay myself and my resources. In most cases, I found myself simplifying things by explaining that I was doing a *práctica* (internship) and that, once I returned to the United States, I would complete my studies and begin work as a teacher. As a result, I became known as *la maestra* (the teacher), and I was addressed as such when I walked through town. Quite often, community members made eye contact, smiled, and said simply, "Susan" or "*Maestra*," without any additional greeting or salutation. On these occasions, I smiled back, unsure of the appropriate response. These were not greetings; they were more like statements of fact. And for several weeks, they left me confused—until a friend in town finally told me something important. "They esteem you," she said. "It is important to them that you are here." And in that comment, the entire spectrum of interactions made much more sense to me: in a town in which *none* of the school's teachers live, I had suddenly become a representative of formal education. I was, in a way that continues to impress and haunt me, a link to the outside world.

In this way, I view my research experience as a kind of *contact zone* in which people from different backgrounds came together for a time, and something new happened (Pratt, 1992). I do not pretend that my presence in the town went unnoticed, or that it did not change the social fabric in subtle ways. It did. During the time that I lived in Villachuato, my neighbors were challenged by the notion of a single woman living alone in an otherwise empty house. On the other hand, it also became possible for them to learn English and to obtain translations for U.S. immigration documents. For this reason, I am a necessary presence in my own research—and part of my findings result from my own reflections on this experience. But neither did I feel that any of this activity deterred from my study. My participation did not harm the clarity of my data; rather, it deepened it. In addition to granting me more contact with people, for instance, the English class that I taught allowed me to see people in a learning environment whom I otherwise wouldn't have seen. I was able to see their reactions and preferences. I got to see how they progressed, who progressed, and why. Indeed, in his historical estimation of the development of ethnographic field research, James Clifford (1988) describes participant observation as a balance between experience and analysis: "'Participant observation' serves as shorthand for a continuous tacking between the 'inside' and 'outside' of events: on the one hand grasping the sense of specific occurrences and gestures empathetically, on the other stepping back to situate these meanings in wider contexts." He also reminds us that this process is always necessarily subjective: "Investigation, looking into something, is never neutral" (p. 34). In this vein, I took part in the community during the time in which I lived and worked in Mexico; and at the same time, I found myself constantly standing back to evaluate those same experiences.

During the year that I lived and worked in Villachuato, from July 2007 to June 2008, I collected several months' worth of classroom observation notes; recorded interviews with students, families, teachers, and administrators (see the appendix); and participated in a full range of community events, including weddings, funerals, religious gatherings, and so on. I followed this work up three times. First, I returned to Villachuato a year after leaving into order to catch up with research participants regarding their stories and ongoing literacy experiences. Second, I traveled to Marshalltown, Iowa, in the summer of 2009 in order to conduct parallel interviews with members of that community, many of whom are family members of individuals whom I had known in Villachuato. Third, during the summer of 2011, I traveled to Mexico City in order to conduct interviews and collect archival materials at the Secretaría de Educación Pública, the federal agency that designs and distributes all of Mexico's public school curricula. In total, data for this book consist of seventy-five hours of classroom observation and eighty semi-formal interviews, most of which were recorded in Spanish, which I later transcribed and translated.

## OVERVIEW OF THE BOOK

The opening chapter surveys recent critical scholarship on literacy and seeks to debunk the assumption that education ties directly to economic development. This work is important in large part because market-driven literacy programs, such as public schools, endorse a *contract* mentality: Students who subscribe to the demands of public education—both physical and ideological—will be granted access to increased earning potential. Indeed, what I call the "literacy contract" orientation has been a powerful component of the capitalist marketplace at least since the early twentieth century. Even so, some groups—particularly those for whom the contract does not always function as promised—have resisted this delayed-gratification orientation toward public schooling. One such group, analyzed at length in my study, are those students who migrate—whether on a permanent or temporary basis—from Mexico to the United States.

Following these theoretical discussions, the second chapter formally introduces my research site, a small town called Villachuato in the Mexican state of Michoacán. From the town's inception as a foreign-owned hacienda through the impact of contemporary bi-national policies like NAFTA, the town has perennially suffered from economically-driven sources of oppression. Today, more than half of Villachuato citizens live in the United States—a significant number of them relocating to Marshalltown, Iowa, where students and their families navigate the process of adjusting their habits, identities, and expectations with regard to literacy, formal schooling, and life goals. From there, the third chapter traces a history of shifting forms of oppression in rural Mexico through the lens of formal education. This chapter argues that, while Mexico's public education system has strategically drawn on traditional rhetorics that appeal to the values of rural culture, its curricula and goals have sometimes been more self-serving than attentive to local needs. This discrepancy may account for lowered motivation on the part of local community members, like those of Villachuato, such that many students do not opt to complete their schooling or move forward to professional training.

Moving forward, the second half of the book presents sustained analyses of the ethnographic material that makes up the majority of my study. Specifically, the fourth chapter samples narrative case studies from half a dozen women whose lives span Villachuato's history from the Mexican Revolution to contemporary post-NAFTA migration trends. An important finding of this chapter is that as access has expanded, literacy has taken on ideologically oppressive facets, such that students in Villachuato often value their social connections more highly than school resources. Further, the fifth chapter delves more deeply into the implicit conflicts that exist between rural Mexican schools and the communities they serve. While many educators in rural Mexico believe that education is both a moral responsibility and the best means of personal advancement, economic conditions often oblige community members to invest first in migration and then to consider possibilities within education. As teachers resist these familial choices, students develop a pragmatic orientation to education, accepting the utility of those school lessons that teach them to navigate commercial and government bureaucracies and foregoing any further value-drive imperative.

So what happens when students from an environment like Villachuato encounter U.S. classrooms? The final chapter treats interview data from a follow-up study conducted in Villachuato's principal receiving community:

Marshalltown, Iowa. While families in Marshalltown do want their children to attend school, the education process is far from linear, and children often find themselves with a split sense of loyalties such that, as members of a transnational world, they are implicated in a new stage of ideological oppression. Moreover, stories from both sides of the border make clear how strong the ties are between migration and education, such that migration is the strongest catalyst to increased literacy gains that currently exists in the extended Villachuato community. Therefore, as I trace out in my conclusion to the book, although teachers on both sides of the U.S.-Mexico border continue to endorse formal education as the best *means* to desired financial *ends*, Mexican migrant families view education primarily as a form of prestige. Specifically, a young person's school success is considered a family's reward for other forms of investment and sacrifice—including migration. That is, education is considered an end itself, rather than a means to something else. Moreover, migration functions as a catalyst of—rather than a competitor to—literacy. Taken together, these transnational experiences of literacy destabilize the existing patterns of thought that have determined the ways that we have constructed, legislated, and delivered public education since the post–World War II period.

# 1. Crisis and Contract / A Rhetorical Approach to Transnational Literacies

**AMERICA IN CRISIS: THE NEW CRUX OF LITERACY AND MIGRATION**

On the morning of March 10, 2010, downtown Chicago's Federal Plaza filled with more than a thousand demonstrators who had come to protest the U.S. government's ongoing failure to make progress on the DREAM Act,[4] a long-standing legislative proposal targeted at educational access for immigrant youth. As a focal point for the event, eight young men and women stood up and publicly proclaimed their status: undocumented. Not having been born in the United States and never having been given papers to remain in the United States, they have no legal right to reside here, despite that fact that they have spent most of their lives here, have been educated here, and in many cases do not remember their home countries or languages. The Chicago event was a kick-off for a larger national demonstration called National Coming Out of the Shadows Week, a movement intended to pressure politicians to take action on the still pending DREAM Act, which, if passed, would help undocumented youth gain access to education beyond high school.

The National Coming Out of the Shadows demonstrations occurred in the wake of considerable national debate about immigration, including Arizona's two new laws that had been passed in late 2009: HB 1080 and HB 2281. The former bill grants police the right to request an individual's proof of legal status, while the second bill eliminated ethnic studies curricula in public schools (State of Arizona, 2010). The two laws sent the country into a tailspin of debate. Was this racial profiling? Was it self-defense? Was it simply a practical and unavoidable component of immigration management? Moreover, the timing of these two sets of events seems more significant than coincidental, as it suggests the extent to which current U.S. citizens remain profoundly uncertain of how to handle immigration—particularly as it relates to youth, education, and our nation's future. Indeed, the passage of Arizona's laws was followed by a hearing at the level of the Supreme Court, as well as the adoption of several related state-level immigration laws in Alabama (2011), Indiana (2011), South Carolina (2011), Utah (2011), and Georgia (2012). These ongoing layers of conflict reveal a deep moral schism in the United States: What is our responsibility—either morally or economically—with respect to educating those young people who live within our borders? Further, if we decide, either for moral or pragmatic reasons,[5] to make a full range of educational options available to everyone who lives within U.S. borders,[6] what forms of curriculum and programming are most effective?

In contrast to conservative trends like HB 2281—and, earlier on, the English-only movement of the 1990s[7]—that curb certain types of curriculum, including curriculum delivered in languages other than English, more progressive responses to these questions have focused on increasing access by supporting diverse curricula, as well as initiatives like the DREAM Act. However, even these well-intentioned, student-focused responses can have deeply ironic implications. As an educator, I have witnessed the complexities that surround our nation's general desire both to manage formal education and to make it broadly available. For instance, in 2008–9, I worked with South Tucson's GEAR UP Project.[8] GEAR UP is a federally funded program that seeks to strengthen college readiness initiatives in school districts with low socioeconomic status. As a GEAR UP staff member, it was my job to encourage students at high schools in South Tucson to plan for college. In support of this mission, my colleagues and I developed college readiness programs for teachers, students, and parents. These programs touched on topics ranging from course planning and study skills to financial aid. However, while the programs themselves accomplished their mission in several instances, it was not at all uncommon for parents to approach me and my colleagues to ask: "What happens if my child doesn't have papers? Can she still go to college?" The answer is never easy. Without legal status in the United States, students are not eligible for most forms of financial aid; and, in many cases, they cannot legally complete a college application. In South Tucson, this meant that dozens of the students with whom we worked were stymied. Even if they followed our advice and programming to prepare for college, they might not be able to go. I found this irony both heartbreaking and striking: Federal dollars were being poured into a program whose success rate was permanently curbed by virtue of federal and state laws that preclude undocumented youth or adults from attaining a higher degree. This ironic clash of interests highlights two related aspects of educational access that are often left unconsidered: Increased access to education typically means increased regulation of those same educational opportunities. Further, during times of both educational expansion and revision of regulation standards, it is not uncommon for a variety of crisis rhetorics to emerge (Brandt, 2001).

At the moment, I believe that the United States has reached a kind of intersection of such crises that now characterizes our national psyche: literacy crisis vs. immigration crisis. On the one hand, we are concerned that our young people are not making enough material gains in education. These arguments are founded on both pragmatic concerns about the overall status of literacy in the nation, as well moral concerns about minority students' inability to achieve at the rates of their white, domestic peers (Gándara and Contreras, 2009). On the other hand, we are concerned about an influx of immigrants, and we are reticent to make conditions overly attractive for them to stay (Bosniak, 1994). That is to say, are we most concerned with U.S. residents' educational achievement—so as to raise our national productivity and to uphold the moral fabric of our country and its values? Or, are we more concerned with "protecting" our borders, our jobs, and our national identity? Each of these debates holds its own set of crisis rhetorics, demonstrating both the significance of each issue, as well as Americans' uncertainty about how to prioritize them (Brandt, 2001; Connors, 1994; Gee, 1990; Trimbur, 1991). However, as I will argue throughout this book, I believe that this intersection is not an either/or scenario. Rather, literacy and immigration are, I believe, profoundly intertwined, as they have been throughout much of the history of our nation.

Throughout this chapter, I trace the conditions and implications of these historical connections. First, I begin with the review of literacy as a cultural construct from the post–World War II era through the present moment. Thereafter, I examine the ways in which literacy has functioned in the U.S. and Mexican contexts, with respect to the specific historical circumstances of each nation. Building on the historical and ideological analyses of these foundational discussions, I close the chapter by presenting the framework that I will use throughout the rest of this book. Specifically, I propose that literacy has been constructed as a contractual entity linking individuals with larger sponsoring agents, typically religious or state-sponsored educational institutions. Further, in the context of the capitalist market place, this *literacy contract* has become a powerful orienting force, influencing the perspectives and practices of both students and educators. Specifically, the literacy contract promises that those students who subscribe to the demands—both physical and ideological—of formal education will be rewarded with access to upward social and economic mobility. However, the literacy contract does not always function as promised, particularly in the lives of marginalized students. Such students are often punished, either implicitly or explicitly, for their lack of success, regardless of whether they failed the system, or the system failed them. As a result, I argue, students from historically marginalized groups often develop an intuitively rhetorical stance toward literacy, as they survey both their context and their resources (i.e., their available means) in order to adopt a strategic stance toward the demands of the literacy contract.

## FOUNDATIONAL ASSUMPTIONS ABOUT LITERACY AND DEVELOPMENT

A focused discussion of literacy in the context of migration best begins at the historical moment when literacy became a topic of international concern. Principally, this shift occurred following World War II—a period during which several former colonies began to take on sovereignty—when politicians and planners were likewise concerned with economic development. Along with this wave of national independence, commercial ties around the world were strengthening, and capitalist first-world nations became concerned with exactly *how* these newly formed states were managing themselves, particularly with regard to economic development (Kalman, 1999). In the context of these debates, social capital—the network of human resources including labor and skills that are necessary to create economic advancement—earned increasing attention. A variety of theorists and policy makers came to view social capital as the "missing link" of development (McAslan, 2002), and this conclusion ignited interest in literacy—particularly as manifested formally in schools—at the global level, as policy planners came to believe that *education* (i.e., institutionalized literacy development) creates more social capital, and, therefore, more development:

> Economists and policymakers at the international level believed that "progress," or more precisely industrialization according to the Western model, was the solution for this economic disparity, and that literacy was the necessary first step to modernization. They believed that illiteracy was much like a disease, and that its eradication would effectively contribute to social and economic development. (Kalman, 1999, p. 37)

In this way, literacy was identified as an important generative *source* of economic development—one that needed to be carefully managed and nurtured so as to promote continued growth.

In order for literacy to be seen as a panacea, it was necessary to construct an understanding of it as both inherently positive and culturally uniform: a static but necessary entity that would function equally well in developing nations as it had in developed ones. This urge to codify literacy is visible from a variety of historical angles, including the representation of bodies like UNESCO, which in 1952 commissioned a board of experts to establish a common measure for literacy that could be used to evaluate international programs. At that point, the committee decided "to recommend that a person be considered literate who can both read and write a short, simple statement about everyday life" (King, 1994, p. 38). This definition was then utilized to determine the relative levels of literacy in various countries, as part of a development effort to determine the ways and rates at which different countries were progressing. While from an economic standpoint investors were interested in the growth of social capital, UNESCO insisted on the importance of literacy to human rights. That is, education should be recognized as a basic human right because, as social capital, it is the means by which individuals gain access to ways of improving their lives (2008). From this standpoint, it became ethically, as well as economically, important to measure literacy levels and improve educational infrastructures where these levels are lacking.

Within a decade of distributing its definition, UNESCO revised it in an effort to reflect the complexity of literacy as it relates to development and power. While basic skills are important, the committee said, they really only signify one kind of literacy: remedial literacy. True autonomy and power emerge, rather, out of an individual's ability to extract and use such knowledge in social situations:

> A person is literate when he has acquired the essential knowledge and skills which enable him to engage in all those activities in which literacy is required for effective functioning in his group and community, and whose attainments in reading, writing, and arithmetic make it possible for him to continue to use these skills towards his own and the community's development. (Oxenham, 1980, cited in King, 1994, p. 39)

This revised definition suggests UNESCO's recognition of both the complexity of literacy, as well as its social importance. However, this conceptualization still rests on an understanding of literacy as a set of concrete skills and an individual's ability to apply these skills. Further, according to this definition, the main issue in spurring development and equalizing human rights is that of delivering these "autonomous" skills to the areas of the world that need them. That is, the principal focus is on expanding *access*. As a result, a central assumption underlying this drive toward access is the enduring belief that formal education will lead to personal and national economic development.

However, despite this longstanding popular conviction that literacy feeds directly into economic growth, several decades of literacy scholars have argued against this presupposition. In particular, literacy historian Harvey Graff claims that the belief in "literacy-as-a-path-to-development" is false. Despite its firm theoretical foundations, Graff (1987) argues that this "myth" of literacy has never been founded empirically; we simply have no evidence that increased literacy leads distinctly to increased economic development at the national or individual levels. Rather, capitalist economic development depends on mass education because it needs a reliable, ongoing source of trained labor. Linda King (1994) reminds us that mass literacy emerges alongside a combined industrial labor model and a capitalist market structure. In this way, there is a tie between education and economics, though it is not the same causal relationship that is highlighted in the "literacy myth." It is not that literacy leads to economic development (Rogers, 2001), but rather that modern industry and trade structures require mass education as a source of ongoing production (King, 1994).

Therefore, as economic models shift and change, so, too, do literacy models. One theory highlighted particularly by literacy scholar Deborah Brandt argues that powerful social institutions—or, in Brandt's terminology, literacy *sponsors*—fund and organize literacy and, in so doing, define it ideologically. Literacy changes, Brandt (2001) argues, when its sponsorship changes. Moreover, this process typically happens during broad political and economic movements. During these periods of transition, different social institutions vie over literacy, and a shift in sponsorship usually takes place. For instance, the first sponsor of U.S. mass education that Brandt identifies is religion, and the earliest American ideologies of education cast it as a means of shaping morally upright people. In the next stage, the state took control of education, and its value in morality shifted to one of civic good: school became a way to train good citizens. Finally, in the most recent manifestation of American literacy, corporate interests dominate education, and literacy has become a means of social stratification and economic competition. In a similar way, literacy can move spatially, as well as temporally. Specifically, Brandt identifies the way in which literacy "migrated" from rural settings in the United States to larger urban centers, where it has become more diversified and complex. In the 1890s, for instance, much of the country's literacy training took place in one-room schools in farming areas, where the explicit purpose of education was to produce good, hardworking, moral citizens. Over time, however, the labor needs of the country shifted, and so, too, did schools. In this way,

Brandt argues, the analysis of literacy trends can reveal much about the de facto sources of power that control the dissemination of knowledge in a given society. Literacy will be shaped and defined, she says, by the particular "market" of which it is a part. In this way, Brandt's notion of sponsorship both highlights the ideological nature of literacy, as well as the deeply rooted power structures that become involved in the control and circulation of literacy.

Analytic frameworks like that of Deborah Brandt enable scholars to consider the ways in which power is produced and reproduced in social institutions like schools that shepherd literacy. In particular, the grouping of theories known as the New Literacy Studies (NLS) challenges a static view of literacy. Brian Street suggests that "in practice literacy varies from one context to another and from one culture to another and so, therefore, do the effects of the different literacies in different conditions" (2003, p. 1). NLS rejects theories (such as UNESCO's definitions above) that posit literacy as a singular, finite unit. Rather, literacy is always culturally specific and ideological:

> Literacy is a social practice, not simply a technical and neutral skill . . . it is always embedded in socially constructed epistemological principles. It is about knowledge: the ways in which people address reading and writing are themselves rooted in conceptions of knowledge, identity, and being. It is also always embedded in social practices, such as those of a particular job market or a particular educational context and the effects of learning that particular literacy will be dependent on those particular contexts. Literacy, in this sense, is always contested, both its meanings and its practices, hence particular versions of it are always "ideological," they are always rooted in a particular world-view and in a desire for that view of literacy to dominate and to marginalize others. (Street, 2003, p. 41)

As Street cautions, one of the major challenges in literacy research is overcoming reductive assumptions about what literacy *is*, and therefore *what it is capable of doing*. This question is particularly important to cross-cultural examinations of literacy because such studies must consider not only one dominant ideology but several. As such, they must consider overlapping systems of social control related to education. In the case of both the United States and Mexico, each nation's history reveals intimate ties between literacy and social organization—connections that are particularly visible via two of the nations' most salient features: immigration in the United States and colonialism in Mexico. In the next two sections, I review these histories with an eye toward better understanding how each nation's economic history has intersected with and shaped public manifestations of literacy within its borders.

### THE U.S. HISTORICAL CONTEXT: LITERACY AND IMMIGRATION

In U.S. history, a significant aspect of debates surrounding economic development—and therefore literacy— has concerned immigration policy. In this section, I provide an overview of historical highlights related to intersections between literacy and immigration in the twentieth century. Ultimately, I argue that the principal crux in the interplay between literacy and immigration in U.S. history has been a gradual shift from literacy being used to regulate immigration (i.e., literacy protects the nation) to a growing sense that literacy must be protected *from* immigration and its related complexities. The sort of literacy crisis debates presented in the introduction of this chapter exemplify this transition.

While some forms of immigration policy have been involved more directly with economic trends (i.e., the need for additional labor, high unemployment rates), uses of literacy to shape immigration policy have typically had more to do with the racialization of immigrants. During the nineteenth century, U.S. immigration was not limited numerically, though eugenics principles were used to determine related policies, and by the beginning of the twentieth century, this trend had materialized in an English-language exam institutionalized in 1906 that immigrants were required to pass (Motomura, 2006). Even so, at that point U.S. borders remained theoretically open: numerical limits and the category of permanent residence as opposed to citizenship would not emerge for more than a decade. The scales tilted, however, during and following World War I, when a fear of outsiders escalated and the United States experienced its first pronounced race-based immigration crisis. At that point, "The fear of racially inferior immigrants led to a push for literacy tests," which were instigated in 1917, followed just four years later by the establishment of the first formal numerical limits placed on U.S. immigrants (p. 125). However, while these literacy tests were theoretically established in order to vet which immigrants had acquired sufficient education to contribute to U.S. society and economy, some such examinations were cast as IQ tests that focused more on innate qualities rather than educational gains and related skills. Moreover, scholars have recently called into question the fairness of these exams. For instance, immigrant children in the 1920s and 1930s were negatively tracked into low-level school offerings based on the results of IQ tests that were administered to them *in English*. Poor test results were then used to justify the placement of Mexican-origin students in remedial classrooms:

> The rationale was that the IQ tests provided the necessary "scientific evidence" that gave those in charge of schools the license to prescribe what was best for Mexican children. These tests purportedly showed that Spanish speakers

failed to achieve academically because they were: (1) non-English speakers, (2) culturally deprived, (3) mentally retarded, (4) bilingual, (5) poor, or (6) not interested in learning. (Reyes and Halcón, 2001, p. 43)

In this way, for the first half of the twentieth century, literacy's relationship to immigration was primarily one of regulation. That is, literacy was used as a tool to vet immigrants—and, in some cases, to typecast them via questionable unfair, or inaccurate measures. As such, literacy was essentially viewed as a social institution that functioned to *protect* U.S. national interests.

During the civil rights era, however, immigration policy—and, in a commensurate way, literacy—experienced a significant shift. The spirit of the times was more amenable to giving support to immigrants, though these same measures ironically tightened immigration. For instance, following the passage of the Civil Rights Act in 1964, significant amendments were made to the Immigration and Naturalization Act in 1965. These policy changes represented the first time that the United States adopted a basic nondiscrimination principle with respect to immigration. Further, these revisions remain the basic outline of today's immigration admissions system (Motomura, 2006). This conversion toward nondiscrimination is congruent with a human rights orientation in the law—both before and after the civil rights movement—to recognize the fact that immigrants have some basic legal rights regardless of their status (Bosniak, 1994). Both of these progressivist trends—nondiscrimination and human rights considerations—took on particular importance toward the latter half of the twentieth century, as the category of "alien" or undocumented immigrants took on increasing significance. As mentioned earlier, it was not until the 1920s that numerical limitations were imposed on U.S.-bound immigrants; until that time, the "undocumented" category as we know it now did not exist. Furthermore, while it became a legal category early in the twentieth century, labor recruiting (particularly from Mexico) and guest-worker programs kept these divisions more fluid until the 1960s, when the Bracero Program ended, amnesty was issued, and the borders were tightened. Ironically, at the same time that civil rights for racial minorities were gaining traction, the categories of legitimate and illegitimate immigrants became more firmly cast, both legally and in the minds of U.S. citizens. From that point forward, there has been a firm division between legal immigrants—who, even if they are not yet citizens, have clear access to basic rights—and illegal immigrants, whose rights and access to social services, including education, are continually under debate.

In the context of these changes, it is significant to note that, at this same time, literacy ceased to function as a tool to regulate immigration. What happened then is interesting, because, as a powerful tool that had been stripped of its particular agency in the immigration context, it then became an entity that needed protection itself. While the United States refocused its efforts on fair, albeit numerically limited, entrance to the country, immigrant students have in many case remained a marginalized group, as some practices have—intentionally or otherwise—tracked them for low performance, while other policies have actually cut undocumented children off from access to education. For instance, the English-only movement in the 1990s—the official platform for which was fairness and access to uniform education for all children—limited linguistic variety in schools in several states by regulating the use of English as the only classroom language, thereby precluding children from using their native language at school (Citin et al., 1990; Lu, 1998). Some critics have argued that this policy creates hardship both for students who are nonnative English speakers, as well as those who remain culturally tied to a heritage language. Similarly, Arizona's HB 2281 represents another such movement to limit diversity in schools, a trend that arguably can lead students to feel alienated and therefore to experience lower achievement. Finally, in its most extreme case, this tradition of sentiments has also manifested in policies that actively prohibit students without documentation from accessing schools. An example is California's Proposition 187, passed in 1994, which was billed as the "Save Our State" initiative and cut undocumented immigrants' access to several social services, including schools (Bosniak, 1994). These composite trends signify a shift in our national orientation toward literacy. As a valuable resource that must be protected and preserved—and reserved for those who are entitled to it—literacy is threatened by outsiders who come to this nation. Rather than regulating—and thereby "protecting" the nation—literacy itself is now considered vulnerable and must *be* protected.

In turn, these policies have reopened debates about the relative rights of immigrants (e.g., do we prioritize human rights or national self-protection?) and, more significant to my study, ongoing considerations about education. As mentioned earlier, progressive responses have particularly focused on access: access to schools, to appropriate linguistic curriculum, and to nonalienating curriculum (Fox, 1999). More negative responses, however, complain that students, even when granted access to education, don't prioritize it correctly— they don't "care" about it as they should. This kind of rhetoric becomes even clearer in contexts of comparisons among minority groups in which some groups are cast as "model minorities" while others, notably Latinos, are cast as low-achieving and irresponsible. This concern further manifests itself as a full-blown literacy crisis when people identify rising numbers of immigrant students in U.S. classrooms and lowered achievement. Whereas once literacy was used to measure innate ability, our turn away from discriminatory practices has effectively shifted attention toward blaming low-achieving students for their own lack of formal academic success.

The concepts reviewed above largely outline understandings of literacy as it relates to the United States as a receiving community. What is often missing from these discussions is a consideration of literacy as a phenomenon in the sending community, as well as in the unique context of transnational movement. To that end, I move next to an overview of literacy as it has been examined and theorized in the Mexican context. In particular, I review the ways in which scholars have identified the power implicit in literacy within the Mexican context, as well as the historic discord in the uses of this power.

## THE MEXICAN CONTEXT: LEGACIES OF COLONIALISM

Whereas literacy as a tool of social management in the United States has focused on vetting foreign individuals who arrived as immigrants, various Mexican scholars have traced the history and implications of the ways in which outsiders have used literacy to subdue and control the native populations of Mesoamerica. Specifically, the Spanish colonial project in Mexico utilized literacy, particularly as disseminated through the Catholic Church, to control and indoctrinate indigenous groups to Spanish language, belief structures, and social norms (Gonzalbo Aizpuru, 2000; Hernandez-Zamora, 2010). Therefore, throughout North America literacy has historically been used to control groups of less privileged persons. As outlined above, these groups in the United States have tended to be immigrants and ethnic minorities; that is, a dominant majority has shown concern about the worthiness of newcomers and minority groups to join either the nation or a particular social class. In contrast, Mexico's legacy has been one of powerful minority groups—originally colonizing outsiders from Europe—controlling large sectors of the population through both economic and ideological means.

Indeed, a wide range of Mexican scholars have identified several historic political struggles over literacy, from colonial legacies (Gonzalbo Aizpuru, 2000; Hernandez-Zamora, 2010; Jiménez and Smith, 2008; Tanck de Estrada, 1989), to government control (Greaves Laine, 2001; Marsiske, 2000), to demonstrations (Cortina, 1989; Flores-Crespo, 2004; Martínez González and Valle Baeza, 2008), to gender inequity (Pereyra, 2001; Riquer and Tepichín, 2001; Rodríguez-Gómez, 1999), to the impacts of transnational migration (Hamann, Zuñiga, and Sánchez Garcia, 2008). Early on, literacy in Mesoamerica was independently sponsored and fostered its own unique, complex means of managing language and information (Bonfil, 1996; Gonzalbo Aizpuru, 2000;

Jiménez and Smith, 2008; Reagan, 2000). However, subsequent colonizing efforts shifted control of language use, information transmission, and educational models. Under colonial sponsorship, literacy in Mexico was utilized as a means of evangelizing indigenous peoples (Gonzalbo Aizpuru, 2000; Kobayashi, 1999), though little attention was given to the needs and interests of these groups themselves. More profoundly, Mexican literacy scholar Gregorio Hernandez-Zamora (2010) argues that early colonizing powers in Mexico actively defined indigenous peoples as illiterate, relegating them to that category as a means of taking power and control. As a result, he explains, literacy—as a foreign-sponsored institution—has for centuries been alienating for native Mexicans: "For five centuries Mexicans in particular have encountered European literacy and education as instruments of conquest and colonialization, economic deprivation, and cultural assimilation and dislocation" (p. 7). Hernandez-Zamora's point is well taken, as numerous scholars have identified ongoing political tensions surrounding education in Mexico (Flores-Crespo, 2004; Greaves Laine, 2001; Marsiske, 2000; Martin, 1993; Martínez González and Valle Baeza, 2008), despite the fact that the nation is now politically independent and public education is managed by the government, rather than by foreign or religious influences.

However, even as literacy sponsorship in Mexico shifted from colonization and the Catholic Church to the new federal government, formal schooling still did not necessarily serve the lifestyles and needs of citizens in all areas of the country. For instance, as Mexico developed into an autonomous state, it has maintained a very centralized education system that arguably functions in large part to serve the state's needs by socializing children at the primary (Jiménez, Smith, and Martínez-León, 2003) and secondary school (Levinson, 2001) levels. Early on, during the late nineteenth and early twentieth centuries, the Mexican government launched a variety of active literacy campaigns, but these campaigns primarily served the interests of urban citizens, often to the detriment of citizens in more rural areas:

> Literacy . . . requires a cultural context on which to prosper, and [many] rural areas of Mexico and other parts of Latin America are composed of small-scale societies dominated by oral communication. The point is not that rural people are illiterate but rather that urban societies have needed to develop universal literacy in order to establish communicative links between individuals participating in a constantly shifting and changing large-scale community. Hence it is only when rural illiterates come into contact with urban culture, as in the case of migrant labor, that they experience the urgent need to learn to read and write. (King, 1994, 48)

As such, the goal of spreading literacy throughout the country—first on the part of Spanish colonizers and then on the part of the central Mexican government—has often been at odds with the needs and practices of indigenous and rural communities. Initially, the colonial economic model actively sought to preclude participation from the majority of the population. Later on, a new capitalist market structure demanded participation in formal education (Martínez Jiménez, 1996), particularly for the purpose of training a labor force, despite the fact that many rural agricultural communities continue to employ a family labor system, rather than enter the commercial market (Monroy, 1999). As a result, local communities are not always served fully by their schools, and those same schools may demand things from students that they are not willing to give. For instance, seeking higher levels of education (i.e., high school or college) may require leaving the home community: a sacrifice that may be neither logical nor attractive to many rural youth.

Therefore, even as access to education has increased in Mexico during the previous several decades,[9] new schools and programs have been very centrally managed, such that, as Hernandez-Zamora argues, many populations of students continue to feel quite alienated by the nation's literacy practices. In particular, he highlights the ways in which the national rhetorics surrounding literacy have changed little since the colonial period. Emphasis continues to be placed on *illiteracy*: What hasn't yet been accomplished, and how this lack is harming the nation. Indeed, those individuals who haven't passed through official literacy channels are labeled as insufficient/illiterate. Hernandez-Zamora (2010) notes that, in this way, in Mexico, literacy has been situated "in the individual, rather than in society" (p. 8). Further, programs have been designed to "eradicate illiteracy": "Since the 20th century, literacy policies and programs have been implemented on the basis of a growing rhetoric about 'alarming levels of functional illiteracy' in the population. Official figures in countries like Mexico count the number of 'illiterate' adults in [the] millions" (p. 21). In this way, Mexico, too, participates in rhetorics of literacy crisis, which is most fundamentally about social participation and control.

But is the Mexican population truly plagued by as much functional illiteracy as these rhetorics would suggest? Many Mexican scholars believe that it is not. Rather, they focus on two related insights. First, they have noted that there is often an implicit ideological division between schools and the communities they serve because schools emphasize one kind of formal literacy, whereas communities practice written literacy in different contexts and for different purposes. For instance, in several related accounts, researcher Robert Jiménez and his collaborators highlight the ways that writing is treated very formally in Mexican primary and secondary schools, such that writing practices are taught and learned for their own ends (Jiménez, Smith, and Martínez-León, 2003; Smith, Jiménez, and Martínez-León, 2003; Teague, Smith, and Jiménez, 2010). In contrast, community members practice writing for different, more casual purposes at home, but they do not consider these practices part of their education in *writing* per se. In the same vein, Jiménez and his collaborators argue, teachers do not draw on home or community texts in the classroom, such that a strong division between home and school literacies endures, particularly in rural communities (Teague, Smith, and Jiménez, 2010). Second, as a result of such divisions, scholars have found that many marginalized segments of the population have focused on limited, practical uses of literate skills. That is, they are not illiterate, as crisis rhetorics from the colonial period onward would suggest, but rather strategic in the ways in which they invest their energies in literate skills that serve their specific needs. Broadly, this trend has been identified with primary school children (Hall, 2006), advanced school children (Levinson, 2001), adult learners (Peredo, 2003), and commercial interactions (Kalman, 1999). Jointly, such studies highlight the varied uses of literacy in Mexico: uses not necessarily readily recognized by official school curriculum. The question, then, is not *whether* these practitioners are literate, but *how* they are employing literacy.

Despite the complexities surrounding how literacy may in fact be used by communities—particularly those with less political and economic power— crisis rhetorics maintain, often identifying such communities as deficient. The following sections of this chapter consider the nature of these ongoing crisis rhetorics, both in the United States and Mexico. However, before moving on, I would like to briefly consider the difference between the ways in which literacy has intersected social control in Mexico and the United States. As outlined above, such control in Mexico has been uniformly embedded. First through colonialism and second through a centralized national system, literacy in Mexico has been used implicitly to control the populace. Specifically, colonial control first constructed illiteracy, and then—through the venue of public schools—the Mexican government convinced its citizens that they needed to become literate through a nationally sponsored curriculum (Hernandez-Zamora, 2010). In contrast, literacy's tie to social control, especially of minority groups, in the United States has shifted from explicit to implicit manifestations. Early on, legislation drew on literacy tests to determine which immigrants would be allowed in. Following the civil rights era, this legislation was eliminated, though implicit uses of literacy continue to determine which groups maintain real access to forward development. While these individual histories are interesting in their own right, of particular interest to my analysis is the fact that, regardless of their differences, both nations have employed rhetorics of literacy crisis to highlight the changes and problems of national literacy manifestations. In both cases, transitions in access (e.g., civil rights in the United States, expansion of public education in Mexico) have inspired rhetorics of crisis surrounding literacy—rhetorics that have led to new formations of implicit control in the capitalist marketplace.

## LITERACY: CRISIS AND CONTRACT

How, then, can we best understand the ways in which literacy is truly functioning in the transnational U.S.-Mexico context, apart from the crisis rhetorics that both nations continue to employ? As a partial answer, I offer an ideological interpretation of how literacy tends to function between individuals and larger sponsoring institutions. This framework, which I call the literacy contract, explains the interdependent relationship between individuals and schools in a capitalist marketplace. Specifically, schools—as the representatives of larger political or economic interests (e.g., government)—require students to comply with a certain set of rules and values, which compel them to attend school regularly, to complete work as directed, and to make personal decisions based on the values endorsed by the school. For instance, schools typically ask students to prioritize professionalization over proximity to family. In return, schools promise upward social and economic mobility. That is, students who subscribe to the demands of public education—both physical and ideological—are granted access to increased earning potential. However, some groups—particularly those for whom the literacy contract does not always function as promised—have resisted this delayed gratification orientation toward public schooling.

In order to understand the workings of the literacy contract, it is helpful to recall the ideological utility of crisis rhetorics themselves. Scholarship has shown that literacy crisis rhetorics serve to preserve existing institutions (Brannon, 1995). If literacy is perceived to be injured or threatened in some way, the institutions that sponsor literacy—often schools or, more broadly, governments—have a solid platform to work from in order to reassert their own worthiness and importance to society. Who would want to do away with or seriously alter mass education at a time when literacy levels are perceived to be plummeting? Further, Deborah Brandt reminds us, these rhetorics tend to emerge during times of transition, when literacy-sponsoring institutions are being threatened by change (2001). They serve, quite simply, as an attempt—sometimes a successful one—to maintain the status quo. In this same way, we can identify the crisis rhetorics currently surrounding U.S. immigration patterns and policies as a means of "putting on the breaks." Indeed, migration scholar Roger Waldinger argues that U.S. immigration policy is both notably noncommittal and incredibly slow to change (Ghandnoosh and Waldinger, 2006). Interestingly, we can apply similar analysis to the Mexican context, though in that case, the legacy of colonialism has meant that crisis rhetorics have been used by a governing minority in order to draw residents into new ideologies and organizational structures. In both situations the net result is the same: a warning of crisis is announced to establish the idea of a problem or deficiency that needs to be "fixed" by a governing institution. This need presumably demands loyalty and participation from those purportedly served by the institution. In this way, "literacy crisis" rhetorics are primarily about compliance.

The way that such crises function in the U.S.-Mexico context is interesting, particularly for the opposing values that drive them in each country. To begin with, in the case of the United States, current literacy crisis rhetorics focus on decaying literacy standards: our literacy levels are going *down* (Brandt, 2001; Connors, 1994; Gee, 1990; Trimbur, 1991). As mentioned earlier, I argue that this perception is crafted in part from the suspicion that diversifying student bodies causes literacy to decline. Thus, change in the status of literacy in the United States is generally considered negative and damaging. The assumption is that at one point we had quality standards, but we are now losing them.[10] In marked contrast, the focus of the literacy crisis rhetorics in Mexico is that illiteracy had plagued the nation for centuries and that literacy levels remain alarmingly low. The impetus here is to *create* change, in the form of bolstering literacy levels via schools' participation. In this context, then, change is considered *good* and the "problem" that needs to be fixed is that paucity of literacy, particularly in rural and indigenous areas of the country. Considered together, then, crisis rhetorics in the United States and Mexico run counter to each other: In the United States, change is considered negative because it damages existing standards, while in Mexico change is considered a necessary means of raising literacy standards.

While U.S. and Mexican literacy crisis rhetorics differ in their directionality, as well as their origins of social management and ideologies, they bear a significant common feature: a focus on *access*. In the United States, this focus manifests particularly in progressivist discussions (as explained above) that argue there is a need for more—and more inclusive—curriculum for minority students. In Mexico, significant investment has been made in reaching students even in remote areas.[11] Both of these conversations, however, are predicated on the assumed causal connection between education and economic development—or, at the very least, on the belief that literacy is a valuable resource. As per Brandt's arguments above, in the contemporary capitalist market structure, literacy has come to function as a resource in and of itself: something that has worth, needs to be protected, and can be bought or sold, given or received. That is, not only does literacy help to facilitate the movement of goods and services in a capitalist market, it is in *itself* a good to be bought and sold. Literacy will be shaped and defined, Brandt argues, by the particular "market" of which it is a part (Brandt, 2001). These arguments reflect the particular ideology that shapes literacy experiences in a capitalist marketplace: literacy is a resource. As such, it has value, and it must be controlled. Therefore, while physical access is undeniably a crucial component to educational participation, I argue that it is a necessary but insufficient condition. Indeed, there are real dangers to overestimating its importance. For instance, if access *does* exist and particular groups of students (e.g. immigrant students, rural students, racial minorities, indigenous students) still fail to excel, the tendency is to point the finger back at them—to *blame the victim* (Labov, 1972). Rather than focusing insistently on a presumed causal tie between education and economic growth, I believe that a more interesting and generative question would be how economics and education impact and alter each other ideologically; or, in Street's terminology, what is potentially transformative in the interactions between education and economic patterns (Street, 2001).

Therefore, in partial answer to this question, I suggest that, in the contemporary context—one that both values and seeks to protect literacy, just as it continues to promise that literacy will lead to valuable outcomes for individuals—literacy has come to function as a *contract*. Organizing units, such as nation-states, provide public education—increasing access in rural areas, to undocumented youth, and so on—and in return they expect individuals to subscribe to the activities and value systems that these institutions endorse. The implication here is a socially endorsed pact: If a nation (or other sponsoring agent) provides reliable access to formal education, then those on the receiving end should participate and appreciate the resource that they have been given (Young, 2007). That is, they should both comply and *care*. If they do, they are promised further rewards—most notably professional success following the completion of school. However, while a contract orientation functions well in a capitalist market wage-labor economy, it does not deliver equally in all settings. As later chapters of this book will demonstrate, in places like rural Mexico, school often demands much more than it delivers, and in such cases students' motivations may slacken.

Despite these complexities, when students fail to perform or to demonstrate adequate investment, whether because their schools do not meet their needs or because they feel dubious about the conditioning that these schools promote, those who remain invested in schools—from sponsoring governments to teachers working at the schools—perceive a crisis. A student's failure to "care" sufficiently, expressed in either attitude or behavior, is conceived of as a breach of contract. For instance, contemporary debates about the relative or perceived failure of students from rural Mexico (in both Mexico *and* the United States) to make strong gains in formal educational settings has tended to focus on issues of choice and commitment. At the site where I conducted my research in rural Mexico, for instance, teachers complained of students making the *wrong choice* by opting to migrate—either domestically or internationally—to work, instead of continuing on with their education. Similarly, in the United States, Latino students and families have often been perceived as *not caring* sufficiently for education (Valenzuela, 1999). In this way, a "crisis" constitutes a pattern (e.g., an awareness of the failure to uphold the terms of the contract, suspicion of the contract, unwillingness or inability to subscribe to the values embedded in the contract, etc.) that breaches the literacy contract. In turn, these same crisis rhetorics are used to maintain the contract's control.

In transnational contexts (Rong, 2009; Salas et al., 2011; Waldinger, 2011), the nature of the literacy contract becomes that much more complex. As Brandt's analysis showed, if political and economic shifts transform literacy, then certainly increases in transnational migration, along with struggles over the control and legislation of that migration, are significant to literacy's ongoing manifestations. Further, as commerce is now the principal literacy sponsor, transnational migration—as an economic condition—is arguably shaping literacy, as well. Broadly, I believe that transnational migration— both as the movement of people, goods, and ideas, as well as the creation and revision of policies guiding that movement—is the next horizon of literacy studies that we need to consider. So, we can see why literacy is valuable in this context, and also how it is changing. On both counts, literacy in the trans-national context lends itself to crisis rhetorics, as dominant society strives to protect and control it, not so much from qualitative change, but from shifts in socioeconomic stratification. Further, I argue that part of our challenge working with minority and immigrant youth is that their experiences and perspectives "breach the contract" whether or not they intend to do so. The irony in the case of immigrants from rural Mexico is that they have been "breaching the contract" in their home country, as well.

## RHETORICAL POSITIONING AS AN ALTERNATIVE TO THE CONTRACT CULTURE

As an alternative to the prescriptive, normative impact of literacy crisis rheto-rics and the commensurate contract culture that they foster, I argue that local actors often assume a more flexible, rhetorical stance toward literacy: one that reads the implicit lines of institutions' rules and finds ways of complying, though tentatively and selectively. A problem of even well-intentioned examinations of immigrant and minority students can be the propensity to cast them as uninformed victims of larger, powerful institutions. One goal of this book is to highlight the levels of awareness—implicit or explicit—that rural Mexican communities carry with respect to their life conditions and opportunities to attain resources and to position themselves socially, particularly within or with regard to institutions like schools.

Other scholars have already identified rhetorical aspects of literacy. In the late 1990s, Patricia Bizzell described literacy, like rhetoric, as provisional and tied to audience, and she argued that both are dialectical in nature (1998). More recently, Shannon Carter has advocated a pedagogical approach called "rhetorical dexterity" that encourages students to apply rhetorical principles of analysis and contextual awareness in order to understand the constructed nature of literacies both in and out of the classroom (2006). With specific respect to Mexican-origin students in U.S. schools, Juan C. Guerra (2004) likewise identifies ways in which these students can learn to manipulate literate activity to their own ends. Focusing on literacy as a rhetorical entity—subjective and relative, and therefore fraught with flexibility and power—he argues that, "To make the most of an educational experience, students must learn how to manipulate language in a school context in ways somewhat different from those used in their respective homes and communities" (p. 58). Guerra highlights the usefulness, particularly, of pragmatic and personal modes of communication like letter writing and autobiographical writing. The goal, then, is not to sacrifice what was learned before, nor to privilege one literate act over another, but rather to learn ways of navigating both systems.

Building on these foundations, my analysis of the experiences of rural Mexicans presented in this book considers the ways in which both community contacts and individual position function as means of establishing rhetorical ground with respect to formal education. In this work, I draw on a common understanding of rhetoric as the process of applying one's available means (i.e., resources) within a specific, carefully considered context in order to strategically achieve a particular purpose (Gross, 1994). Traditionally, these fundamentals have been applied to written and spoken language. However, various contemporary scholars have applied it to visual images (Kenney, 2002) and social performance (Crable, 2006; Hawhee, 2006). In this vein, I believe we can cast literate activities in the same framework in order to better understand how individuals make choices about how to enact themselves as literate beings. In support of this framework, I draw on theorists such as Pierre Bourdieu, who argues that social positions are constructs (e.g., teacher/student relationship), and the combination of position and repetition accounts for an individual's identity. That is, social position leads to positional identity, or how students come to see themselves a certain way (e.g., successful, smart, dumb, not suited to school, etc.). In reality, though, the picture is more complicated because in fact, individuals inhabit a variety of positions, so the intersection of habits (what Bourdieu calls *habitus*) and contexts (fields) is occurring all the time in a variety of ways, which means that people have to respond to them all the time. Therefore, they are constantly making decisions—implicitly or otherwise (Fairbanks and Ariail, 2006).

As individuals make informed choices about what to pursue and how to behave in a given context, they act out literacy on a daily basis. Therefore, I argue, literacy is a practice that is *enacted*, rather than simply acquired. A focus on literacy-as-enacted emphasizes action, or the fact that literacy is dynamic and changing, rather than static. Literacy has meaning through such activity because it gains significance via other people, and the way in which all persons position themselves, individually and collectively, with respect to other people. Further, a rhetorical conceptualization of literacy emphasizes the role of individual agency within the larger context of a community or institution—a perspective that is particularly important to discussions of less-privileged literacy actors because it casts them as active, discerning participants rather than disempowered victims. However, such rhetorical positioning is achievable only if individuals are both aware of their context, as well as aware of—and able to deploy—the resources at their disposal—or, in the vocabulary of rhetorical analysis, *available means*. As my research findings demonstrate, members of communities in rural Mexico have historically gained access to awareness and resources—both material and ideological—through social connections. Moreover, in recent decades, these connections have extended across the U.S.-Mexico border as family members have migrated north, whether on a temporary or permanent basis. Because ties between Villachuato and its receiving communities in the United States remain close, migrating family members often call regularly, send remittances, or make personal visits home.[12] Indeed, even in the context of the recent economic downturn in 2008, these connections remain strong, stalling only mildly during the worst years of recession (Alarcón, 2009; Cohen, 2010; McKenzie and Rappoport, 2010) and quickly restabilizing (Bayona Escat, 2012; Consejo Nacional de Población, 2010; Ratha and Silwall, 2009).

One remaining question, then, is how community members benefit from this additional social capital. First, there is certainly a broader resource base. As migrants send money home, increased financial capital becomes the means by which Villachuato residents can build farms, start small businesses, or send children to school. Second, in the vein of Peggy Levitt's notion of social remittances (i.e., the values, expectations, and behaviors that migrants bring with them into their new situation and bring back home), the stories and artifacts that migrants send home expand the community's awareness of the variety of local and global contexts of which it is a member (Levitt, 1998). Third, given these additional material means and amplified critical awareness of context, members of the Villachuato community are better able to work strategically to position themselves—in the spirit of Bourdieu's analysis—in the ways that make the most sense for their own needs and desires. In many cases, such positioning and use of resources in these communities have taken the shape of resistance and/or self-preservation in the threat of oppressive conditions. Considered together, these outcomes suggest that one effect of the remittances—financial and social—that migrants send home is that they position community members at home to function rhetorically, rather than reactively, to sources of social oppression. Indeed, this transnational context particularly highlights the ways in which literacy is enacted because the overlapping contexts involved highlight the fact of differing ideologies. If we begin to consider things in this way, then it behooves us to approach differently our questions about literacy access and achievement. Not only are we asking what is the meaning of "success" (i.e., purpose) (Valdés, 1996), but also *how* people are making choices about how to present themselves. We may see, for instance, children who have attended school in both Mexico and the United States advocating one thing in one place and another in another place. And, as such, the very rhetorical nature of literacy becomes quite clear.

**CONCLUSION**

As this chapter has outlined, there remains considerable concern—sometimes elevated to a crisis pitch—about the ways in which literacy plays out in both Mexico and the United States. From both scholastic and policy perspectives, related debates have tended to focus strongly on access. However, the above historical analysis of literacy in both the United States and Mexico reveals a strong connection between access and regulation. Specifically, access becomes an apparent theme once literacy has become considered a resource in the capitalist marketplace. In turn, once literacy is identified as something valuable, competing institutions seek to control it. As a result, access alone may be considered a good beginning point for student-focused education and policy that seeks to even the playing field. However, because of the tie between access and regulation, progressive educators should foster awareness of the ways in which literacy values are implicitly manifesting certain types of social control. In the United States, social control via literacy has shifted from explicit legislation to implicit social conditioning, via the literacy contract. In

Mexico's case, an equivalent form of control has been functionally embedded through both the colonial period and the early decades of Mexico's statehood. In the latter context, which now likewise holds to a capitalist market structure, this implicit control has also taken the form of a contract orientation, as the government promises educational access, and students are asked to comply with the delayed gratification schema of schools. However, this equation, particularly in rural areas, is not that simple. In particular, the literacy contract is faulty in two principal regards. First, it does not always deliver; or, if it does, the demands/sacrifices it makes may not be on par with what it gives. Second, it does not take into account the other resource bases that may be available to a given community, nor the way in which those resources may impact people's decisions regarding literacy choices, including both their self-representation in schools, as well as their explicit participation or lack thereof in school. As later chapters of this book will show, increased access leads to increased and diversified forms of regulation, which can in turn lead to both oppression and resistance. Indeed, as my data show, many students in rural Mexico learn both implicit and explicit forms of resistance to the demands of formal education. Further, as I demonstrate in the next chapter, they are successful in these endeavors in part because they are accustomed to centuries of oppression and resistance. However, once students arrive in the United States, their approach to education—including habits of self-sustaining resistance—become confused and diluted because of the new iteration of literacy contract—its glowing promise and its practiced decades of implicit control—that they encounter there.

2. "Aren't You Scared?" / The Changing Face of Oppression in Rural, Migrant-Sending Mexico

*A*ren't you scared?

This was the most common phrase that I heard from community members in Villachuato, not only during my initial weeks in the town but throughout the ten months I spent there. "A big house like that," people would say to me. "And you're all alone there. Aren't you scared?"

I settled in Villachuato to conduct research on Mexican migrant students' educational backgrounds because of a personal connection: an old college friend whose family originated from Villachuato. My friend, Nicole Ramírez, is the last of ten children and the only member of her family to attend formal schooling past high school. When I mentioned my research plans, she encouraged me to consider Villachuato as a site, both because of its strong migratory ties to the United States and because of her own family's continued ties to the town—ties that, she persuaded me, would serve as the kind of social capital that a foreign researcher would need in order to connect with the community in ways that would make a research endeavor successful. She was right. Less than a week after my arrival, I had been invited into three different homes, and a number of other people—all women and children—had greeted me or struck up conversations with me on the street. They knew the Ramírezes. The most financially successful of Villachuato's migrant families, the Ramírezes have done much over the years to help community members back home. Their strong reputation in town was undoubtedly helpful to me, opening doors and encouraging trust where it might otherwise have been much more difficult to come by.

All the same, the distinction between me and my neighbors was pronounced. I was a foreigner, and a woman traveling alone. The latter fact in and of itself made me markedly different: Most women in Villachuato do not leave their town, and they certainly do not do so alone. Moreover, the house I lived in—alone, for the vast majority of my time in Villachuato—was tremendous: six thousand square feet, it held enough bedrooms for each of the Ramírez family members to have their own sleeping quarters, should the entire family visit Mexico all at once. *Ten rooms*, I counted—*twelve, thirteen*. The house was huge: block-like and labyrinthine all at the same time. It wasn't a stretch to feel overwhelmed and a bit skittish: Bats nestled in some of the rafters; an array of new sounds drifted in the windows as I slept. So, early on, my neighbors' question had seemed appropriate. *Scared?* Yes—a bit. But I was determined to succeed in Villachuato, so I did my best to set my own fears aside and to deflect inquiries with a gracious smile: "Oh, you know, it's not that bad," I explained. "I know my neighbors well, so I don't feel so alone. And I only stay in a small corner of the house, anyway." For the most part, it worked; I believed my own answers. But the question didn't stop coming. "Aren't you scared?" women on the street would whisper to me, nodding toward the looming house. "Aren't you scared?" children would giggle when they ran up to greet me on the street. Scared, scared, scared—*aren't you scared?*

### DANGER, FEAR, AND THE IMPACT OF PARTICIPANT OBSERVATION

In some ways, my neighbors were right: My stay in Villachuato was at least theoretically imbued with physical danger. For instance, while I sat at the bus stop at the edge of town (figure 2.1) a few days after my arrival, a group of men in a pickup truck trundled to a stop in front of me. Eight eyes settled on me. I glanced back briefly, then looked away; their stares were intimidating. For several minutes, the pickup truck sat there idling. The day was bright all around us. Telephone wires crisscrossed their way over the street; the lilt of a radio thrummed in the distance: *norteño* music. I was aware, in that moment, that I was neither completely vulnerable nor completely safe. The bus stop sat along the highway, just at the edge of town. Across the street, an *abarrotes* (local supplies) store was open for business; surely, someone was inside. From time to time, another vehicle passed us by, slowed almost to a stop as it made its way over the speed bumps that lined that section of the highway. At the same time, the air around me crawled to an uncomfortable stillness. At that point, I knew almost no one in town. Those whom I did know were back at the Ramírezes' house, several blocks away. I had no cell phone, no weapon. I was, quite literally, defenseless as the men's eyes climbed slowly down and back up my body. Later, I would write in my notes: *I feel like I have been visually raped by four men.* At the same time, I knew that nothing had really happened. As a foreigner, I understood that I stuck out, and that I would attract attention from time to time. But those men's stares, I thought, had been intentionally threatening. I had stood there alone, and they had taken the opportunity to express a sexualized form of power.

Figure 2.1. Bus stop in Villachuato

A minute later, though, they were gone. No one looked back. I kept my eyes focused forward, pulling my backpack more closely to me. I had already begun dressing down: wearing loose jeans and plain shoes, a zippered sweatshirt and little or no make-up. I shook my head to clear it, trying to come to terms with what had just happened. That interaction had indeed been threatening, hadn't it? It had been *real*?

Throughout the next month, several other vehicles slowed past me in and around town. Always, they contained male residents whose stares were as frightening and unsettling as the first ones had been. I was disturbed; I was worried. But, having no clear recourse other than to leave the town, I tried to shake it off. I went on with my work. At the same time, I met more people in town, and I began to feel more connected and secure. My research was under way at the schools, and I began offering free English classes for adults in the evening. After some weeks, I realized that the pickup trucks had ceased. When they shifted past me now, no one paused to cast meaningful glances at me. I was relieved, though still not entirely at ease. Clearly, I understood, there were powers in that context that could impact me in significant ways—that could limit my activities, or could potentially hurt me.

Indeed, the years 2007 to 2009—the time during which I conducted the bulk of the research for this book—there were real forces to fear in rural Michoacán. Drug networks in the area had begun shifting in response to political pressures, sending gang members to live incognito in residential communities like Villachuato. During the year before my arrival, two such men had lived in Villachuato, though they had moved on by the time I arrived. Even so, a body had been found in a stream that runs along the edge of town not long before I moved to Villachuato. The man, I was told, had been involved in gang activity. Several months later, during my tenure in Villachuato, a young man in a neighboring town was murdered in the middle of the night when he allegedly tried to escape his membership in a drug cartel. While those particular victims were directly implicated in criminal activities, there were other whispered dangers, as well: bandits that lurked along the highway, kidnappers that targeted the wealthy and held them for ransom. I began sleeping with a cell phone dialed to my neighbor Roberto's phone number. I asked him to take me out to the fields to learn how to fire a gun. Whatever the extent of the reported dangers, I thought, certainly some of them were true. And I recognized that I attracted attention; my presence in the community was no secret.

*Aren't you scared?* Months after my arrival, long after the pickup trucks had ceased and I had resided in rural Michoacán for quite some time without being kidnapped or physically harmed, the town continued to ask me: *Aren't you scared?* People told me that they felt sorry for me, living alone as I did in the big house. I had offers—which indeed I accepted from time to time—to go sleep in other people's home. *So you're not alone*, they told me. And I thanked them.

*Aren't you scared? Aren't you scared?* It became a noxious question. A nauseating question. I tried to smile and wave it off. But that simple question took hold of me in ways that, in hindsight, have astounded me. Having traveled broadly, and having lived alone in other Latin American countries, I had considered myself a seasoned, confident traveler. Typically, I made careful note of local practices and tried to curb any of my own behavior that would have been considered offensive, but I had generally maintained my own habits. Not long into my stay in Villachuato, however, I hesitated to complete some of my most basic daily routines, including exercise. How many more men might stop to whistle or stare at me if I went running alone along the path at the edge of town? Out there along the river that divides the town's residences from its farmlands, I would have no defense. There was no police presence, and no hospital. If something had happened to me, I truly would have had no recourse. That reality was sobering, and I leaned on my new network of female friends for support. For instance, instead of running along the scenic river at the edge of town, I followed a small group of young women to an unused lot toward the center of town to run one-eighth-of-a-mile laps around a gravel space that was spotted with broken bits of glass. Further, instead of wearing shorts in the warm central Mexican weather, I wore heavy, full-length sweat pants because I was told that only children and men wear shorts. Given these conditions, I found it difficult to keep in shape, difficult to remain feeling confident and independent.

The effect was that, yes: I *did* become afraid of my surroundings, and of my position within them. I felt vulnerable in a way that increased my sense of connection to my immediate community. Like the other women of the community in which I was living, I became less likely to leave the town and more comfortable when I did not. Several of my habits changed. I realized quickly, for instance, that women do not drink in public—not even when they are offered a bottle of beer at a wedding or town festival. I recognized, too, that they do not go out alone, not even to walk the three or four blocks to the central church plaza. In that context, I felt that I was being distinctly managed. Sometimes explicitly and sometimes implicitly, I was taught to assimilate. Joining my neighbors for mass, for instance, I was told not to cross my legs in church. Or, going out with a group of girls in the evening, I was taught to link arms with friends in order to maintain cohesion with the group. Further, there were more deeply rooted facets of assimilation—the most profound of which was that of fear. Fear held me in check. It prevented me from wanting to go out at night, or of leaving the town at all. It made me feel completely dependent on my neighbors for my well-being and my safety. It made me feel vulnerable, and not quite in control of my life.

This composite effect, I have considered in hindsight, reveals important implications about the ways in which the town organizes itself. That is, my difference—and the town's and my own need to come to terms with that dif-ference—exposed me to processes of social management that are central to Villachuato's history and ongoing character. Control, I learned firsthand, is ex-pressed socially in Villachuato. Further, the manner through which this control was expressed—by collectively managing people's behavior via their thoughts, reactions, and expectations—suggested to me a Foucauldian sense of socially expressed discipline. That is to say, the town of Villachuato, as I experienced it, has ingested oppression for so long that it now controls itself via social expectations. Some of this pressure has materialized in gendered double-standards that have had a particularly negative effect on women. While a complete analysis of the ideological foundation of gender norms in the town is beyond the scope of this project, I can say—both anecdotally via my own experiences and descriptively via data in subsequent chapters—that it exists as a strong force. In an area that was historically controlled by foreign economic interests which left the local community struggling and oppressed, that same control—and, arguably, oppression—is now expressed socially via a variety of gendered norms and other social expectations. In this way, physical and economic oppression has been felt for so long in this place that there is a mistrust of outside influence, even though they have constantly been impacted by external pressures.

## VILLACHUATO: FOUNDATIONS AND CHANGE

Power and oppression have been endemic in Villachuato literally from the town's origins. An artificial community in the sense that it was built by sixteenth-century Spanish colonists and populated with residents from surrounding areas, Villachuato was developed as a foreign economic interest, and it has never quite functioned as an independent community. As a hacienda, Villachuato originally functioned to produce food supplies for neighboring commercial hubs, most significantly Puruándiro. This large town, which numbered fifteen thousand by the mid-nineteenth century, had been peopled for some time, and the rich agricultural areas around it, of which Villachuato is an important part, had good yield. Lying between the foothills of two mountain ranges driving west towards the sea, Villachuato lies in a fertile valley and, therefore, became an important area of commercial agricultural production under Spanish colonialism. For some three hundred years, the Villachuato hacienda was one of the main suppliers of food to its much larger neighbor Puruándiro, cultivating large stores of grain products, beans, chilies, and corn (Romero, 2002).

The hacienda system was a well-tuned mechanism of exploitation: the most efficient means that the Spanish conquistadors found of controlling local populations and utilizing the land for commercial ends (Villegas et al., 1995). As the hacienda culture continued to grow in the area around Puruándiro, increasing numbers of indigenous people were displaced. Additional calamities like agricultural plague and drought eventually ensured the failure of small-scale farms in the region (Romero, 2002). By the mid-eighteenth century, when the Villachuato hacienda was at its peak, most of the indigenous people who remained in the region were employed by the monopolizing hacienda owner. Today, Villachuato—which means "town at the foot of big hills"—is a *rancho*: the kind of small agricultural community that, Marcia Farr (2006) reminds us, has been overlooked by U.S. scholars. Because we tend to romanticize indigenous communities as the "real" Mexico, we have often neglected to consider and analyze the *rancho* farming communities that make up so much of central Mexico and account for a large percentage of outbound migration to the United States. Indeed, although the state of Michoacán has a strong, enduring tradition of Purépecha indigenous communities, these groups live southwest of Villachuato, in the higher hill and lake country south of the state capital. As a farming community in the plains, Villachuato maintains no ties at this point with the displaced indigenous people that centuries ago were brought to work at the town's hacienda.

According to current residents, their ancestors lived like slaves under the hacienda system, tied down because of low wages and personal debt (Villegas et al., 1995). The discrepancy between classes was severe. "They had a father to say mass," one-hundred-year-old Esperanza remembers of the hacienda and its private services. "And they had a bread maker to make their bread. They had everything. They made a lot of money. And the people from here took care of everything. . . . And all the animals around here belonged to [the hacienda]. So many that sometimes they went around to buy more, but they already owned everything. *Everything.*" Like similar haciendas of the time, the Villachuato homestead (figure 2.2)—the remains of which still exist as a communal landmark—was well stocked, including houses for the various owners and management, a church, offices and a company store, a school, production equipment and storage, and communication facilities (Romero, 2002). Moreover, historical documents about this region describe Villachuato as one of the wealthier, more technologically advanced haciendas of the region—a condition that would likely have created resentment among residents and exposed them—for good or for ill—to worldly advancements.

Figure 2.2. Façade of the Villachuato hacienda

Eventually, this level of exploitation led to significant political changes: first, the independence movement of the early nineteenth century, and a century later, the Mexican Revolution. Essentially, these twin movements were stages in a two-part process to free Mexico from foreign interests, first at the political level and later at the economic level. The roots of the first movement began to emerge in the southern region of the Mexican state of Guanajuato, very close to Villachuato itself. However, the hacienda system as such survived Independence in the sense that, even though Mexico became politically sovereign, much of its land and industry were still controlled by foreign interests. Later on, in the early twentieth century, rebel groups throughout Michoacán and neighboring states began to take up the battle cry that eventually led to the Mexican Revolution. What is sometimes forgotten about this war—an aspect that is important for understanding the revolution's legacy on a place like Villachuato, was its regional character. While its great icons like Pancho Villa and Morelos remain strong, even in foreigners' imaginations, the truth of that war was that it was generated, fought, and recovered from on a very local scale, the effect of which was that post-Revolution Mexico was a fragmented country with several centers of local pride and identity (Rockwell, 1996). Neither was the result of the war immediately liberating—or even safe-guarding. For largely unremarkable rural areas like Villachuato, the revolutionary years and the decade thereafter were essentially a time of martial law. As Esperanza remembers these times, the conflict between the revolutionaries and the government was often a wash, with both sides flooding the town to demand food and supplies:

ESPERANZA: The *chinacos* (local Revolutionary soldiers) kept to the hills. They were just people, except that they armed themselves, and went around like that. Sometimes with a horse. [You know], in case the government came by, [so they could] assault them. But there were times that it happened the opposite way. There were times when the government got them.

MEYERS: And was it dangerous for you in the town?

ESPERANZA: Yeah, a little bit. Sometimes my mother would tell me: Don't stand up! Don't stand up! Because bands would come up on the ranch going with the *chinacos*, and they rode their horses up into the hills. And sometimes they threw their lassos into the houses. [Or] they just maybe killed a horse. That's all they really did. They didn't do anything. But before, yeah. They did things. But not here. In Puruándiro, in San Francisco. Over there, yeah, they did terrible things. Just as bad the *chinacos* as the government.

Given these conditions, Esperanza reported, the townspeople themselves often acted under their own jurisdiction, since the hacienda managers had lost power: "[Once] they killed a cow, and the people divided it up among themselves. The meat. And they ate it. And sometimes the *chinacos* came and asked for things from us. Because they needed it for their cause. And they would just take it. Some meat, or whatever." Indeed, in many ways, this communal aspect of Villachuato remains quite similar today. Although the town is now officially registered as part of the political territory of neighboring Puruándiro, there are no police in the town and no elected officials or designated political presence. As such, the town in many ways governs itself. And, therefore, the connectivity among neighbors continues to be strong and important to the town's ongoing survival.

## LIFE AFTER THE REVOLUTION

This decade of tumultuous years did, however, finally result in the awaited liberation that came with land ownership. Following the close of the Mexican Revolution, one of the more radical results to ensue was the wide redistribution of land all around the country. A new system, designed to decentralize land ownership and to improve the lives of those actually working the land known as *ejido*, essentially a communal landholding arrangement, was implemented:

> An ejido is formed by several small landholdings, each of which is assigned to a member of the ejido, although some of the ejidos also have common lands. Most of the members of an ejido are small farmers, and a high proportion of the ejidos' lands in Mexico are rain fed [and] dedicated to staple production. Prior to the *ejidal* reform, the *ejidatarios* were not allowed by law to sell or lease their lands, nor even to hire workers, although they did so. (Yúnez-Naude and Paredes, 2006, p. 215)

However, as with so many other things, the ejido system only worked in some aspects. To begin with, it took several more years than intended for the people of Villachuato to receive their landholdings. Although an agrarian reform law was inaugurated in 1921, the distribution of lands was not uniform (Villegas et al., 1995) and did not reach Villachuato until the 1930s. Further, according to one local informant whose parents had told her the story, several members of the community took it upon themselves to approach the new government and request the promised land distribution:

> Well, some *señores* from here—they went to Morelia, to get it worked out. They asked for land shares. One man named Francisco (Pancho) Contreras, and another one named Librorio Ramírez. They went to Morelia to get things

fixed up, so that we could have our shares of land here. [They were] *campesinos* (rural townspeople) . . . after the revolution, they went . . . to fix things. So they'd give us the land. And they came around asking for money: Give us something; we're going to Morelia. And my mother gave them some, so that they could go. And they went on foot, because they didn't have enough money. So they went on foot, all the way to Morelia. It took them a whole day.

According to Veronica, who did not attribute a date to her story, Villachuato did, at some point, attract the attention of Lázaro Cárdenas, the engineer of the new government, who visited the town to see to the redistribution of lands:

> VERONICA: [Someone] came . . . and took the lands away from the hacienda. [Then] the government had them, and then gave everyone their little piece of land. Lázaro Cárdenas came, my father said that he came. . . . [Father] was sick that day, and he went home for lunch. And when he came back, the others told him: Lázaro Cárdenas was just here. That he came to help. To give everybody their two hectares. Or three. Three was the most that they gave to people. But *Lázaro Cárdenas*. Who knows how he happened to come here?
> MEYERS: And was it better for you after you had your own lands?
> VERONICA: Well, it was more peaceful then . . . they divided up the lands . . . but men started to get drunk . . . the people who were in charge, who had come from Morelia . . . and they started to charge money for the lands.

Once again, the suggestion of these conversations is that Villachuato has continued to receive visitors from the outside who beg, con, or outright steal their resources. Oppressive force, in this way, took on a less systematic though no less significant impact on the community's lives, such that the community itself continued to hold strong internal ties and to remain suspicious of outsiders. Furthermore, once the revolution was over and families had been assigned their allotted lands, life in Villachuato was not easy. "The plague came," Esperanza told me, remembering her childhood shortly after the revolution:

> And then the flu, which felled a lot of people. So many people died. . . . I was maybe seven years old, when the plague came through. And I believe it was three years after the first one, the second one came. It killed a lot of people. A lot of people died. One came after the other, the plagues. People would get sick in their stomachs, and they had blood there. And they died from that.

In addition to problems with sanitation and other environmental hardships, there was a critical oversight in the general ejido land design: Although the land had been reclaimed from wealthy, exploitative foreigners, the new inheritors of this land—the rural Mexicans—were still so poor that most families lacked the resources to work their new land:

> ESPERANZA: No, we didn't have the tools, yet, to work the land. No, it was better for them to plant in the *cerro* [the hill]. Planting their corn. It wasn't until later that they started planting the lands.
> MEYERS: And how did that happen? How did they start?
> ESPERANZA: Well, once they started to have enough money to buy things. . . . They bought the materials. . . . Yeah, little by little, they got together the money, so that they could go buy the necessary tools for planting. Here there wasn't anything like tractors or anything—nothing, nothing like that. And if you didn't have your two horses, you couldn't hook them together and plow.

Certainly, their lives improved, but very slowly—and not always in the ways that they expected. Further, an important theme here is that of intention. While the ejido system was intended to provide rural Mexicans with the means to make their own lives, this oversight in resources (i.e., how to transition from essential slavery to small-scale capitalism) will be important to remember when we consider the promises that are made in schools—and the real likelihood that people do or don't have to use the knowledge learned in school to improve their lives in the context of the town of Villachuato.

By the end of the post-Revolution era, the challenges that Villachuato citizens faced had shifted. No longer did they live under slave-like conditions for the benefit of a single landowner or manager. Politically, they belonged to Mexico, rather than Spain; and economically, they were autonomous, at least in name. That is, the visibly oppressive aspects of their lives dissipated, even if poverty remained indelible. However, as these visible forms of oppression fell away, more subtle and complex forms began to be expressed as Villachuato became increasingly implicated in large-scale transnational relationships.

**OLD INFLUENCES, NEW HORIZONS**

Two events toward the end of the twentieth century, the Ejido Reform in 1992 and the signing of the NAFTA agreement in 1994, had particular impact on communities like Villachuato—impact that has bound the community to outside influence and, therefore, to a variety of complex channels of oppressive force. The first event, which opened ejido lands to lease and sale, was intended to create opportunity among farmers, as they would theoretically now be able to increase capital by selling lands or borrowing against them. However, the actual sale of lands has been far less than policy makers had anticipated. By 2001, only 5 percent of ejido lands had been sold, suggesting either that the market for such lands is low, or that farmers were not interested in selling. However, one important implication of the ejido reform ties directly into the subsequent signing of the NAFTA agreement in 1994: "Opening of the ejido sector to foreign direct investment, and elimination of the prohibition against formation of production associations between foreign private investors and ejidatarios" (Yúnez-Naude and Paredes, 2006, p. 220). Therefore, one risk to the small farmers under NAFTA and the ejido reform is that they may be pressured to sell lands, such as the family plot pictured in figure 2.3, to the interests of large, multinational companies. However, what is proving to be the larger threat to the small-scale farming industry under NAFTA has been competition with foreign-produced goods.

Figure 2.3. Farmland outside Villachuato

Corn cultivation is a major segment of small-scale agriculture, commercial and otherwise, in Villachuato and throughout Mexico. The staple of the Mexican diet, white corn, "has remained the major crop produced in Mexico: during 1983–1990 it accounted for almost 48 percent of total supply of the six major basic crops and 57 percent of the area cultivated with these crops" (Yúnez-Naude and Paredes, 2006, 228). However, under the NAFTA agreement, Mexico has been flooded with a huge supply of cheaply produced yellow corn from U.S. megafarms. And while yellow corn is, theoretically, used for livestock feed, the impact on corn cultivation in Mexico has been significant, with thousands of farms failing under NAFTA: "The problem lies in the fact that corn is still the basic food for millions of poor Mexicans and an important segment of its production is by small farmers" (228). And these small farmers, having only obtained the tools to work their land within the past few decades, do not have the scale and organization to streamline operations and produce a product as cheaply as that of the U.S. commercial farm. Therefore, because of the combined effects of the ejido land reform and pressures of NAFTA trade, many small farmers in Villachuato and other towns are finding their livelihoods are no longer sustainable. And, without many other good options within their own country, they are heading north: "rural out-migration (both within Mexico and to the United States) increased significantly during the 1990s compared to the previous decade. . . . This may reflect several . . . factors, including the reform of the ejido system of property rights" (224).

The spread of Mexicans northward has created interest in a vast array of venues, including the particular relationships between sending and receiving communities, Villachuato being an example of the former. While early migration from Villachuato targeted the Santa Ana area of California, it shifted during the 1990s toward the Midwest, including Nebraska, Minnesota, and Iowa, with a particularly large number of Villachuato residents feeding directly into the small agrarian town of Marshalltown, Iowa. Jiro Ramírez, a former resident of Villachuato who was among the California wave of migrants explained to me that this trend was partly financial: as housing prices soared in California, the seasonal fruit-picking labor market located along the state's grapevine and the Sacramento basin likewise became saturated. The Midwest, in turn, boasts much more affordable housing, as well as year-round work in the meat-processing industry, and therefore has attracted increasing numbers of new migrants (Kandel and Parrado, 2005). Therefore, despite the unpleasant work and much more severe weather conditions, many citizens of Villachuato have shifted their migratory attention toward the Midwest, particularly states like Iowa, Nebraska, and Minnesota. This pattern has remained true, despite the recent economic downturn in the United States beginning in 2008. Although the rate of new arrivals has slowed somewhat, outbound migration from Villachuato has continued, and those migrants already in the United States have remained abroad, rather than returning to Mexico (Alarcón et al., 2009). In part, this ongoing migration pattern can be credited to the strength of existing migration networks (McKenzie and Rapoport, 2010), though scholars have also noted that any negative impact of the 2008 recession on migration flows had leveled out by 2011–12 (Bayona Escat, 2012).

However, both the need for stable work and the success of relocation in the Midwest rely on other factors. First, it is important to note that, in addition to real estate prices, migrant patterns themselves have changed: instead of coming to the United States for temporary stints to harvest fruits and vegetables and return home for the winter months, migrant laborers from Mexico are now becoming permanent in the sense that they take on year-round employment, bring their families with them, and buy homes. In large part, this shift is attributed not to migrants themselves but to policy changes that are making border crossing increasingly difficult (Cohen, 2010). Specifically, the termination of the Bracero Program in 1964 subjected workers coming from Mexico to much closer scrutiny (Cerrutti and Massey, 2004).[13] Alongside this change, the coyote industry (i.e., human smugglers who, for a fee, help migrant workers make their way illegally across the border) has grown. And as border crossing itself has become more difficult, the coyote service is both more sought after and more dangerous, and prices have increased. Whereas, fifteen years ago, families from Villachuato crossed the hills around Tijuana without incident, community members in the area reported that a single crossing now costs anywhere from $2,000 to $5,000, an amount that takes migrant workers well over a year to pay back. Furthermore, increasing numbers of deaths are being reported in the deserts of Arizona and California and along the Rio Grande (Humanitarian Volunteers).

### PURO VILLACHUATO

Despite the legacy of oppression that has shadowed the town's history, the general feeling today in Villachuato seems fairly positive. People go about their daily lives in a consistent rhythm, rising at about 7:00 in the morning to make tortillas and go out to the fields. Siesta takes place from 2:00–5:00 P.M., during which time the town's various small shops and commercial interests shut down. The storefront businesses cater to locals' needs: produce and canned goods, dry goods, locally produced bread and tortillas, paper supplies, knitting supplies, and drinks. The stores are all family-operated and feature a counter at which customers ask for supplies. There are no restaurants other than the small, temporary *puestos*—taco stands that enterprising individuals set up in the evenings. Social outings consist of walks to the plaza—three blocks away, in my case—where children play video games in one store front, couples sit talking closely by the well-trimmed shrubs, and men lounge idly by pickup trucks in the evenings. Other than national and religious festivals—of which there are several—the only social excursion is a dance held every Sunday evening in this same plaza. On those evenings, an average of one to two hundred people arrive and walk circles around the plaza, dance, or sit talking on benches. Once per year, these numbers swell intensely during the annual festival that is hosted just after Easter, when large numbers of Villachuato migrants return temporarily from the United States to join their families in a week-long celebration complete with live bands, carnival rides, horse races, cock fights, and rodeo events.

But mostly Villachuato maintains its identity as a small, quiet rancho located among the rolling hills and valleys of northwest Michoacán, about six hours due west of Mexico City and a thirty-hour bus ride from the closest U.S. border crossing. Just grazing the edge of the Sierra Madre del Sur, Villachuato has historically been considered a rich agricultural basin. Today, small-scale agricultural operations continue to produce commercial crops of corn, livestock feed, and strawberries. Situated along a highway, Villachuato consists of a number of *bajadas*, or cross streets—the largest of which is pictured in figure 2.4—that function as highway off-ramps and continue into town to become residential streets. The highway itself is narrow and unlined, with neither guardrails nor shoulders. Residents of Villachuato walk along the highway to reach destinations such as bus stops or the secondary school. The only precautionary measure of pedestrian protection is a series of worn speed bumps that slow cars near the more important bajadas. The highway itself was paved approximately eight years ago. Now, it is possible to reach nearby Puruándiro (the nearest commercial hub) in twenty minutes. Before that, it took more than an hour.

"Well, it certainly has changed," one woman in her fifties, who moved to Villachuato twenty years ago when she got married, told me:

Figure 2.4. Villachuato's *bajada principal* (main street)

Because when I got here, well . . . there wasn't a [plaza]. There wasn't a *centro*—they put that in later. And the newer school; they also put that in later. They've changed a lot. . . . The houses didn't used to be so tall—they were much shorter. Little houses. And well, the streets weren't paved. They were pure dirt and mud. Everything was really messy. There used to be really big ruts full of water. Sometimes, you couldn't get across because there was so much water.

"Here for instance," she explained, gesturing around her family's narrow, concrete-walled kitchen. "We didn't even used to have this table covered up. Water came through the roof. . . . sometimes a lot of water came. The table, and all the food, would get all wet. And I had to go running with my things inside," she laughed. "I had to grab up the tortillas and beans so they didn't get flooded with water. Yeah, that was how things were," she explained again. "I'd tell the kids: come on, grab up the beans, they're getting all wet! But things got better when we got some [building] materials—a bit of plywood to put up there." The difference between these two architecture styles, based on available construction materials, is pictured below. Today, some 20 percent of Villachuato homes are made of adobe mud bricks, while the remaining homes have upgraded to manufactured materials.

Another resident, a woman in her late thirties recently returned from two decades living in the United States, remembers her modest childhood home that stood on the same grounds where now the family has built a white-washed house of concrete and wrought iron trim:

Figure 2.5. Adobe-style home in Villachuato

I remember, before we had this house, we had a small, adobe brick house, you know, and it was very small. It only had, you know, two bedrooms, and a small kitchen. And I remember most of the homes being bricks, or made of just bricks and covered with . . . cardboard. And um, the people used to be very poor. There were no sidewalks, no pavement [laughs]. And there was only one family in this neighborhood that had, you know, a regular brick home. And they considered that family to being rich. And it was just like it is right now, just brick. . . . It wasn't even like fixed. And that was the only family that had a TV. I remember, it was a small black and white TV, and I remember we all used to gather at a certain time to watch this comedy show, and it was like, fifteen, twenty kids in the house watching that show [laughs] on that tiny little black and white TV. Because people were so poor, they could not afford to have anything like that. And I do remember that our kitchen was made of bricks and covered with cardboard. I remember seeing the holes in the cardboard, in the mornings, you know, how the sunshine rays come inside through the holes.

So, Villachuato is changing. Comprised of approximately four thousand inhabitants (Grey and Woodrick, 2002), the town would likely be twice that size if everyone who was born here stayed. As it is, most families report that half or more of their relatives are living somewhere in the United States, most of them committed to jobs in agriculture, construction, or meat-packing. And many of these without legal documentation. The money sent back from these

Figure 2.6. Home constructed of manufactured materials in Villachuato

undocumented migrants complements government funds to build roads, put in street lights, and improve school buildings. It has refinished the church (figure 2.7), and installed a plaza in the center of town, where fifteen years ago there was nothing but an undeveloped field. Now, Villachuato residents have a place to converge on Sundays afternoons; they have a place to celebrate Independence Day. They have potable water, phones, pavement, and a stable supply of food—thanks to an increasingly socially-minded government, and a huge number of missing residents.

Figure 2.7. Villachuato's newly painted church, spring 2008

And it is really these absent residents—what is *not* present, rather than what *is*—that truly characterizes Villachuato today. The migrant culture in Villachuato has been strong since at least the 1970s, sending migrants first on a seasonal basis to California and increasingly now on a more permanent basis to America's heartland: Nebraska, Iowa, Minnesota. Even now, despite the U.S. economic downturn of 2008, these patterns remain, particularly because many migrants from Mexico don't want to leave the United States, as they fear that they will not be able to return (Alarcón et al., 2009). So today, this phenomenon characterizes nearly every aspect of life in Villachuato, despite a strong sense of tradition and cultural identity. Many children are missing fathers; many young wives do not know when they will see their husbands again; families are split in half; most vehicles in town have U.S. license plates; and children playing soccer on the street wear sweatshirts with English emblems that they don't know the meanings of. The culture in this way is slowly shifting.

While nearly everyone I spoke with admitted the importance of migration to the town's growth and prosperity, several citizens also complained of the influence of drugs and gang culture; the town, they say, is no longer as safe as it was. "I never used to worry at night," one woman told me. "But now, yes. I don't sleep as well." Teachers, too, have their complaints. Migration, they say, encourages school desertion. "The kids have a conception," one teacher told me. "That they are going to finish primary school and go to the United States *mojado* [wetback]."

So the problems and improvements in Villachuato are both expanding, and at the same time, the culture of the town is shifting, both in worldliness and dissolution. Villachuato is a place that tries very hard to maintain its identity and traditions, and at the same time can no longer survive without external influences. And perhaps the most convincing evidence of the irony in which Villachuato now finds itself is the collection of empty houses found throughout the town. As much literature on migration shows, a key motivation for migration is to accumulate capital for the completion of a project (e.g. starting a business or building a home) in the home country (Durand and Massey, 2004). The motivations of Villachuato migrants are no exception. The vast majority of homes in the town have been improved by remittance dollars—which continue to channel into Villachuato, despite the challenges to inbound U.S. immigration following 9/11 in 2001 and the global recession of 2008 (Cohen, 2010). And, while some families do return to inhabit these houses, it is true that many homes—often the largest and most elegant among them—remain empty. Reflecting on the relative merits of migration, one Villachuato citizen told me:

> It's good and it's bad. . . . because, you know, most of the homes that they build—beautiful two-story houses—most of them are empty, because the families are over there. Sometimes, you know, they start bringing their whole family over until everybody's gone. And they leave their homes behind. . . . But their dreams never die. You know, they have their places here because they're hoping that one day they might come and stay. And it's sad because I've seen so many houses that they're falling apart. There're cracks everywhere, they're falling apart, because they're been empty for years. Alone, you know, for so many years. And all that work, and all that money spent for nothing.

But it happens, she says, again and again. Families go north, assuming that they will come back. But they get entrenched in life in the north, she says: "And they just get so used to the American way of life that you know, it's hard. It's hard for them to leave everything behind and come back."

## CONCLUSION

It makes sense that the people of Villachuato value strong community ties and that they find implicit ways of curbing outside influence as they did in managing me, a foreign researcher, through an unshakable sense of fear. I find the legacy of that fear powerful not only as a means of forcing me to assimilate to local behavior patterns but also in the sense that it suggests ways in which oppression and power have taken on more embedded, symbolic manifestations in the town. Moving forward, I will outline my analysis of the ways in which power and oppression have played out historically and locally with respect to education.

The political and economic history of Villachuato characterizes many of the communities that send outbound migration to the United States (Durrand and Massey, 2004). It is a complex history, economically and ideologically; and, as I trace out in the remaining chapters of this book, I believe that it has a strong impact on the educative experiences of students in these areas—including the impact that these experiences could have on those students who migrate to the United States Subsequently, as I move through my analysis of the data from this study, I am particularly interested in the ways that such ideological pressures impact individuals' experiences of literacy. However, because these relationships are so highly contextualized in the transnational migration flow between the two nations, this project likewise takes a strongly historical bent, as I seek to trace out the development of literacy norms and practices from the formation of the public school system in Mexico through recent migratory trends that continue to send significant numbers of students north, despite economic uncertainties and a tightening of immigration policies in the United States since 2008.

## 3. "They Make a Lot of Sacrifices" / Foundational Rhetorics of the Mexican Education System

In fall 2007, the new seventh grade language arts textbook that arrived in Villachuato featured a smiling teenager playing on his laptop. In the background, other children listened to music, read a variety of books, and worked on computers. At the time, regular phone service had existed in Villachuato for less than a decade, and internet was almost completely inaccessible. Home computers were extremely rare, and only a third of middle school students received some form of computer training. The disjuncture between Villachuato's lifestyle and the design of these new textbooks suggested a clear if unintentional message: students in rural communities are not necessarily the primary audience of Mexico's centralized public education curriculum. In Mexico, curriculum—including textbooks—is regulated by the Secretaría de Educación Pública (Secretary of Public Education, or SEP), which is located in Mexico City. Impressively, SEP produces new textbooks each year and distributes them to every student in the country.[14] This commitment to supplying all students with their own set of textbooks each year represents a considerable financial investment—one that originated in the 1940s when education leaders were particularly concerned about access. Unquestionably, these books are significant, perhaps more so in rural areas like Villachuato, where libraries and book stores are inaccessible and school texts may literally be the only books that a child will ever own. In practice, however, the centralized nature of these books' production has meant a potential disconnect between curriculum design interests and Mexican citizens in rural areas. That is, official knowledge is quite literally negotiated and produced in another place and time. While the implications may be subtle, as I tried to understand the apparent impasse between students and educators in rural areas like Villachuato, it seemed to me that subtle messages like the one that the above textbook sent impacted students by reminding them that the values espoused by their schools were not necessarily congruent with the needs and experiences in their own lives. As an outside observer, I could only imagine the gradual loss of interest that I would feel as a student if the curriculum that I encountered had such limited relevance to my life.

Textbooks represent one example of the potentially complicated dynamics of Mexican rural education. Another example of the disconnect between school resources and community recipients in Villachuato is that of the design of the town's middle school itself. Designated as a *secundaria técnica*, the town's middle school is intended to provide students with applied scholastic preparation rather than the high school and college-bound skills that traditional *secundarias* provide (see note 9). SEP's design for secundaria técnicas includes three curricular foci: agriculture, fishing, and office work. The specific model employed in a given area depends on the demand for work in that area. Given the fact that Villachuato's only industry is the family farm, its secondary school should focus on agriculture. However, the resources required to develop workshop space for crop cultivation and animal husbandry are extensive, so the school reverted to a less expensive focus area: a version of the professional model, featuring drafting and architecture, with limited computer classes (M. E. Rojas Solis, personal communication, September 15, 2007). So, while there are no such jobs available in Villachuato—indeed, there is no external employer/commercial wage labor available at all—secondary students take classes in architecture, and they receive no school-sponsored training for the kind of agricultural and domestic work that will constitute most students' labor realities. Given these disjunctures, I began to understand why it was that most students in Villachuato ended their school careers after middle school—the end of compulsory education in Mexico—or earlier. The secondary school curriculum—the highest level of school available in town—serves them in some ways but has significant limitations in others.

At the same time, teachers who work in the town expressed to me their frustration that more students don't decide to go on to higher levels of study and professionalization: a pattern that expressed itself as its own kind of literacy crisis. Students, I was told, are making the wrong decisions. In particular, many of them (or their families) decide to migrate north in order to earn money rather than remain in Mexico to pursue their formal education:

the "correct" means of personal advancement. In this way, many teachers in areas like Villachuato perceive of migration as a significant threat to students' participation in local schooling. "Migration," the secondary school director told me at one point, is a really big problem here." In contrast, rural teachers expect young people to remain in their home communities long enough to complete primary and middle school. Thereafter, they encourage students to migrate temporarily to an urban center in order to continue pursuing their education at the high school and college levels. However, because there are no professional employment options in towns like Villachuato, such a move becomes permanent. The handful of students from Villachuato who go on to study at the high school level, for instance, are only able to use their professional degree if they remain in an urban center. In this way, education becomes a significant sacrifice—one that potentially never quite pays off.

Early on, then, I became aware of a strong tension between Villachuato's schools and the community that they serve. At the same time that my daily life taught me about community closeness, I worked at understanding this tension between community members and their schools. Why *were* students dropping out of school? Was it because of migration, or other factors? Moreover, was this decision as devastating as school leaders seem to believe it is? The next several chapters consider these core questions from a variety of angles, beginning in this chapter with a historical overview of the variables and influences involved in the development of a public education system in Mexico. In this historical context, I consider, following Hernandez-Zamora's assertion, how education in Mexico has, since its colonialist foundations, been alienating for a majority of Mexicans (2010). Following this line of thinking, my analysis of my own data does indeed suggest that a key reason why students don't continue their education is that they find their educational experiences alienating. One project of this book, therefore, is to trace *why* and *how* these patterns of alienation have occurred. In large part, I argue, these tensions are a result of the highly centralized nature of the Mexican education system: a system that formulated as such because of three related historical patterns. Below, I trace out the development of this system, highlighting the impact of (1) the legacy of colonialism, (2) the strain of post-Revolutionary nation building, and (3) the pragmatic realities of the need to build a comprehensive public education system very quickly.

In particular, this discussion traces the roots of a *literacy contract* (i.e., an implicit agreement in which schools require student compliance and promise economic reward in return) in Mexico, which I argue took shape following the Revolution: a time at which formal public education was introduced into the most outlying areas of the nation, and at which the nation's market structure was shaking off the last vestiges of foreign control in order to function as a capitalist market structure: a structure that scholars argue depends on the continual supply of trained labor (King, 1994; Levinson, 2001; Marsiske, 2000; Monroy, 1999). However, while developing urban centers functioned according to this economic model, significant sectors of the countryside continued to survive based on indigenous collectives and small-scale family farming. This family labor model does not interface with the demands of capitalism, including the delayed gratification of education. However, Mexico "sold" this kind of thinking to its rural citizens via rhetorics with which this population was intimately familiar: religious rhetorics of sacrifice and redemption (Dewey, 1926). In this way, I suggest that the priorities of SEP's national programs, which developed following the revolutionary period, do not always mesh with the needs and priorities of rural communities. This disjuncture, I believe, impacts students' decisions to leave school, as much as does migration or any other factor. However, my interest here is not to critique the Mexican education system but to account for the disjuncture that students feel.

To that end, I take a descriptive approach, surveying the development of public education through precolonial, colonial, and postcolonial periods so as to outline a framework for thinking about the impact of contextual forces on Mexican education and the ways in which these patterns continue to impact rural students' experiences and decisions today. From there, I consider more recent factors, including teacher training and centralized curriculum. Along the way, I offer brief parallel analyses of developmental phases in U.S. school systems, in order to contextualize my discussions and to highlight the similarities and differences between educational histories and structures of the two nations. Commensurate with historical frameworks like Deborah Brandt's theory of literacy sponsorship (2001), phases of educational history in both the United States and Mexico can be tied to prominent moments in political shifts and military action. Specifically, as each nation fought for increasing levels of political autonomy and worked in commensurate ways to define a national consciousness, it likewise expanded and defined its education system, such that formal education in both nations has historically been tied to the civic formation of individuals (Churchill and Levy, 2012; Glenn, 2012; Martínez Jiménez, 1996; Meneses, 1983). An additional similarity is the process that both nations engaged in—though in different ways—to separate public schooling from its initial involvement with religious sponsorship of Protestantism in the United States (Churchill and Levy, 2012) and the Catholic Church in Mexico (Hernandez-Zamora, 2010). In contrast to these areas of overlap, the most crucial distinction between the educational systems of the two nations is that the U.S. system has largely been decentralized (Glenn, 2012), whereas Mexico's system has been highly centralized (Arnaut, 1998). These two contrasting approaches are rooted in the material differences between the United States' foundational emphasis on self-governance as opposed to centuries of colonial control in Mexico. In the former case, early American colonialists focused their efforts on building a new national consciousness and infrastructure, but they did not include indigenous groups in their plans for education and government (Cremin, 1980). In contrast, once Mexico gained political and economic autonomy, mestizo populations were firmly established, and the national government targeted all populations, including indigenous groups, for education and civic engagement (King, 1994; Meneses, 1983). These distinctions, I argue, continue to create subtle differences between the ways in which students—particularly those with less power—may respond to education in each national setting. For instance, as a partial demonstration of the ways in which this history manifests itself in Mexico, I close this chapter with a final anecdote that explores the town of Villachuato's contemporary response and resistance to authority: a pattern that suggests that loyalty is felt most strongly at the community level than through ties to church, school, or other institutions. This last conclusion will have further implications for my analysis of additional social and education-based data in further chapters as I consider how citizens in rural Mexico have encountered education in their home communities, as well as in U.S. schools.

## FORMAL EDUCATION IN RURAL MEXICO THROUGH THE REVOLUTION

While rich formal education traditions can be traced throughout Mesoamerica (Jiménez and Smith, 2008) beginning with the Olmec civilization from 1500 B.C.E. to 150 C.E. (Reagan, 2000), the first external literacy sponsor was the Catholic Church. As part of Spain's colonizing efforts (Gonzalbo Aizpuru, 2000), the Church functioned as the conduit for an ideology that helped create compliance with the new econonomic model of colonialism: a model that allows for participation by a minority and actively excludes the majority of the population from econonmic participation. One of the steps in this process, argues Mexican scholar Gregorio Hernandez-Zamora, was the creation of a category of illiteracy. That is, the colonialist efforts, as manifested by the Catholic Church, categorized indigenous groups as "illiterate," both to solicit control of the nation and to convince the newly illiterate populace that they needed the educational services that the Church, and later the State, provides (2010). In this way, educational institutions in the colonial period focused little on the needs of local populations (Gonzalbo Aizpuru, 2000; Tanck de Estrada, 1989), nor on the existing traditions of knowledge making and transmission that already existed among indigenous groups (Bonfil, 1996; Jiménez and

Smith, 2008). Rather, they created a sense of literacy crisis so as to establish their own importance. As explained earlier in this book, the parellel concept of literacy crisis in the United States emerged not out of a senes of deficit, but rather from a sense of falling standards. That is, while the latter half of the twentieth century has inspired concern about school quality, earlier moments in U.S. history have looked more hopefully at education (Trimbur, 1991). For instance, during the colonial and revolutionary periods in the United States, foundational discussions about nation building and self-governance included debate about the best format and contents of education, ultimately leading to a utilitarian orientation toward education and a strong level of control at the state level (Cremin, 1980; Glenn, 2012).

As numerous Mexican scholars have pointed out, however, the history of their nation is imbued with a sense of struggle for control over education (Arnaut, 1998; Flores-Crespo, 2004; Greaves Laine, 2001; Marsiske, 2006; Martínez González and Valle Baeza, 2008; Meneses, 1983; Rodríguez-Gómez, 1999), as well as ongoing legacies of the often negative impact of powerful sponsoring intitutions on the lives of individuals (Gonzalbo Aizpuru, 2000; Tanck de Estrada, 1999). Early on, building on the ideological foundation described above, religious schools were founded throughout colonized Mexico as a means of spreading both the Catholic faith and the Spanish language. Moreover, while missionaries' core intention was religious conversion (Flores, 1966), general literacy instruction became necessary as they realized that, "era necesario enseñarlos primero a ser hombres y después a ser cristianos" (it was necessary first to teach them how to be men and then how to be Christians) (Kobayashi 1999, p. 14). To that end, the missionary schools of sixteenth- and seventeen-century Mexico included basic lessons in reading and writing, but they likewise treated European handicrafts, animal husbandry, music and literature (Flores, 1966). In this way, the goal was complete colonialization: to convert people not only to a new faith, but a new set of cultural customs and values. Further, the particular blend of religious orders that arrived in New Spain is significant. Among the most important of these were the Dominicans, a highly authoritative order who were among the first to arrive, and the Jesuits, who worked extensively in rural areas and were interested in teaching practical reasoning and life skills (Martínez, 1981). Both of these influences would be later expressed in the creation of a public education system that, on the one hand, claims a pragmatic focus but that, on the other hand, maintains a highly centralized structure which often overlooks the needs present in individual rural sites. Interestingly, although the education system in the United States developed a much more decentralized model, scholars have similarly noted the reliance of this model on religious rhetorics of morality. In particular, the Puritan tradition emphasized redemption but promised it only to a few. Relying on these rhetorics, the U.S. education system arguably continues to emphasize the importance of the work ethic at the expense of those students who, for whatever reason, do not succeed within its structure (Churchill and Levy, 2012). In this way, such rhetorics are used in the United States in order to "blame the victim" for his or her school failures (Valenzuela, 1999).

The second major historical stage in Mexican education took place between the Independence movement (1810–21) and the Revolution (1910–20). During this transitional timeframe, the state became the custodian of education and established its goal of realizing universal education within Mexico. The most important figurehead of this era was Benito Juárez: a man of indigenous origin who eventually rose to take the presidency of his newly independent nation in 1858. Well aware of the importance of education to nation building, Juárez declared education to be both a right and an obligation of all Mexican citizens (Martínez, 1981; Martínez Jiménez, 1996). Although schools were expanded under Juárez's leadership and subsequent presidencies, the new nation lacked the economic resources to extend education to its entire population. Part of the source of these difficulties included the geographic diversity of the nation and its population (Arnaut, 1998), as well as continued influence of foreign interests. That is, although Mexico had won its political independence, European and American interests were still largely dominant in Mexican economics (Villegas et al., 1995). Among these factions, the Catholic Church itself still owned enough land to be able to wield strong political influence (Martínez, 1981), which was a strong source of friction in the new nation, as liberal factions within the new government sought to negate the Church's economic and ideological influence (Martínez Jiménez, 1996). In this content, Juárez worked to separate Church and State in many important social institutions, including education. However, educational growth was slow throughout Juárez's presidency and subsequent leadership during the nineteenth century. In particular, during the long, problematic presidency of Porfirio Díaz (1884–1911), which eventually led to the Mexican Revolution, little investment was made in rural education, such that growth in functional literacy rates remained low throughout the nation (Martínez Jiménez, 1996). By the turn of the twentieth century, only half of the Mexican population had attended some form of schooling, and only 30 percent of Mexicans could read and write in Spanish (Martínez Jiménez, 1996; Rockwell, 1996; Vaughan, 1977). Further, those who were educated under this system were primarily the elite, urban members of society (Bernardino, 1978). So, while public education existed between the wars, equal access to it did not. Moreover, the political struggle over control of education continued through this period, even though the colonial influence had—officially speaking, at least—ended. Similarly, in the United States the period between the American Revolution and the Civil War was characterized by a strong desire to expand formal education, although the nation's increasing land mass made it difficult to reach all citizens. In the context of this period of political prosperity and expansionist mentality, pioneer families pressed westward and championed a sense of self-reliance: a value that continued to characterize an emphasis on local control and parent involvement in education once subsequent decades brought formal schooling into broader geographic reaches of the country (Cremin, 1953).

The period following the Revolution, roughly 1920–30, represents the most important stage in the creation of a formal system of public education in Mexico: a period still known as the "golden age" of rural Mexican education (Arnaut, 1998). Following the battle cries for "land and education" (Hughes, 1950), many rural citizens were still left waiting for access to education, as well as for a true agrarian reform (Jiménez Alarcón, 1975). In response to the former issue, José Vasconcelos, the minister of public education following the Revolution, championed the expansion of rural education in particular, as well as the establishment of public offices to better manage education throughout the nation (Arnaut, 1998). Vasconcelos was commissioned to do this work in part because the new leadership after the Revolution recognized, as Juárez had before them, the importance of a national education system: "Illiteracy is one of the greatest obstacles to our goal of attaining common ideals for the different cultural groups that constitute our nation and to the achievement of economic and social well-being among our workers and farmers" (Federal Security Agency, 1945, p. vii). Implicit in this statement is an assumption of the importance not only of cultural unity and economic development but also of political control (Moreno Fernández, 1985). If illiteracy (i.e., the lack of reading and writing skills in Spanish, as opposed to indigenous literacy skills of any kind) was perceived of as an obstacle to nation-building, the related assumption was that nationalism relies on a degree of both hierarchy and homogenization (Arnaut, 1998; Martínez Jiménez, 1996; Meneses Morales, 1983). Indeed, this orientation, even if implicit, is congruent with contemporary theories of the role of education in the reproduction of social hierarchies: Schools in the capitalist system impart skills and culture, creating a homogenized yet stratified work force (Althusser, 2001), and students internalize school values and behaviors as a form of symbolic social standing (Bourdieu, 1998). As students move through their formal education, then, they become a part of larger patterns of social reproduction as they learn both labor market skills and state allegiance. Therefore, as Mexico's new public education system developed along a centralized model—influenced both by previous colonial patterns and new national needs—it both expanded school access (Arnaut, 1998) and functioned in part to organize the new nation's social strata in the context of a developing capitalist market structure (Meneses Morales, 1983; Moreno Fernández, 1985). Further, schools' promise to offer a better post-Revolutionary livelihood to the nation's youth constitutes a developing literacy contract orientation. However, as I will explain below, the fact that industrialization, and therefore wage labor, had not reached many rural areas throughout the country meant that the demands and promises of the literacy contract were at times incongruent with local realities. In contrast, the Industrial Revolution in the United States, followed by the nation's increased political significance as a world power following World War II, meant that public education had reached a period of high prosperity and promise by the first half of the twentieth century. While rural families in the United States report feelings of alienation similar to those identified in Mexico (Brandt, 2001; Brooke, 2011), the nation's ongoing urbanization, along with the prosperity of the postwar years, outweighed these perspectives. By and large, the literacy contract that was developing during the early twentieth century in the United States boded well. Increasing sectors of society—including women, African Americans, and the working classes—were gaining access to higher levels of education, as well as the economic rewards that it promised (Cremin, 1980). It wasn't until that same education system began to reach its material limits during the 1970s and 1980s that rhetorics of relative crisis entered into public debate (Berliner and Biddle, 1995).

Despite the incongruence between labor training and opportunity in Mexico during the early twentieth century, a process of enculturation related to the literacy contract began to take place in 1921, when José Vasconcelos officially took charge of the newly reconstituted Secretaría de Educación Pública (SEP) and began to design a national curriculum for use throughout the new nation. Despite Vasconcelos's enthusiasm, and his continued dedication to rural development (Arnaut, 1998; Jiménez Alarcón, 1975), this work was not without its challenges, as two-thirds of the population still lived in rural areas, and 65 percent of Mexicans were illiterate (Ramírez, 1982). Moreover, the education system itself remained underdeveloped, and there was no sustained means of training teachers: "In 1922, approximately 100 untrained teachers were struggling to maintain a few federal rural schools" (Federal Security Agency, 1945, p. vii). At the same time, under the new constitution, primary education was made obligatory, and many new schools began to be constructed in rural areas. It was at this point that, thanks to the expansion of school infrastructure and teacher training under Vasconcelos's leadership (Arnaut, 1998), communities like Villachuato finally began to have access to at least a primary education, including basic reading, writing, and arithmetic skills. However, it is important to note that Vasconcelos's crusade toward education access was not entirely altruistic (Meneses Morales, 1983). Indeed, the new state had a strong nationalizing agenda that it actualized in large part through the public schools—an implicit agenda that caused considerable political debate during the process of the creation of a centralized education system following the Revolution (Arnaut, 1998). To this day, however, Mexican public schools retain their tie to nationalism. For instance, schools hold elaborate weekly civic ceremonies in lieu of class time (figure 3.1).

Figure 3.1. Weekly civic ceremony at Villachuato Secondary School

In order to appreciate the role of this nationalizing project, it is important to understand the nature of the Mexican Revolution itself. The Revolution did not operate as a single, concentrated force, but rather as a series of localized conflicts and staged resistance efforts at the regional level. As such, the Revolution was a loosely connected collection of guerilla efforts, rather than a carefully staged war with a united front. The result was a liberated but very fragmented nation, and loyalties were most strongly felt at the regional level (Rockwell, 1996). One of the principal efforts in the aftermath of the war, then, was a movement to nationalize: Finally independent of both foreign political and economic control, Mexico had to pull together its identity and loyalties so as to build a new democracy (Meneses Morales, 1983) and a sustainable domestic market (Moreno Fernández, 1985). Congruent with Althusser's theory of schools as important political tools (2001), the spread of public education in Mexico took on utmost importance: "The educators and anthropologists of the 1920s who articulated the ideal of the *Escuela Rural Mexicana* proposed a 'civilizing mission' to transform rural society" (Rockwell, 1996, p. 304). This approach, however, is not unlike the colonial creation of a category of illiterates. In the same vein, rural knowledge and practices were not valued in the new capitalist marketplace, so a national literacy campaign was conducted in order to convince rural citizens of their need for formal education (King, 1994). Furthermore, according to a literacy contract mentality, this civilizing mission would necessarily have been predicated on an assumption that rural areas would begin to participate in industrial labor models, such that they would both need to train laborers and that these same laborers would benefit from their participation in the open market. However, because so many rural areas have remained disconnected from large-scale commercial systems, the literacy contract held little promise for them, and in many ways, rural communities have not complied with its terms.

In the remainder of this chapter, I pay special attention to the period following the Revolution, both because it is historically important as the period during which Mexican education was formalized and because it is ideologically important to the way that this education system and its commensurate contract orientation—despite its incongruence with many rural conditions—was spread nationally. As Deborah Brandt's analysis has shown (2001), sponsorship of literacy in the United States shifted from Church to State in the nineteenth century, and scholars have identified ongoing vestiges of religious rhetorics in our school discussions (Churchill and Levy, 2012; Glenn, 2012). Similarly, Mexico's patterns of sponsorship have followed the same trajectory, although the transition to secularism occurred more recently, and the same kind of rhetorics continue to characterize education in Mexico, as well. For instance, in order to build a new infrastructure, the Mexican government relied on familiar vehicles and rhetorics, particularly religious ones, to spread its nationalizing agenda. Like the Jesuits and Dominicans before them, the new rural educators *were* a kind of missionary force—albeit with a new secular agenda and message (Santiago Sierra, 1973). Indeed, as Vaughan (1977) suggests, this kind of strategy makes sense, as the influence of religion remained dominant up through the beginning of the twentieth century, such that loyalties, especially in more rural areas, remained tied to the Church and family. However, as formal education gradually centralized under the new government, education itself became increasingly migratory, such that young people were obliged to leave their home communities in order to seek the personal advancement that education implicitly offers. That is, because quite often no commercial employment options exist in areas of rural Mexico like Villachuato, and becoming educated for a profession means sacrificing geographic proximity to one's family and home community. Therefore, in order to motivate people to pursue formal education, the newly formed SEP had to both normalize and glorify the process, which it did in part by employing religious rhetorics of self-sacrifice and personal salvation. In particular, these rhetorics prize the process of sacrificing one's identity affinity and geographic location within the home community in favor of pursuing formal education, which presumably improves one's personal satisfaction and professional opportunities. As I will show later in this chapter, the rhetorics that rural educators still use to describe their careers, challenges, and goals is that of a missionary presence that aims to convert and "save" rural communities—even when the curriculum that these teachers advocate is not congruent with the community's actual needs.

## A SCHOOL WITHOUT WALLS: THE ROOTS OF
## RURAL EDUCATION IN MEXICO

In both Mexico and the United States, significant stages in the development of a national public education system coincide with equally significant moments in the two nations' political histories. As just described, this process in Mexico can be divided into the period prior to Independence (pre-1810), the period between Independence and the Revolution (1821–1910), and the period following the Revolution (post-1920). In the United States, historians of education history have divided similar time frames into the colonial period (1600–1779) during which time ideological frameworks were laid; the period between the Revolution and the Civil War (1779–1865) when a government-sponsored education system began to be developed; the Civil War through World War I (1865–1918), a series of years when education expanded to serve more groups, including African Americans; and the contemporary period following the world wars, when education expanded through measures like the G.I. Bill (Butts and Cremin, 1953; Glenn, 2012). Although the specific ranges of years vary between the two nations, the basic stages of development are fairly similar, as each nation gained increasing political and economic autonomy and, in turn, developed mass education programs both to prepare young people for the labor market and also to train them in civic values. In the United States, these values focused on democratic participation and local decision making (Glenn, 2012), while in Mexico they evoked Mesoamerican ideals of collectivism (Bonfil, 1996). Moreover in the United States, the need to prepare laborers was particularly strong in the wake of the Industrial Revolution (Butts and Cremin, 1953), whereas in Mexico, the civic purpose of education was more strongly felt during the early stages of new nationhood (Meneses, 1983).

As noted above, two of Mexico's principal needs following the Revolution were to develop an economic base and to unify a national consciousness (Montañez, 2007). On both counts, education was an important medium that needed to be expanded—most notably in rural areas, where the majority of Mexicans still lived and few schools existed. However, there were at least two important issues to be dealt with regarding education: how to recruit and train teachers in rural areas and what to have them teach (Hughes, 1950). In particular, the latter question was quite crucial because, up to that time, rural education had been largely controlled by the Catholic Church, and the new government wanted to regain cultural and political control of rural areas (Santiago Sierra, 1973). However, at the beginning of the 1920s, there was almost no government-sponsored schooling in rural areas, and little to no teacher training in those areas. Moreover, in order to spread a new nationalism approach to rural education, it was important to secure cooperation from rural communities themselves (Méndez, 1981). To that end, the new SEP office had to determine not only what things were important to teach people, but also what kind of curriculum and delivery modes these communities would accept.

In order to address these issues of school distribution and acceptance, José Vasconcelos administered a program to send professional teachers and practitioners out into rural communities in order to determine the latter's needs, and what kind of education would best suit these needs (Ramírez, 1982). These groups of educators, then, had two principal goals: first to investigate communities' whereabouts, conditions, and needs; and second to begin basic instruction, so as to build an infrastructure of schools and teachers: "Supervising teachers, called *missioners* [italics mine], went out individually to work with those who were serving as teachers, to give support for the new schools, and to do all the things necessary to make the rural schools an institution which would actually teach the rural people new patterns of living" (Federal Security Agency, 1945, p. vii). These teams of educators, called "cultural missions," worked on literacy classes for children and adults, teacher training for community leaders, and the creation of community infrastructures, including school buildings, drainage systems, and health services (Santiago Sierra, 1973). These activities, particularly the building of school and community centers, were completed with the help of the townspeople themselves. These centers were intended to serve all levels and interests of the community; they became known as "the house of the people" (Hughes, 1950, p. 11). In this way, the cultural missions functioned as Mexico's first rural normal schools (Dewey, 1926; Santiago Sierra, 1973).

An important leader of this work, Rafael Ramírez was the product of one of the Porfirian normal schools of the late nineteenth century (Ramírez, 1982). In contrast to his own conservative training, however, Ramírez was strongly influenced by Marxist thought and particularly by Dewey's and Rousseau's conceptualizations of education. He supported, therefore, a vision of participatory education focused on community needs. At the same time, he recognized the difficulty of designing localized programming in Mexico because of the nation's extreme cultural and topographical diversity. Even so, under Ramírez, the cultural missions—similar to contemporary place-based models of rural education that scholars like Robert Brooke advocates (2011)—worked as much as possible to attend to local needs, and to take education out of the school building and into the fields and related work places, producing the foundation for later models of vocational and agricultural curricula. As such, he advocated "a school without walls": localized education that attends to specific community needs and works with individuals to help them solve their own problems (Ramírez, 1924, cited in Hughes, 1950). In this way, Ramírez's pedagogy reflected his belief that economic and social advancement is intimately tied to education. In order to get ahead in life, Ramírez argued, rural citizens need to learn to think critically. That is, the goal of rural education for Ramírez was, "que el hombre piensa en el *por qué* hace tal cosa, *para qué* debe hacerlo, y *a quien* beneficia con el productor de su trabajo" (that people think about the *why* of a given thing, the question of *to what end* of doing it, and *who* benefits from the product of such work) (Bernardino, 1978, p. 52).

Ramírez's efforts were successful in the sense that they helped create community interest in education, an important foundation for the broader federal project of delivering national curriculum. In contrast, while Ramírez's work with the cultural missions was innovative and socially aware, these more liberal aspects of the project did not endure as revolutionary zeal waned. According to rural secondary school director Francisco Reyes, the grassroots energy of Ramírez's local efforts could not compete with the development of a larger, more organized and politically powerful education system (personal communication, April 18, 2008). Severely diminished by 1938, the cultural missions were largely replaced by another educational system that had been developing alongside them: the nation's normal schools. In essence, the cultural missions had functioned as traveling normal schools for a decade and a half. However, under the new, more stabilized government, it became increasingly possible to develop and deliver a uniform curriculum to the variety of urban and rural schools that had been built throughout the country. Indeed, by 1942, the curriculum at rural and urban normal schools had been synthesized into one model: a unified curricular model that more effectively served the nation's own ideology and agenda of civic loyalty and economic productivity. In this way, the attention to local issues in education disappeared from the Mexican consciousness and becoming educated increasingly meant that young people were obliged to relocate to urban environments, as has also happened in rural areas of the United States (Brooke, 2011). What is interesting to note, however, is the way in which both programs—first the cultural missions and later the normal schools themselves—rely on the same kinds of religious rhetorics, casting teachers time and again not simply as educational agents, but as important missionary representatives of a larger state agenda.

Therefore, while the new educational mission initially focused on the needs of rural communities (including curriculum that was tied to local activities), it was eventually replaced by a centralized system that served the State's nation-building interests and functioned more efficiently in fostering rapid expansion of education throughout the country. This new centralized system, however, was also built on the earlier foundations of the concept of illiteracy that was established during the colonial period: a belief that rural and indigenous knowledge practices do not "count" as literacy, and that the lack of a more valuable institutional literacy must be corrected in these communities (Gonzalbo Aizpuru, 2000; Hernandez-Zamora, 2010). In this way, education was developed for an industrial market (Monroy, 1999; King, 1994), even though rural communities didn't have access to wage labor. This incongruence created problems, as rural communities were asked to adopt values—and to make commensurate sacrifices—that are the foundation of mass education in a capitalist market. Many of the frictions described in the latter chapters of this book have their roots in this general historical disconnect. For now, though, I turn my attention to the ways that this legacy has played out in the lives of rural Mexican teachers. Specifically, in this next section, I draw on Bradley Levinson's concept of the process required to become an educated person. In many contexts, Levinson argues, becoming educated means that an individual must relinquish his or her initial identity, drawn from the values of the home community, and replace it with a new professional identity (1996). The next section considers this process in the lives of teachers who work in the Villachuato community.

## A CIVILIZING MISSION: TEACHER TRAINING FOLLOWING THE REVOLUTION

Teacher training constitutes an important component of the development of the Mexican education system that also reveals an important distinction between systems in Mexico and the United States. Principally, it is interesting to note that the systemization of teacher training through the development of a robust system of normal schools in Mexico coincides almost exactly with the discontinuation of normal schools in the United States. While the United States experienced a relative "golden age" of normal schools from approximately the 1870s through the 1920s (Fraser, 2007; Ogren, 2005) these schools were diverse, and, given the nation's decentralized education system, the rigor of such training varied widely throughout the country. Following World War II, increased demand for education at all levels sparked interest in "all purpose state colleges," and the university system took over the responsibility of training the nation's teachers (Fraser, 2007). Not long before the United States discontinued its normal schools, during the 1920s and 1930s, Mexico began building a large, standardized system of normal schools to train teachers for its newly established centralized education system (Arnaut, 1998).

According to SEP's self-authored history of public education in Mexico, the most difficult conquest "es la intelectual y moral de un pueblo entero. . . . El secreto está en la educación de las masas populares y el factor principal en las escuelas normales" (is that of the intellectual and moral fiber of the people. . . . The secret is in mass education, and the principal factor is the normal schools) (Méndez, 1981, p. 447). Written in 1981, the SEP's consideration of its own origin betrays a strong awareness of the power of education to unite a nation and the importance of a workforce that is willing to deliver the message. SEP found that workforce in its teachers—and it found the means of forming these teachers in a centralized system of normal schools. In this way, teachers became the evangelists for the "civilizing mission" of public education: they were trained under a specific orientation "to subordinate the three Rs to the betterment of rural life" (Rockwell, 1996, p 304). Moreover, by both internalizing and fostering the nation's new conceptualization of the educated person, these teachers spread a new ideology commensurate with liberated Mexico's goal of unifying the nation through the development of "a cooperative, class-conscious, solitary peasantry" (Knight, 1994, cited in Rockwell, 1996, p. 304). Normal schools are, therefore, an essential component of the Mexican education system because of their particular post-Revolutionary history and because they are still the principal method used to train teachers. Rather than attending postsecondary classes in a university setting, aspiring teachers in Mexico attend four years of normal school training focused on the grade level they wish to teach: preschool (kindergarten), primary (grades 1–6), or secondary (grades 7–9). Thereafter, rather than applying for jobs directly, graduating teachers are assigned to a school based on the qualifications and needs of the teachers' union and SEP.

Based in part on foreign influences like John Dewey's progressive education models and in part on the existing Porfirian normal schools, the new generation of normal schools developed slowly, emerging first in urban centers (Jiménez Alarcón, 1975) and spreading gradually toward more rural areas until it became broad enough to replace the migratory "missionary" model of educational training (Santiago Sierra, 1973). In rural areas in particular, these schools were important because they allowed people without prior access to formal teacher training to become professionalized (Cardinal Reyes and Bolaños Martínez, 1981), but they also resulted in the stratification of professionally versus nonprofessionally trained teachers (Arnaut, 1998). Moreover, given the geographic diversity of smaller communities, many of these schools were designed as boarding schools—a feature that had the added effect of removing students from their home communities long enough to reorient them toward a new value system (Rockwell, 1996). Congruent with Bradley Levinson's explanation of identity development mentioned above, higher levels of education in Mexico require students to sacrifice the values and assumptions of their home community in exchange for a new identity based in the ideologies of the education system itself, which, in turn, responds to specific economic pressures. This is, he argues, the real process of becoming an educated person: adjusting one's identity, rather than acquiring a certain set of skills or knowledge (Levinson, 1996). And in fact, the early literacy goals of rural normal schools in Michoacán and elsewhere were formative, rather than comprehensive: "Más importante a la Escuela Normal el aspecto formativo que el informativo" (More important to a Normal School education is the formative, rather than the informative, aspect; Vela 1975, p. 13). Moreover, this identity shift occurs through exposure to the discourses present in the new environment: discourses concerning the nature and value of education (Arnaut, 1998). In the case of rural Mexicans attending post-Revolutionary normal school training, these discourses reflected the importance of education to personal development and social responsibility (Martínez Jimenez, 1996). However, because urban centers provide more varied economic opportunities, schools' values (i.e., the promise that formal education will lead to increased life chances) were more in tune with reality. In rural settings, on the other hand, the identity shift that young teachers made tended to be more jarring both because they were often physically removed from their home communities and because the values they learned as educators was sometimes incongruous with the realities in the communities that they had come from.

Recent data that I drew from teachers working today in rural areas like Villachuato and its neighboring town, Puruándiro, the county seat, demonstrates the enduring nature of this process of identity transformation. Of the teachers I interviewed, all but two were from rural areas of Michoacán, and nearly all were trained at state-operated normal schools in the region.[15] Likewise, nearly all of the teachers I interviewed came from the kind of large families (between five and nine siblings) that were common in this area up through the 1970s, and the majority of these families were led by stay-at-home mothers and fathers who worked either as *campesinos* in the fields, or as craftsmen (e.g., shoemaker). As a result of this reliance on a single wage earner, families often could not financially support their children's education. In many cases, teachers-to-be had to work at the same time as attending school, which meant that the process took longer. In other cases, they had to wait a period of time while another sibling used the family resources to become educated before pursuing their own studies. "There were so many of us, and not very many resources," the secondary school director in Puruándiro told me. "So, some of us got to study, and others of us had to rest. Once some of them had gotten through, they could help the others."

Once these young professionals finally obtained their teacher training, they did, as Bradley Levinson predicts (1996), begin to identify more with their new, professional community than with their community of origin. The director in Puruándiro was, like so many educators in the area, among the first in his family to become educated. "My parents basically didn't study," he told me in a hushed voice:

> In those times, it was very difficult to do so. My father has told me that he went to primary school, and didn't quite finish. He just went to learn how to read and write, and that was sufficient. And my mother, the truth is it pains me to tell you this, but she doesn't know how to read or write [laughs, embarrassed]. And we're all professionalized [my siblings and I]. So, as you can see, she really worried about us—preparing us. Because she told us that her life experience was very difficult, and she wanted us to prepare ourselves for something better. To be able to defend ourselves. And the most important thing was to learn something.

The juxtaposition of embarrassment and appreciation with which he narrates his story suggests an important tension in his loyalties. While he understands his parents' hardships and appreciates his mother's work to make possible a better life for her children, he is, at the same time, ashamed of his illiterate parentage. Having actualized their own hopes for him, he has reached a higher social level, one that brings with it a new set of values, the most important of which is literacy itself. In this way, this school director's experience is an excellent example of the kind of identity shift that Levinson argues is part of the process of becoming an educated person. At the same time, it likewise suggests to me an enduring pattern of religious themes embedded in Mexican education. That is, having made the necessary sacrifices, educational professionals like this man believe that they have attained personal salvation through the realization of a professional life.

Indeed, these themes of sacrifice and redemption are the first evidence of a missionary-like rhetoric that endures in rural Mexican education. According to the logic of this religious rhetoric—which functions congruently with the logic of delayed gratification embedded in the literacy contract—achieving an education requires young people to sacrifice connections to their home community, but it also promises professional reward. Moreover, this kind of rhetoric was apparent not only in rural educators' stories of their own training, but likewise in their discussions of students. Describing the hardships of students from Villachuato who pursue their education at higher levels, the secondary school director admits,

> I only know a few people who have their kids at the university in Morelia. Very few. Like four or five. And do you know what these kids do? They work—they work a lot. Waiters, shipping. All that. It's hard for them to study. They have to go and rent—they don't have houses. There are some student houses, and they're full of people. So, they go and they make a lot of sacrifices.

Implicit in this school director's conversation with me was his belief that this kind of hard work and self-sacrifice is *how it should be*. Commensurate with a literacy contract mentality, he believes that young people *should* make sacrifices for education, most particularly because it offers them a better life. To this end, he spoke glowingly of the few students who have continued on, admiring their work ethic and the wisdom with which they have made their life choices. In a related vein, another teacher explained to me that there is much more hope for students now: "Well, the world is much more up-to-date now, you know. So it's not likely that kids will only go to primary school anymore. They're going to keep studying. And to get work. We have to study, right? To get work. To do better in life." Statements like this one assume that formal education leads students to acquire professional jobs; however, there is no paid employment in Villachuato beyond agricultural day labor. Further, because the majority of the students with whom I spoke do not wish to leave their family and their town, the promise of education is incongruent with the values and life choices in Villachuato, and many townspeople remain unmotivated to prioritize formal education. At the same time, the assumption that education honorably involves self-sacrifice and personal reward is evidence of a continued association between education and religious values that has characterized Mexican education through the colonial period and the cultural missions following the Revolution, and up through the current structure of SEP and its normal schools. Furthermore, this association, which I argue was actively drawn upon in order to win rural communities' compliance with Mexico's new public school system, represents the foundation of a literacy contract orientation in Mexico. As a wage labor market expanded throughout many areas of the country, a contract orientation toward education likewise developed, though dressed in the familiar religious rhetorics of moral uprightness and delayed gratification that had characterized earlier eras of Mexican education.

## MEXICO'S CONTEMPORARY CURRICULUM AND ITS IMPACT ON RURAL STUDENTS

What I have traced thus far is the creation of a public education system that paralleled Mexico's transition into an independent wage labor economy. During the decades between Mexico's Independence movement and the Revolution, the vestiges of colonialism meant that foreign economic interests continued to dominate much of the Mexico economy, such that the budding nation's full conversion into an open capitalist market with commercial opportunities occurred most fully following the Revolution. In this way, the State's national literacy campaign took place alongside this economic transition. Furthermore, given these twin processes, Mexico's new school system did begin to take on a contract mentality with respect to literacy, though it was manifested through older, more familiar rhetorics of religious sacrifice and delayed gratification. It should now be clear, then, that there were several historical reasons for the development of a very centralized education system in Mexico: deep roots in colonialism, the State's post-Revolutionary need to create a national psyche, and the logistics of creating a massive public education system in a very narrow window of time. These are some good reasons, and not necessarily an agenda of control. All the same, this is a history of some significant political struggles (Greaves Laine, 2001; Montañez, 2007), and I do believe that this legacy has certain effects on the ways in which education plays out for some groups in the population. In the remainder of this chapter, I briefly consider the impact of this history on the way that curricula have developed, and I introduce some patterns of behavior in rural settings with respect to interfacing with authority. In subsequent chapters, I move more deeply into ethnographic accounts of education at the local level, in the context of the broad history laid out here. Finally, toward the end of this book, I consider how this history, as well as contemporary patterns, impacts the experiences of students who migrate to the United States.

Alongside all of this history, curriculum itself has, of course, had its role: one that is perhaps best traced through the nation's highly standardized textbooks, which I mentioned at the opening of this chapter. These SEP-pro-duced textbooks have been distributed to every child in the nation since the 1960s: a policy that officially emerged out of a response to the government's realization that, although schools were now available in rural areas, many students did not attend because they could not afford the supplies. Therefore, in order to incentivize students to go to school—which, of course, helped to foster an ongoing nationalizing agenda—the central government established a system of free books (in addition to school supplies, and in some cases scholarships for uniforms, food, and transportation). Even today, those who work in the textbook branch of SEP passionately describe the benefits of free books, which include a national identity, as well as the importance of equality (L. Barba, personal communication, July 17, 2011). However, despite the long-term success of this project, the history of national textbooks has not always been without conflicts. Indeed, as Cecilia Greaves Laine points out in her historical study of the roots of the free textbook system, the initial planning stages of the project were rife with tensions that elevated to the level of national uproar about the content and control of books that would be issued to every young Mexican. Although that conflict—as evidenced by the fact that private religious schools protested the adoption of the nationally produced books—was, most significantly, evidence of ongoing tensions be-tween the government and the Catholic Church to control education (2001), it also suggests a profound awareness of the significance of centrally produced information and curriculum that it utilized throughout the entire nation. Indeed, while much good certainly comes from these free textbooks—par-ticularly for students who might not otherwise have access to education—I contend that a centralized curriculum necessarily has its challenges, given the diversity of student audiences in a nation like Mexico. Indeed, as a brief overview of Mexico's curriculum and textbooks will show, the further that SEP's programs have developed, the more estranged rural communities have felt from the school process.

A broad historical read of the textbook archives in Mexico City reveals three principal curricular trends: mechanics and civic education (1960s–80s); canonical works and artistry (1980s–1993); and social constructivism and stu-dent processes (1993–present).[16] First, when SEP began distributing textbooks during the 1960s, the texts distributed revealed a clear link to a nationalizing agenda (Montañez, 2007). For instance, the sixth grade language arts reader published in 1960 was a chapter book about a boy who takes a road trip to various parts of Mexico, highlighting the nation's diverse geography, linguis-tic and cultural traditions, and industries. The use of formal education to transmit civic information is quite clear in this instance. At the same time, the presentation of information in this book is interesting because it likewise clearly considers a rural audience. For instance, themes like airplanes and long-distance travel are presented in such a way as to introduce them to communities that do not have access to travel and specialized technologies. However, while the reading materials in the 1960s sought to better inform rural citizens of their nation and of the broader world, the applied work was more mechanical in nature. The accompanying book of exercises assigned to sixth graders in 1960 focused primarily on drills and handwriting practice, an area of emphasis that endured, at least in practice, at many schools, particularly those in rural settings (Jiménez, Smith, and Martínez-León, 2003).

By the 1980s, however, the curricular focus had shifted significantly, losing both its tie to an explicit nationalizing agenda, as well as to its consideration of rural lifestyles. In 1985, the sixth grade language arts reader was an anthology of national and international authors consisting of brief readings from a variety of genres on a variety of topics. The book presents no central message, except for the general emphasis on the importance of literary appreciation and the practice of reading. In the introduction to the book, the author extols: "Read! Read well!" Here, then, is an emphasis on art for art's sake. This period of curricular history in Mexico is perhaps the most divorced from needs on the ground, though it does begin to press toward ideas of the pragmatism of reading (e.g., the author indicates that the practice of reading will help students learn to speak well). That is, this curricular phase begins to identify the utility of literacy for the sake of the individual, rather than predominantly for the sake of nation building. Further, this orientation begins to take on an almost rhetorical awareness of the connection between literacy training (i.e., reading) and an individual's ability to speak/present oneself in privileged circles (i.e., cultural capital). This shift was likely positive for rural communities in the sense that it highlights pragmatic aspects of literacy, though likewise negative in the sense that it identifies literacy as individualistic—an orientation that runs counter to the communal values of rural livelihood.

Finally, by 1993, a major pedagogical shift brought a social turn to the Mexican curriculum. Whereas earlier curricula had focused on mechanical skills and canonical texts, this new constructivist model shaped students' work into projects, thereby focusing their attention on social contexts and issues and requiring them to employ critical thinking and problem-solving skills. Indeed, by 2010, primary and secondary school textbooks had begun to directly reflect several components of a writing-process pedagogy: investigating, summarizing and responding, drafting and revising. In addition, there is new a focus on auto-evaluation (i.e., reflection). While one might expect that such curriculum would appeal in a pragmatic sense to students in rural communities, in practice this curricular conversion has been quite complex. In several of the states that have the highest numbers of rural and underprivileged students (Chiapas, Oaxaca, and Michoacán), political tensions have prevented the delivery and distribution of textbooks, as well as the adoption of new curriculum and the commensurate professional development training of area teachers. In addition, community members themselves purportedly resist such changes. In meetings with both SEP officials in Mexico City and school leaders in rural Michoacán, I was told that many parents just want their kids to learn quickly and efficiently how to read and write. They aren't interested in experiential learning; perhaps they don't trust it. While I was not able to cross-check this pattern directly via additional interviews, much of the data that I drew in the Villachuato community corroborates this understanding: What parents want is for their children to be able to *defenderse* (defend themselves) in life, able to use the tools of reading and writing. In addition, either for political or pedagogical reasons, many teachers have resisted these changes, such that, in my observations of Villachuato language arts classrooms, I witnessed a strong emphasis on grammar drills and handwriting exercises.

As curricular developments have progressed in Mexico's centralized public education system, the emphasis has drawn further and further away from rural communities. While an initial emphasis on civic engagement took pains to appeal to rural audiences, subsequent curricular plans—and their commensurate politics—haven't maintained that emphasis. As a result, rural communities have been increasingly alienated from the schools that serve them. And, as I argue later in this book, I believe that there is resistance toward taking on the full ideology of schools. That is, it's not that parents don't want their students to learn how to think critically—or, indeed, to have this tool— but they are resistant to taking on the full mindset of schools, because the schools don't truly serve them. They recognize at some level that the literacy contract is a danger to them because it asks young people to relinquish the values that hold the community together and make the local economy (i.e., the family farming unit) work. So, the contract mentality itself is a threat to rural life, and the mask of religious rhetorics doesn't work to fully dissuade the community from this fear—in large part, perhaps, because even religion itself has never had full sway. In the last section of this chapter, I briefly consider the community's response to institutional authority, which does not take precedence in such settings.

## COMMUNITY RESISTANCE TO INSTITUTIONAL AUTHORITY

In Villachuato, a community that is almost 100 percent Catholic and that has no other access to books than those that SEP provides, one might expect that a school promoting values of sacrifice and salvation would be well received. In many ways, community members in Villachuato do indeed accept their church and schools at face value, though at the same time, they seriously question and sometimes openly resist the authority and underlying ideologies of both institutions. In order to understand this ironic dualism, it is important to note that Villachuato, as a satellite unit of a much larger municipal seat located some twenty miles away, is without direct political leadership. There is no state presence in the town, other than an appointed treasurer who oversees the spending of funds to improve roads and install street lights. Nor is there any police presence or strong political identity within the town. The most important leadership figure, then, is the Catholic priest. Indeed, all major events in town—from private weddings and funerals to large-scale annual celebrations—are conducted under the auspices of the Church. Most townspeople—particularly women—attend mass regularly. Even so, my observation of religious events in the town suggested to me that their parallel importance was their function as a social gathering. In many ways, the townspeople of Villachuato adopted the Church authority as a means to structure these interactions; but they were willing to challenge that same authority if ever the Church's wishes shifted too strongly against their own.

The juxtaposition of masses and biblical doctrine with other social practices provides several examples of the ways in which Villachuato citizens utilize religion as a structure for social engagements. One important example is that of the large number of women's rosary groups that meet throughout town in the later afternoon/early evening. The women who attend these gatherings are typically married and spend their days at home cleaning and preparing meals while their husbands work in the fields. On the whole, there are many fewer opportunities for women to leave the home. Between five and six o'clock every day, however, many women set down their domestic and child care responsibilities and join together at a friend's home to recite the rosary and read daily scripture. There is no male presence at most of these gatherings, and the town priest is certainly not present. Rather, these rosary circles become a way for female friends to connect with each other as they practice their faith and afterward engage in a general discussion of the day's events. The religious purpose to their activity grants it importance, such that their husbands are not able to argue with this time spent away from the home. In a related example, the month or so between the Catholic holidays of Epiphany (January 6) and Ash Wednesday (forty days before Easter) becomes a time for community sharing in Villachuato. A regional custom of "waking up the baby Jesus" becomes an occasion for friends and neighbors to gather together to share an evening meal. In this example, the religious component of the gathering falls farther into the background as groups of friends and neighbors—again predominantly women—spend roughly two hours visiting and eating before engaging in a brief recitation of the rosary that is accompanied by small fireworks, confetti, and the distribution of gifts and cookies. In both of these examples, the Church is a kind of informal *sponsor* of social gatherings amongst friends and neighbors; and, while the religious component to each activity remains important, it was clear to me as an outsider how these events functioned covertly as a means for increased social autonomy, particularly for women.

At other times, the juxtaposition of religious and social elements is even more striking. In the next two examples, formal Church celebrations are augmented by large-scale social activity—sometimes to the point of provoking the Church's critique. First, December 12 is an important religious holiday in Mexico: the Día de Guadalupe (feast day of Mexico's virgin saint). Mass on this day is typically held at four or five in the morning, such that the congregation leaves the church thereafter just as light is breaking. When I left church in the company of friends after the Día de Guadalupe mass last year, I assumed that we would return to our respective homes to rest and spend time with family. In the plaza adjoining the church, however, I discovered a live band, stalls of freshly boiled corn rolled in mayonnaise, and men passing around plastic cups of punch—spiked with tequila. These festivities, begun at seven in the morning, did not end until much later that afternoon. Throughout the day, a parade was held, firecrackers were lit for sport, and large quantities of alcoholic punch were consumed. In this sense, the Church holiday was the motivating factor for a social gathering; but thereafter that gathering in many ways took on an identity of its own.

The use of Church feast days as a catalyst for large-scale public gatherings is even more clearly demonstrated during the town's annual fiesta celebrated during Easter weekend each year. This festival is the largest in the region and attracts outside vendors who bring in carnival rides, rodeo events, and several large music bands. Festivities last several days, and the town nearly doubles in population, as family members who live and work in the United States make the journey home for the fiesta. Among the popular activities celebrated each year is the tradition of *bañarse en cerveza* (bathing yourself in beer). During this event, the main streets of town swell with revelers who agitate beer cans and open them to release a spray of foam that bathes the crowd. The final destination for this informal parade is that same small plaza area that adjoins the town church, where the young people in town converge to dance and continue drinking and bathing in beer. As this event has grown in popularity and size during recent years, however, the town priest has become increasingly vocal about its inappropriateness. "He doesn't like us to dance," a young woman in her twenties explained to me. "Because he says it's not right to do that for Easter. But we like it—everybody does. Everybody dances." In an effort to prevent the dancing that is central to fiesta activities, a set of fountains was installed in the plaza during February of 2008. My friends, many of them women in their midtwenties who rely on the fiesta as their most significant opportunity each year to meet potential husbands, came to me in horror. "There isn't going to be any place for us to dance," they told me. And in fact, they had drawn up a petition to extract the fountains which, they believed, had been installed through some political pressure on the part of the priest. Thereafter, in the largest organized political event that I witnessed in the town, a series of town meetings was called to discuss the situation. In the end, the fountains were removed, and fiesta drinking and dancing continued as usual—despite the priest's displeasure. In this very clear demonstration of loyalties, the town chose its own interests over that of the Church. The community, therefore, made its priorities known: It is not institutional authority that takes precedence, but rather the collective context that draws them more closely together.

## CONCLUSION

This chapter has shown that one significant problem with rural Mexican teachers' belief that formal education is the single best means to self-improvement is that this paradigm, which emerged historically through Mexico's progression of literacy sponsors from the Catholic Church to the post-Revolution SEP, both masks the larger agendas at work in and around Mexican public education—colonialist power, national cohesion, and capitalist development—and often functions as an empty promise for local communities. Rural communities' motivation toward education (or lack thereof) has in many ways been tempered by the history of educational access in Mexico. Early on, colonial interests created a category of illiteracy (Hernandez-Zamora, 2010), which later gave the post-Revolution government a platform on which to build a public education system. This system promised to eradicate illiteracy in the nation, and to provide citizens with the tools that they need to survive. While this promise functioned in the interest of a wage labor market structure, as well as for those citizens living in urbanized areas where such markets exist, rural citizens' interests did not mesh with this model. Moreover, Mexico's strong need to build a national consciousness following decades of disintegration and war encouraged a strong ideological push toward education, particularly via the use of religion-sponsored rhetorics that supported the principles of a literacy contract orientation: self-sacrifice with the promise of future redemption and reward. The moral uprightness that is the tone of these rhetorics encouraged students to part ways with their identity and values from their home community and to relocate geographically. Further, by employing religious messages of self-sacrifice and redemption to describe formal education, school leaders glorify formal education and deemphasize its potential connection to social reproduction and hierarchies. However, this strategy can backfire when community members recognize that the relative "salvation" that formal education promises asks them to sacrifice geographic proximity to their family and home community—a sacrifice that, in many cases, they are not willing to make. The scope of this history has similarities to that of the United States, particularly as the U.S. education system has grown larger, and local participation has become more limited (Glenn, 2012). In the United States, where decentralized education is still the model but not always the reality, students—particularly those who have already experienced forms of alienation through education—may indeed find themselves at odds with their schools.

In Mexico or the United States, the weight of the sacrifice that schools require, the complexity of the ideological demands of sponsoring institutions, and the strength of ties between cultural value systems and economic structures—the latter of which do not always serve minority groups—all potentially contribute to rural communities' resistance to the literacy contract. There has been an implicit sense that education does not have the community's best interest at heart, and therefore students—much to the dismay of teachers—have often declined to continue pursuing formal education. Rather, as a means of seeking economic opportunity, many students and families have migrated either domestically or internationally in search of commercial employment. And, while Villachuato teachers often expressed to me an either/or mentality regarding migration and education, the truth is that education itself requires permanent migration, as it forces students to relocate to urban centers and to leave their home community behind. The next two chapters will explore further examples and ramifications at the local level of this "failure" of the literacy contract—a failure that, I argue, is nearly a foregone conclusion of the contract itself. Thereafter, the book's final chapter will consider the weight of this legacy on those students who migrate to the United States and matriculate in the schools there. Broadly, whether in Mexico or the United States, students' involvement and success in education is not simply a question of caring or commitment. The challenges of the education system itself, and the particular histories that guide it in different sites, create strong blocks in some cases to the well-being of young people who might otherwise choose to continue on. There is, most profoundly, a gap in the contract that continues to exist, because the contract cannot deliver at the same level as the investment it demands.

# 4. "They Didn't Tell Me Anything" / Community Literacy and Resistance in Rural Mexico

## FIESTA TIME

Once a year, just before Easter, the otherwise quiet town of Villachuato comes alive. During the preceding weeks, streets and homes begin to fill with extra cars—their license plates from Iowa, Minnesota, California, Nebraska—and family members. As relatives from the United States flood into the town, English adds itself to the cadence of daily life, and children compare notes with their cousins about life "on the other side." Toward the center of town, the streets fill with food vendors, baked goods, housewares, and jewelry for sale. Beside the old hacienda façade, an otherwise vacant lot becomes a carnival, complete with mechanical rides and competitive games. Two blocks away, in an empty field that is sometimes used for softball matches at other times of year, metal grandstands are erected and a rink is installed for a series of well-attended rodeos.

Villachuato's fiesta is well known throughout the general region of northwestern Michoacán. It is the town's claim to notoriety, and it is a remarkable display of festivities. Eight-foot-tall puppets are danced through the center of town, and Modelo beer cans are shaken and sprayed over the crowd so that dancers are literally "bathed in beer." In the evening, crowds throng inward to dance to the music of live bands. A week later, video clips of these festivities appear on YouTube so that family members living in the United States can take part in the festivities from afar.

The excitement of this festival, as well as the added influx of visitors—many of them young men who live and work in the United States for most of the year—makes *la fiesta* a central point of conversation among the young women in town. And with good reason. Given Villachuato's strong trend toward outbound migration, relatively few young men live there full-time, so the fiesta season represents an important opportunity for courtship. Indeed, several weddings are held each year during the weeks following the fiesta. Some of these weddings are planned in advance (as in the case of couples who have been courting long-distance for some time), and some are more spontaneous. Equally, some of these unions result in women returning to the United States with their new husbands—quite often without papers and without the expectation to work outside the home—while in other cases men return to work in the United States and women move in with their new in-laws in Villachuato.

In this way, the fiesta dynamic highlights the gendered reality of Villachuato: Men come and go, and women remain at home. And, while discussions about the fiesta fill the entire year, highlighting the longing that families and would-be lovers feel to be more connected with community members living in the United States, the wake of the fiesta can leave some young women in compromised situations. During the year that I lived in Villachuato, for instance, one of the young women in my social group eloped with a man a few days after the fiesta. They went to live briefly in the empty house that he kept in Villachuato, and he promised to take her back to California with him. However, when he left a few weeks later, he went alone. At nineteen years old, Eugenia went back to live with her parents, where she worked in their small storefront painting nails and embroidering handbags. After that event, she no longer joined our social group for outings because now she was a married woman.

### "NOT A SEÑORITA ANYMORE": GENDER NORMS IN VILLACHUATO

In Villachuato, a community that is nearly 100 percent Catholic, social expectations are conservative and gender divisions are strong. While men work and/or migrate and are often seen publicly on the street, women's lives take place primarily inside the home. Typically, a young woman is expected to help her mother with chores and then to get married, move to her husband's home, and take care of children and domestic responsibilities there. Indeed, the gender demarcations in the town are apparent even at a visual level. At any social gathering, the women comprise the dominant position, in both numbers and spatial importance. At the weekly dances held in the plaza on Sunday evenings, women sit on benches or link arms to wander casually around the perimeter of the plaza, while the men stand off to the side watching the show.

The same activity is true at weddings and funeral wakes, parades, and any other public gathering. Even on the streets at night, male and female neighbors come out to visit with each other, but never in mixed circles.

The effect of these practices creates a kind of woman's world, which I was immediately taken into. In contrast, it was all but impossible for me to gain access to the men's world. To that end, I gave up that part of the research equation, choosing instead to focus my energies on the women and their dynamic (see Ralph Cintron's parallel process and outcome with male research participants in *Angel's Town: Chero Ways, Gang Life, and Rhetorics of the Everyday*). Women are each other's social lives in Villachuato, particularly because the majority of their days are spent within the home. Mothers, daughters, and daughters-in-law prepare meals together, clean the house, and wash and iron clothes by hand. In the evenings, when they come together to talk and do cross-stitch, they most often unite with neighbors from the same immediate block. Even for younger women, "going out" for the evening usually means walking three or four blocks to the plaza, buying an ice cream cone, and coming back. Given this backdrop, my arrival in town was notable, and the women of my immediate neighborhood took me into their social circles right away, such that I began to partake in these quiet evenings on the stoop or out to the plaza to buy ice cream or roasted garbanzo beans.

Along with these social friendships also grew research relationships. As people began to know and trust me, they began to share their stories. "There is a lot of machismo here," my friend Carla told me. "But it is getting slowly better." When she was twelve, her father would not allow her to attend the secondary school, because he told her that the girls who went there only wanted to chase after boys. Carla told me that story with a note of resentment in her voice: While her brothers were allowed to go to secondary school (although two out of three did not finish), she was not. In a related story, I learned how Lucía, now in her late thirties, came to the United States a decade ago. Among the youngest of eight children, she was one of the few women in town who became educated, taking a bus daily into Puruándiro to enroll in postsecondary secretarial and accounting classes, her mother selling pigs to pay for her education. However, once she graduated, her father refused to allow her to seek work in Puruándiro—the only option, since there are no offices or businesses in Villachuato. "I already had to put up with enough gossip with you in school," he said. "People talk—they say you go there to see some man. I've had enough." So, even though the income would have helped the family, and despite the mother's investment in her daughter's education, the young woman stayed at home—until an opportunity arose, and she moved permanently to the United States.

In comparison to previous generations, however, examples like Carla's mark a strong progression toward women's autonomy. A generation ago, things were much worse. Elvira, a woman now in her forties, explained to me, with a sardonic tone to her voice, how these things used to happen in the town:

ELVIRA: If you went out with a guy, you were his girlfriend, and you couldn't go with any others. You weren't considered a *señorita* anymore—that was it. People were really ignorant back then. There was a lot of ignorance.

MEYERS: But it was normal, that people thought this?

ELVIRA: Yeah, it was normal before. Well [laughs] . . . they say that before that, they used to just go around and take women and marry them.

MEYERS: Really?

ELVIRA: Yeah. They said, "You're not a *señorita* anymore." That's really ugly. . . . Yeah, they weren't *novios* [boyfriend/girlfriend] or friends or anything. They just took her. Because the guy liked her, so they went and took her. And they told her: "You have to get married." They didn't even know each other. And imagine that.

While outright forced marriage is no longer practiced, there is still an insinuation of seduction and female exploitation. A young man is sometimes said to have *robado la novia* (stolen his girlfriend) and taken her home to live with him. While these unions tend to end in formal marriage, and are often consensual, the conditions of some unions are questionable, as when Jacqueline's fourteen-year-old friend left secondary school to go live with a twenty-seven-year-old man. In another instance, a teacher from the secondary school in Villachuato told me that they had lost a student: a thirteen-year-old boy who had "gone off" with his girlfriend. Even my next-door neighbor, a twenty-year-old young man, "stole" his girlfriend during the time that I was living in Villachuato. While this union was entirely consensual, it did lead to the early termination of the girl's studies. Brenda, a seventeen-year-old girl who was within three months of finishing high school, was one of only a handful of young women in town who were able to pursue studies beyond secondary school. However, during her first weeks living in her new husband's house, she was primarily concerned with the question of how Juan preferred his sandwiches: toasted bread, or no? When I asked, she told me that, no, she would not be going back to school. She looked at me blankly, and I could tell. She didn't have to say it: What would be the point?

Coming to terms with these women's lives was challenging for me both as a researcher and as a friend. My early impression of the women I socialized with was something of patronizing sympathy. I felt sorry for them. Where could they go? Nowhere. All they had was marriage. Moreover, because of the huge outpouring of northbound migration, there aren't enough men in the town to go around. Reports of girls fighting over boyfriends are common. Even so, the two women in their midtwenties who became my closest friends in Villachuato showed no particular interest in marriage. Their lives, they felt, were slowly improving. Cynthia, for instance, is one of the few women in town to hold a job; she commutes each day to Puruándiro to work as an administrative assistant in an office collecting taxes from businesses. And, after being denied secondary school, Carla, who says that she has always had a strong sense of curiosity and love of learning, has obtained her secondary certificate through an equivalency exam. Now, she takes any and all temporary classes that pass through Villachuato: first aid training, English classes, computer tutorials. Indeed, Carla's sister Myra related her story to me: "It was hard to decide to get married, because I had to give up all of my freedoms." Indeed, it is not at all uncommon for young women to give up any independent financial activities once they get married. Even in larger areas like Puruándiro, I heard from several teachers that their mothers, once getting married, gave up the teaching profession. In some cases, women who were more highly educated than their husbands give up their professionalized work in order to become housewives.

Given the difference between these women's lives and my own, it was important for me to listen carefully to their reports of their own lives and to keep these perspectives in mind as I have moved through the analysis for this book. While it was at times difficult not to judge or respond emotionally to patterns that I witnessed—women hiding birth control pills, abusive spouses that couldn't be escaped, girls being precluded from school while boys were able to go—I have worked to remain true to the spirit of these women's perspectives: the areas that still anger them, and the areas that they feel are improving. These perspectives are particularly significant because gender is such a helpful lens through which to examine how literacy has functioned in areas like Villachuato. As the town's most oppressed group, as evidenced by their physical confinement in domestic spaces and fewer life options as compared to men, women have drawn on each other and on literacy in order to avoid violence, forced marriage, domestic isolation, and depression. In the case studies below, I trace Villachuato's literacy development historically via the lives of six women, beginning with a woman who lived through the Mexican Revolution up through Nicole Ramírez, my link to the Villachuato community, whose literacy background straddles the United States and Mexico. These composite perspectives outline the profound complexities that women—and indeed all members of communities in rural Mexico—face with regard to literacy and migration.

However, despite women's often complex relationships with formal education, most international attention on gender and education in developing countries has focused on expanding physical access (Fennell and Arnot, 2008; Pagán, 2001). Based on the contents of the narratives below, however, I believe that such a focus is insufficient, if not dangerous. Indeed, as some U.S. feminist scholars have identified, state-sponsored literacy can have both positive and negative impact on women's lives (Naples, 2003); therefore, literacy can serve as both a source of oppression or a "hope for escape" for women from low-resourced backgrounds (Rockhill, 1987). At minimum, these scholars argue, the relationship of women in developing nations to official literacies is highly complex (Mohanty, 1991), such that physical access alone cannot guarantee uniformly positive, predictable, and sufficient outcomes. Similarly, Mexican scholars have highlighted the complexities that women face with respect to both education and migration, and they have identified the ways in which women's experiences of both have been historically overlooked. For instance, some Mexican scholars have highlighted the ways that migration can be liberating (Ángeles Cruz and Rojas Wiesner, 2000) or not (Gómez et al., 2007). Either way, women have largely been left out of previous scholarship on Mexican migration, even though they represent an important individual pattern (Furlong, 2010). Furthermore, women's roles in education, whether as students (Riquer and Tepichín, 2001) or teachers (Rodríguez-Gómez, 1999), have often been overlooked. Even more significantly, several scholars have identified the ways in which education—and its impact on women—in rural areas of Mexico has historically been understood (Bonfil, 2001; Pereyra, 2001).

In partial response to these oversights, the stories that follow unpack historic and contemporary complexities that women in Villachuato have faced regarding literacy, migration, and intersections of the two. In particular, the experiences of women from Villachuato illustrate ways in which literacy was in fact most liberating when access to formal schooling was at its lowest levels. As access expanded in and around Villachuato, so did manifestations of ideological oppression expressed through schools. In contrast, women's consistent form of self-preservation—whether in terms of accessing literacy or of deflecting the potentially damaging influence of literacy institutions—was social networks, both in the town and, as migration in the area increased, beyond the immediate spheres of Villachuato. The support and migration remittances available through these social networks served both to raise awareness (Anzaldúa, 1999; Furlong, 2010; Lugones, 1992) and to offer women a means to resist those broader social forces that impacted them negatively. Finally, in some cases, these same social ties likewise granted women alternative means to literacy and the agency that it can lend to individual lives.

## "WRITE ME A LETTER": EARLY AWARENESS OF
## THE UTILITY OF FORMAL LITERACY

Esperanza, one hundred years old and the town's oldest inhabitant, is an early example of a woman whose life was characterized by the complexity of literacy. In particular, she is one of the clearest examples of a woman who utilized formal literacy in order to subvert oppressive social and gender norms, even though she herself never learned to read or write. Born in 1909, shortly before the Mexican Revolution reached the town of Villachuato, Esperanza had no access to formal schooling, and her life therefore has been characterized primarily by physical labor. While this in itself is not unique given her generation, Esperanza's story is notable because of the amount of work that she, as a woman, performed outside of the home. As a girl she reports having gone habitually to the fields with her father to prepare the horses and milk the cows. Later on, for much of her married life, she likewise relied on fieldwork and animal husbandry to support herself and her nine children, as her husband often left her to fend for herself while he migrated north to work in the United States Even now, Esperanza's reputation in town is one of hard work and strong-mindedness. Men a generation younger than her attest to her strength—admitting that she could work the plow better than most of them—and they continue to respect her mastery of this work.

Beyond her physical strength and endurance, Esperanza's sense of self and self-preservation are likewise strong—a characteristic perhaps most notable in her descriptions of the method of her various courtships. Although neither Esperanza nor her suitors were formally literate (i.e., able to read and write), their courtships interestingly were conducted through letters, which Esperanza reports that a neighbor was able to read and write for her. While this practice was common enough at the time for a formal marriage proposal, it was also not uncommon for men of Esperanza's generation to simply 'take' women, rather than propose to them. Esperanza protected herself from this form of injustice both by refusing to leave the house alone, and by exploiting literate practice and insisting on its importance to determine specific actions. Regarding the first man who asked for her hand through a letter, she says she denied him:

> He needed to go take a bath. He came round [to see me], but he needed to take a bath. And I said to myself: this just won't work. And I told a neighbor: write me a letter. Write me a letter, and tell him "no." And yeah, he wrote me the letter, and told him that. Oh, he got mad. And he wanted to take me off anyway. He had his father come and talk to my father, to try to get my hand. But I said no. I said, that's bad. It's bad to ask and not take no for an answer. I wouldn't go along with that.

The latter part of this passage indicates Esperanza's understanding of the potential injustice being waged against her. Indeed, as several feminist and critical literacy scholars have suggested (Anzaldúa, 1999; Crowther, Hamilton, and Tett, 2001; Lugones, 1992), an individual's awareness of the way in which she is being oppressed is the foundation of her ability to become more self-empowered. In this case, although Esperanza did not want to marry the man in question, he tried to force her into marriage. However, calling upon the formality of the situation—the formal request and denial—Esperanza protected herself by insisting on the credibility of the written word, suggesting that it was the most important determinant of action. In this way, even when she was not the active literacy practitioner, literacy allowed her to remain single for a longer period of time and to be more selective when she finally did agree to get married. This experience suggests that literacy power can be extended through social relationships, as it was between Esperanza and her neighbor, and that such power, once harnessed, can be used for one's own self-defense. In this way, formal literacy can be utilized in order to resist potentially oppressive social practices.

In a contrasting example, Esperanza pushed the uses of literacy even further, demonstrating her understanding that literacy is, in the end, a social construction that can be drawn upon when it is useful and cast aside when it is not. For instance, when the man that she finally married likewise sent a proposal letter, she demanded instead that he come see her in person:

> I said, "He has to come and bring me the letter *himself*." So he came and said, "Would you please do me the favor of accepting this letter? I will wait for your answer." And I said, "Ok." And then I went to my neighbor, Pancho, and I said, "So, what does this letter say?" And he said, "Well, it says that he loves you." And then [my future husband] came back, and we talked through the gate: him outside, and me on the inside. That's how it was. But after awhile he got mad, because I wasn't telling him an answer to his letter. But, oh well. And he brought me another one. And I said, "Pancho, read me this one." And after that, I wrote back to him [to accept].

In this example, Esperanza's actions suggest an even fuller understanding of both the power and malleability of literacy, particularly as a symbolic or ideological entity. By refusing to allow her husband to hide behind the formality of a text, she demonstrates her awareness that writing, as a constructed means of communication, is only one way of doing business. While the formality of writing can be helpful in some situations—as in refusing the previous suitor—there are other moments in which it may be better to call into question its elevated status. As a woman calling the shots with her husband-to-be, Esperanza empowered herself by, briefly, disempowering literacy; it was, she suggested, insufficient in the case at hand. In this way, her actions suggest a kind of suspicion about the official status given to written literacy, as well as an awareness that it can be manipulated to suit one's own purposes. Moreover, the lesson implicit in her experience is that literacy—at least at its ideological level—can in some cases be harnessed as a form of liberating agency.

### "I WAS SUCH A BURRO": LITERACY AS A MEANS OF SELF-DEFENSE

However, while Esperanza may have resisted exploitation through the resourceful manipulation of literacy—if not a mastery of formal literacy itself—not all of Villachuato's citizens fared so well. In this next narrative, Patricia likewise identified formal literacy as a resource that could be useful to resist the powerful forces of poverty and sexism. However, because of the severe limitations in her life—primarily expressed through a lack of generative social networks—Patricia was unable to harness literacy power for herself directly; rather, she focused on facilitating her daughter's access to such power. So, while literacy figured as an important influence in her life, her relationship to it was primarily one of investment and delayed gratification.

A sharp-minded and slightly embittered woman now in her early seventies, Patricia is roughly the age of Esperanza's oldest daughter. Like many of her contemporaries, Patricia was forced to leave school early in order to work at home. The oldest of ten, she is the daughter of an alcoholic father and a depressed mother. "She would get terrible headaches," she told me, describing her miserable and neglected mother. "And cry and cry from her room. She screamed and screamed for us. And because I was the oldest, I had to do something about it. I had to make tortillas, and beans—everything. All of my childhood, all of my youth. It was like a bad movie. We suffered so much." In this way, Patricia was, from an early age, aware of being oppressed. Later on, men, too, figured into the injustices that she suffered. Unlike Esperanza, Patricia was not able to resist a forced marriage:

> I was married at fourteen years old. I was really young. I never thought that I would have children. I was really living my life without any kind of thought up until I was married. But my señor didn't ask me—he took me by force. I was out at the mill, and they took the tools from my hands and dragged me up the hill. I didn't have anything for getting married. It wasn't anything more than he said: "I like this girl." And then he dropped me on the ground. And they took me by force. That was how I got married. Because if it wasn't for that, I wouldn't have gotten married so early.

Throughout, Patricia's narrative is riddled with such stories of silence and violence. There was little, it seems, that her parents or anyone else set out to tell her beforehand:

> When I was expecting my first, Carolina, I was so dumb. I just noticed that my dress was getting tight. So I went to my mother and I told her that I needed help getting more clothes, because nothing would fit me. But she just looked at me and told me that I was probably expecting a child. And I asked: really? And she said: 'Yes. You're pregnant.' But they didn't tell me anything else. When I got married, nobody told me that I was going to have babies, or that I would suffer certain things. Nothing—they didn't tell me anything.

Later on, however, Patricia did begin to hear stories about the ways in which other people lived, and these stories sparked her interest in formal literacy:

> Well, I knew that my grandparents had gone to Baja California, looking for land. And they were successful, and some of my cousins ended up having jobs and careers, but I didn't know them until I was much older. And I was so surprised at their lives—what had happened to them. And now their children are educated, and some of them are professionals, like engineers. That's when I started to think about things—before that, I was just a burro. And finally I asked my dad: Why didn't you have us educated like them? But he just told me it wasn't worth it, because I wasn't intelligent enough. So it was like that: My dad never had any expectations for us; and my mother didn't either. But yeah, my cousins got educated, and it made me think. Because now their kids are all going to school, too. And they're getting their education.

Similar to Esperanza's neighbor, who likewise gained his literacy skills through travels outside Villachuato, Patricia's cousins' experiences of another place and its resources served as a form of social remittance (i.e., information garnered through the experience of migration and communicated back to the home community) that channeled back home via familial correspondence (Levitt, 1998) and altered her thinking about possibilities for her own life. In this way, Patricia began to understand that formal literacy is something that, if one can obtain it, can do much to protect a person from violence and injustice. From that point on, she worked her way into a small operation raising pigs, and she managed to hold onto the money, as opposed to giving it to her husband. Eventually, she was able to send one of her youngest daughters, Lucía, mentioned above, to accounting school. And, even though Lucía was not able to utilize her accountant training in Mexico, she was eventually able to immigrate to the United States, where she now works and sends her three children to private school. Lucía's stable career and family life, as well as her position in middleclass America, is a self-identified success story that has very much characterized Patricia's latter years.

In this way, Patricia identified formal literacy as the power that could best protect her daughter. Because she was more isolated, the process of obtaining education took longer; in particular, Patricia had to secure personal financial means first, before sending one of her children to school. As such, her narrative challenges the belief that literacy itself is the force that leads hardworking individuals from poverty to economic advancement. Rather, relative stability was necessary first, and then literacy—purchased for a price— became the power that set her daughter apart socially. The significance of this conversion is perhaps most evident in Lucía's father's reaction to her studies. Recognizing the fact that his daughter had obtained a means of raising her social status (i.e., a professional career), he used shame (the suggestion of an affair) in order to restrain her. That is, in order to combat rising levels of social power—as experienced through literacy—in the women of his family, Lucía's father utilized his own social power to shame and curtail his wife and daughter. The very fact that he sought to undo his wife's work, however, suggests the very real power that she and Lucía had begun to access. Like Esperanza, they had discovered that formal literacy, if sufficiently accessed and harnessed, could increase their personal power and autonomy. In this way, their experiences—like those of Esperanza—support feminist and critical literacy beliefs that awareness of social power structures is an essential prerequisite to resistance, autonomy, and self-advancement. Further, in their case, family members who had migrated domestically became the means for the beginning of this awareness (Furlong, 2010).

### "SHE WOULDN'T BUY ME BOOKS": THE DENIAL OF LITERACY

Unquestionably, many of Patricia's hardships were a direct result of poverty. Born shortly after the Revolution, Patricia's generation came of age during a time when families in Villachuato finally had land, but resources were still scarce. Most families, like Patricia's, would have struggled to send their children to school; and social violence like rape and wife abuse were not uncommon. However, as the women of Patricia's generation came of age, the relative standard of living in Villachuato did improve, as did physical access to schooling. Today, the majority of Villachuato men and women in their forties report that they attended most or all of primary school. Even so, for several members of the community, access to literacy remained limited—if not by physical means, then by more abstract mechanisms of poverty, including psychological distress, as in the next two stories. For instance, like Patricia, forty-year-old Elvira reports that her mother didn't teach her much about life. Instead, she sought *consejos* (advice) from the other women in town. Describing her first learning experience, she said that she had to find a way to learn how to wash clothes:

> ELVIRA: [I had to] help my mom.
> MEYERS: And who taught you?
> ELVIRA: Well, over there with the señoras—they taught me. We would go over there to the washing area, and we'd wash there.
> MEYERS: And how did you feel about doing that?
> ELVIRA: Well, happy. At first I was really happy. I liked it. . . . [I]t was nice to know how to do something.

Elvira's mother, an age-mate of Patricia, suffered the loss of her own mother at an early age. Although the official history cites her grandfather as accidentally killing her grandmother with a shotgun, Elvira insinuates that the death may not have been so accidental. Furthermore, he all but abandoned the four children from his first marriage when he went off to marry a different woman in town. These four neglected children lived as orphans, and by the time Elvira's mother began to have her own children, of which Elvira is the first female child, she was an embittered woman who resented her children for what they had:

> My mother was really bad. She didn't leave me alone. When I started going to school, she wouldn't get me a notebook. She would only get me little tiny ones with six pages. And she told me that was it. And when it came time for September, she wouldn't get me a uniform. She never bought me one. For all the rest of the kids, yeah, she did. But not for me. She just wanted me to stay home.

As a result, Elvira was only able to finish three years of elementary school, despite the fact that the family had the financial resources to support her through more. The result of this denial of education and personal liberty left Elvira feeling both restless and rebellious. Like many other women in rural Mexico (Furlong, 2001), Elvira's lack of material resources motivated her to think about leaving home. Speaking of the years between school and marriage, she said she had other plans for her life:

ELVIRA: Well, I never thought about getting married. I wanted to get out of here.

MEYERS: How?

ELVIRA: Leave the house. Leave.

MEYERS: Who knows where to?

ELVIRA: Yeah. I just wanted to get out of the house. And I was scared of getting married. I thought, well, if I get married, it's just going to be the same thing. So, I didn't want to get married. But my mother told me, "Get yourself married!" But I didn't want to. I told her, "No, I'm not going to get married." And then she said, "Well, where are you going to live, then?" And a [female] friend and I decided that we would go north, go to the United States Yeah. That's what we would do.

MEYERS: And how did you decide on that goal?

ELVIRA: Because I didn't want to get married. And here, the people say that you have to get married. But what I didn't want to do, I didn't want to serve up food for some old guy. I didn't want to do that. So that's why I didn't want to get married. I just wanted to have a kid of my own, and go on my way.

Eventually, Elvira did make it to the United States for a period of four years, although by that time she was married and had three small children. While she was unable to go on her own as a single woman, the family's decision to go north and make money to build their home in Villachuato was very much embedded in these early dreams of hers. Moreover, the result of this trip had important implications for literacy—not so much for Elvira but for her children. One son who attended English-speaking public schools for those four years is now living in the United States permanently. Even more interesting is the case of Elvira's daughter Cynthia. Returning to Mexico after eighth grade, Cynthia eventually finished her Mexican secondary degree through an equivalency test, and then went on to study both at beauty school and in computer training classes. Now, she has a secretarial job in an office in Puruándiro and cuts hair in the evenings from her home. During my time in Villachuato, I didn't meet any other woman in her age bracket who was so highly trained—and I didn't meet any other woman at all who held a job in Puruándiro.

Cynthia's achievements are significant in an area in which almost no women work outside the home, and school dropout rates remain high. During my interview with Cynthia, she described the influence that her experiences in the United States had on her motivation to pursue higher levels of education:

MEYERS: Why did you decide to study computers?

CYNTHIA: Because I had really liked computers a lot in the past.

MEYERS: Where did you learn to use computers before?

CYNTHIA: Up there in Iowa.

MEYERS: What kinds of things did they teach you?

CYNTHIA: Typing, and how to turn the computer off and on.

MEYERS: Why did you like it?

CYNTHIA: Because the teachers noticed that I was good at it, and it really intrigued me.

Even though Cynthia speaks fondly of her experiences in the United States, she was very clear with me that she intends to stay in Mexico. "I love my town," she told me repeatedly. "I *love* it here." In this way, Cynthia is an individual who has subverted expectations of her on both sides of the border. In contrast with the negative images that U.S. educators often have of Mexican students (Valencia and Black, 2002), Cynthia is a motivated young woman who pushed her educational achievement to the limits of her immediate environment. And, within her community in Mexico, Cynthia refused to remain in the stay-at-home gendered role expected of her. Instead, she brokered the cultural capital that she had accrued in Iowa and used it to increase her personal options in Villachuato. Throughout this process, Cynthia enjoyed the emotional support and approval of her parents—particularly her mother Elvira, who had likewise subverted gendered norms throughout her life.

Similarly, Elvira's is also a multigenerational story of success: Cynthia now has the life of independence and education that Elvira so wanted for herself. However, while Patricia faulted her parents for their neglect and mourned her loss of schooling, Elvira actively resents the steps that her mother took to limit her education. In a composite sense, then, these first three narratives indicate the variety of ways in which poverty limits access to literacy, including some that are not physical. One important lesson thus far, then, is that literacy opportunities require much more than physical access, as has been the focus of so many international campaigns. However, as autonomy and resources have increased in Villachuato, oppression has become more ideologically and psychologically based. This form of oppression played out locally in Elvira's life—that is, at the level of family—and it plays out at the social and institutional level in the following narrative about Myra's challenges with school. Despite these hardships, though, Elvira and Cynthia did find means of accessing literacy—primarily through their experience migrating temporarily to the United States—and, once obtained, that literacy did indeed have a positive effect on their lives.

## "IT WAS A DREAM I ALWAYS HAD": FINDING ALTERNATE MEANS TO LITERACY

In this next narrative, Myra, too, suffered the psychological consequences of complexities related to literacy. However, while in Elvira's case, limits to literacy occurred at the familial level, Myra's story indicates the way in which schools themselves can function to limit a student's opportunities. Therefore, rather than seeking out literacy as a means of improving her life, Myra was obliged to resist and avoid formal education and its damaging impact on her. In contrast to the first three women's stories discussed above—in which women implicitly identified the constructed nature of literacy, the socially embedded power therein, and their own ability to harness some of this power—Myra's story differs dramatically. While she had access to a formal education, the power of school-acquired literacy impacted her negatively at first, such that literacy itself was a form of oppression to be countered. Baffled by her negative experiences in school, Myra found herself compelled to resist literacy at an early age; although, years later, she was able to draw on social ties in order to reclaim a more positive experience with literacy.

A sensitive girl, Myra was a creative, interested young mind who got caught in the gears of an oppressive school. Almost from the beginning, her school career seemed destined for disaster. Her first problems had to do with being left-handed, a characteristic that called attention to her and made her feel confused and ashamed:

> Well, I've always been left-handed, you know, ever since I was a little girl. Yeah, left-handed people aren't very common. And in the group I was in, there were only right-handed people. And they told me, "No, you can't write with that hand." And I said, "Yes, I do. I write with this hand.". . . But all those kids watching me like that . . . it made me nervous. Every time we had to do a writing assignment, it was bad like that.

Later, when she was put in a class with an aggressive teacher, things got even worse:

> I had to leave school, umm . . . I think I was in the fifth grade. I had to leave because a teacher hit me once because I didn't know the multiplication table for "6." He hit us for that. And after that, I had problems with the teacher. I was scared of him, and I didn't want to go to school anymore. So, the next year I didn't go. . . . I finished fifth grade, and I did well. And I was supposed to go on to sixth. But I just didn't want to go anymore. . . . So I lost that [last] year, and I couldn't finish primary school. But you know, I always held onto

the desire to finish it. I saw all the rest of the kids graduating, and I thought to myself, "Oh, I could have been one of them.". . . So, to finish school was a dream that I had ever since I was little. It was a fantasy that I always had.

In this way, Myra understood that her school environment was oppressive and unjust (Riquer and Tepichín, 2001), and her single means of resistance as a ten-year-old girl was to leave that school entirely. While that act of defiance was, in a way, a means of voicing her disdain for the way that she was treated, it also came with a price. The experience left her quite damaged. By the time she reached the age of twelve, depression sunk in; and for several years, she refused to leave her home:

Pretty much once I stopped going to school, I stopped wanting to go outside. And after a little while, I wasn't going to church anymore, or to the dances [in the plaza] or even to the store. . . . From here [indicating the kitchen/living room complex of her house] I only went out to the bathroom or to feed the animals. But I never left the house. I didn't go anywhere. I didn't have a single friend; I was totally enclosed.

The fear that Myra exhibited suggests an extreme agoraphobia, which she herself attributes in large part to her own failed school experience. Retelling these events, this now well-adjusted and highly social young woman speaks with anger at her treatment in school—and with a certain gratefulness to her neighbor Cynthia, introduced above, who eventually convinced Myra to attend adult education classes with her so that the two young women could earn their primary and secondary equivalency certificates:

One day Cynthia said to me, "Why don't you finish school?" And I was like, "Look at me, I'm so old now. I couldn't go to the primary school like this." But there in Puruándiro, they were giving *abierto* [open enrollment] classes. But I didn't think I could go just then. But she told me, "No, look. They give you the books and the classes, and you do your exam. And after that, if you pass, it's all fine." It was like a dream that I had from when I was a little girl [to finish school]—a kind of fantasy that I always had.

The results of Myra's adult education classes were dramatic. From a depressed adolescent scarred by a damaging school experience and therefore terrified of leaving her home, she became a socially active young woman who often went out to participate in town events, took on a job picking strawberries, and left the town itself to go sight-seeing with girlfriends in other parts of Mexico.

Throughout these activities, Myra utilized social resources in order to access an alternative route to the social status that can come with formal education, and the success of that endeavor has had very important effects on her life.

In this way, Myra is an example of a woman who, finding institutionalized literacy an oppressive force in her life, disengaged herself from it—drawing instead on social networks (especially of neighbors who had migrated internationally and brought back increased forms of institutional knowledge) to sustain her and to offer her alternative recourses. Indeed, her experiences support previous findings regarding the ways in which formal schooling often does not function as intended in rural settings within Mexico (Bonfil, 2001). All the same, it is important to emphasize the fact that Myra suffered for her resistance: four years of isolation and depression. Hers is not an easy story; her experiences with literacy are complex (Mohanty, 1991; Rockhill, 1987), even as she professes her eventual success and self-satisfaction. Even so, it is useful to note that, similar to the previous three stories outlined above, Myra's expanding sense of awareness of her resources and abilities is likewise rooted in her social ties.

### "YOU KNOW YOU CAN DO THE WORK": SOCIAL NETWORKS FOR SURVIVAL

While the importance of social ties remains strong in the final two narratives, this next story considers the way in which school may not be damaging so much as irrelevant to the lives of youth in rural Mexico. For Maribel, a self-proclaimed "wild girl," school held no particular promise that could keep her attention. Leaving secondary school due to boredom, she likewise left Villachuato, choosing to live instead with an aunt in Puruándiro. "My mother didn't like it," she said breezily of her move. "But I was already there." After remaining in Puruándiro for several years, Maribel eventually abandoned formal education altogether, finding beauty school as disappointing as the secondary school curriculum had been. Instead, she turned to retail work—where, as an employee, she proved just as strong-minded and self-assured as she had been as a student and daughter. "When you work in the pharmacy and stuff, you're supposed to wear make-up, you know, for being more . . . professional and stuff. And I was like—I didn't like to use make-up and stuff." So, she refused to adjust her personal appearance, even when her boss offered her a raise if she would comply with the dress code. But Maribel didn't worry about it; she looked the way she wanted to and felt secure in her job because she was a reliable worker and her aunt knew the employer. In this way, Maribel has consistently made life choices—including eventual migration to the United States—that reflect a strong sense of self, a reliance on good social connections, and her own willingness to work.

Maribel's social connections are an important distinguishing marker in her story (Alba and Nee, 2003; Portes and Zhou, 1993). In contrast to the other women surveyed, Maribel had access to the neighboring town of Puruándiro at an early age. This contact with a larger community and a more extended resource base made her more aware of her options in life. Instead of picking strawberries a few times a week, as Myra did, she could move to Puruándiro and take a full-time retail job—an experience that expanded her worldview and provided her with work experience, both of which became important to her when she decided to migrate to the United States. Furthermore, whereas Myra's two younger brothers were the first in her family to go north, Maribel, the sixth of eight children, already had several siblings in the United States by the time that she was reaching her teenage years. Her siblings' experiences making repeated illegal "jumps" across the border constitute an important knowledge base that Maribel was able to tap into. Indeed, in her descriptions of her own illegal border crossing, Maribel suggests that the experience of having heard her siblings' stories motivated her to complete that treacherous process. Given the experience of having lived for a time in another place—Puruándiro—she had some conceptualization of "otherness" in life: the possibility of making another, better life for yourself elsewhere.

> When I got up there [to the border], I was so scared. And my brothers, they said, "You see that over there? The lights over there—that's where we're going." And we were at the, you know, the border. And I was like, "No, I don't wanna go." And I looked back at Mexico, and I was like, "No, I don't wanna go back there either."

Once she arrived, Maribel, like many women who migrate to the United States, found migration ultimately more liberating than education (Ángeles Cruz and Rojas Wiesner, 2000). Early on, she realized two important related lessons. First, any schooling that she did have didn't matter very much. As she explained, the work she did in California was physical, and it was easy to learn how to do: "You know you can do the work." Second, any lack of education, especially in English, was not a real hindrance to her. Instead, what mattered most to her survival were the social networks to which she was tied. Recounting the process of "jumping" across the border, she describes an exhausting and unpleasant experience in which she was helped by her brothers, who both knew the steps to follow and already had contacts on the United States side of the border:

[The] jump takes like a week. . . . [And] we were always going to eat tacos every day, you know. Drinking water and eating tacos. We didn't have much money. But, it's still. . . . Well, you don't need much. You're nervous all the time because you're so stressed. And um, we were living in the shitty, cheaper motels [in Mexico]. It's pretty shitty, because they're full of all the people who are trying to get across. And um, after that, we lived in a trailer [in Arizona] and in the trailer we didn't have to pay anything because my brother got that covered. And when we stayed a couple of days in Los Angeles where there were people to help us, we didn't have to pay, either, because it was somebody's house. We stayed there like three or four days.

Figure 4.1. Landscape near the U.S.-Mexico border

Arriving finally in the agricultural basin of California, Maribel describes the work as physically demanding, but not difficult to master:

Yeah, it's hard. You get up at like three or four in the morning so you can get to work by seven [o'clock]. Because you gotta be ready to get your ride, whoever is gonna pick you up. The bus, or whatever. You gotta be ready. So you get up, at maybe four in the morning. And your day depends on how much work they have in the fields. Sometimes it's [longer or shorter, but] you always make it to home by four, [or] maybe even three-thirty. So then you kinda like take care of your body: take a shower, and go eat and . . . get ready for the next day, just like that. Yeah.

Once she had reached her destination, it was her social relationships, rather than any kind of literate base, that helped her:

> Like . . . my sister . . . and I had one friend [too]. She was working there before . . . so she taught me how to do it. So when I had too many lettuce heads in my basket, she told me. She was always right next to me. And she told me do this and that—like that, you know? And she told me to do it fast. "Don't waste too much time with the lettuce," she told me. "Just do it. Take it out, close the box, and send it on." Yeah, she taught me. We were friends for a long time.

So, while education may purport to promise self-satisfaction in life, Maribel found her satisfaction in the independence that she had in this new place:

> I liked working . . . and I liked getting my check every weekend. I liked it, 'cause, you know, I got a check. . . . Sometimes I worked Saturdays and Sundays, too, for another company, and I got another check for those two days. So, I like, had money to pay for where I was living; and I had some to send to my mom, and some to go out and have fun. I liked going with my friends back then. Going out to eat in restaurants and stuff.

Even the language, the only aspect of migration that Maribel found difficult, she gained socially—rather than institutionally—once she began dating the American man whom she eventually married. Now the mother of two, she continues to work in manual labor jobs and awaits the immigration paperwork that will allow for expanded options once she becomes a legal worker. She is satisfied with her life, she says, and prefers residing in the United States, with its increased social and economic options. In Maribel's case, then, her access to life opportunities and satisfaction came through social networks and migration, rather than education (Pereyra 2001), even though she had reliable access to formal schooling in Mexico. Interestingly, though, while formal education has not played an important role in her life, Maribel wants to see her children become educated: "I want them to go on to college and finish and do something kinda, you know, like—something that they like. But, I don't know what they're gonna like. But yeah, I want them both to finish school. And then get jobs and all that stuff." Like Nicole's dynamic with her family in the final narrative below, Maribel hopes for an additional outcome from her life as a migrant: a professional life for her children, particularly one that carries with it some amount of social prestige.

While Nicole did eventually achieve the kind of professional self-satisfaction that Maribel advocates, her path toward that goal was not smooth; and, like so many of the other cases included here, it was Nicole's social ties that saved her. While Nicole's parents were originally from Villachuato, they have been living in Los Angeles for nearly forty years—with the exception of a handful of years when the family returned to Mexico, including Nicole's third-grade year, which she spent at the primary school in Villachuato. The last of ten children, Nicole is one of two siblings born in the United States, and she is the only member of her family who has gone on to college and to pursue a professional career. Emerging from the same background as the preceding five women, Nicole's success was the product of both serendipity and enduring hard work—as well as resistance to the negative and prescriptive judgments that were imposed on her during her education in Los Angeles area schools.

Early on, Nicole identifies as having been a "super motivated little kid." However, much to her own surprise, her progression through school saw her steadily losing spirit, focus, and opportunities. In her own self narration, she continues to emphasize the fact that she does not fully understand *how* this transition happened, but she is able to clearly identify the point at which she lost her motivation:

> And then, like, junior high came, and I started caring less. I mean, I started doing things that, you know, an average student [would do]. But, like, in elementary, I only got As and Bs. You know, really rarely any Bs. But in junior high, [I had] like Cs, and Ds. And, you know, I did enough to get by, and I think—one of the things that I think about now that I think I really hate about myself is that I learned, um, just enough to get by.

Nicole continues to feel amazed by her own academic decline during adolescence, even though she now understands that the schools she attended communicated to her that she was not destined for high achievement—and, therefore, may as well not even try. In high school, for instance, Nicole was discouraged from considering college, even though her grades were sufficient and she herself had the will to go. Instead, she found her school counselors resistant: "Like, you know, I remember filling out the FAFSA form. And asking [my guidance counselors] questions and they actually said, you know, don't even bother. You know, don't do it. It's useless."

Fortunately, because her family, having just benefitted from an unforeseen financial windfall, encouraged her to do so, Nicole *did* fill out a college application on her own and was admitted. Nicole's family helped her get through college, even without financial aid, and eventually she went on to law school. Today, she is a practicing attorney. Her success is testament to her ability to resist the ways in which institutionalized literacy—in this case, in the form of Los Angeles public schools—worked against her, categorizing her as a minority woman not destined for anything more than a high school diploma.

Similar to Myra, Nicole experienced oppressive school forces, and, for many years, she suffered from low self-esteem because of them—particularly because she did not understand them. Also like Myra, much of Nicole's means to self-transformation came through social channels—in this case, from her family. Even though she describes her parents as functionally illiterate, Nicole explains that they always encouraged her to pursue her studies. Moreover, the specific values of a migrant family taught her a great deal, she says, of the work ethic and vision that later bolstered her through a professional career:

> During the summers pretty much from when I was about five years old, we would go and work in Northern California picking fruit . . . [I]t really taught me the value of hard work. I was a really good tomato picker. . . . And I remember my dad always, um, congratulating me, or just you know, showing me how proud he was of me. That really stuck with me, and made me want to like, try harder, and do really well. [Also] it was during those trips that we would drive down to Fresno, or Bakersfield, and while we were there, that my dad would talk to me about being a lawyer . . . which was really weird, 'cause I don't think that he knew what a lawyer was; and he definitely didn't know what it would take to get there. But yeah, I mean, I knew that I wanted to be a lawyer since I was, you know, seven. And he would just be like, you're gonna be a lawyer. And he would like call me *la abogada*.

In her own self-analysis, Nicole told me that she credits her professional success almost entirely to these influences from her family. Despite her parents' own formal illiteracy, it was their encouragement that spurred her to pursue postsecondary education, even when school mentors told her not to bother. Consistent with the other case studies presented above, Nicole's social connections were the most important influence in her life that led her to resist oppression—in this case, racial profiling at her U.S. public high school—in order to ultimately access literate power and professional opportunity. However, in contrast to feminist and critical literacy arguments that identify awareness as the necessary precursor to self-empowerment (Anzaldua, 1999; Lugones, 1992), Nicole's path to success reflects more of a sense of family-inspired self-confidence, rather than an understanding of the prejudices that impacted her early educative experiences. Indeed, having completed her postsecondary degrees, she is now able to analyze in hindsight the power structures implicit in schools. However, this awareness came as more of an afterthought than a precursor to personal success, suggesting that the most crucial influence on Nicole's literacy development was that of positive interpersonal relationships.

## CONCLUSION

The six representative case studies presented in this chapter suggest some of the noteworthy experiences that rural Mexican women have had with institutionalized literacy during the twentieth century. While the stories are neither identical nor exhaustive, some of the major overlapping features indicate, for instance, a significant connection between literacy and oppression, as well as the importance of social ties in creating the conditions to enable women to resist oppression. In the first two narratives, oppression throughout and following the revolutionary period in Mexico was experienced physically and politically. For Esperanza and Patricia, there was little access to literacy training; and, when these women or their children were able to access formal education, it became a means of combating other oppressive forces, including poverty and forced marriage. However, as political and economic conditions improved, and access to formal education increased, oppression took on more symbolic, self-regulatory forms, such that literacy itself often became a vehicle for oppression. In some cases, these oppressive undercurrents took on a damaging psychological dimension—as in the case of Elvira's mother and of Myra herself—experienced at either the local familial or broad, social level. As a result, Myra's and Nicole's stories—and to some extent Maribel's—illustrate young women who initially struggled to resist the negative impact of formal education on their lives. In all six of these cases, interpersonal relationships played an important role in their resistance, as exposure to other people's experiences or direct assistance from friends and family—increasingly expressed through domestic and international migration—became the means through which these women resisted oppressive forces in their lives and, in some cases, found alternative means to literacy.

These composite stories suggest, therefore, that a narrow focus on physical access to schools, such as that typically endorsed by a "contract" orientation toward education, is not sufficient to diagnose and resolve the challenges that women in the developing world face with regard to literacy achievement. These findings also complicate both the assumption that literacy is neutral and reliably leads people away from oppressive conditions, and the concern that alternate forces like migration may be detrimental to processes of literacy acquisition. In the case of the women whose stories are presented here, social influences—particularly those that involve lessons from migration—encouraged the kind of self-awareness and institutional critique that ultimately led to increased personal agency. In some cases, this awareness led to resistance toward interpersonal or institutional forms of violence, and in other cases, it led individuals to find alternative means to literacy. In either case, the women presented here did not follow the prescribed courses of action for their lives, whether with regard to literacy, domestic relationships, or professional work, and so on. This very process, as I will analyze more deeply in the next chapter, is most fundamentally a process of positioning oneself rhetorically with respect to literacy and other social forces. Indeed, throughout the course of the next two chapters, I will press these ideas further by outlining community members' contemporary responses to formal literacy, as well as the assimilation process that students experience when they migrate to the United States.

# 5. "So You Don't Get Tricked" / Counternarratives of Literacy in a Mexican Town

The library in Puruándiro (figure 5.1) is a one-room collection of books, computers, and children's theatrical materials. Although the five computer stations boast free internet access and large, flat-screen monitors, the book collection itself is modest, comprised of eight or ten thinly populated shelves, ranging in material from religious studies, to science, to literature. Stopping by for archival materials, I was offered five books: the full extent of historical material available about Puruándiro and other municipalities in the surrounding area. Two of these books were self-published histories; one was a religious text; one was a guide to municipalities of the state; and one was a printed copy of website materials. All were well worn, the worst of them nearly falling apart. Moreover, when I asked to borrow the books, I was informed that the only way I could get a library card would be to bring a friend from Puruándiro to vouch for me. Without a Puruándiro citizen who would sign on my behalf, I could not take the books home with me. I shrugged. "It's OK," I told the librarian. "I have time. I'll read the books here." But the implication stayed with me: for students from Villachuato, who do not have a library of their own because the town's library (figure 5.2) was never finished, research materials are nearly inaccessible.

In an even broader sense, the modest amount of information available about Villachuato, the difficulty of accessing it, and the clear investment in technology over traditional texts all suggest important implications for

Figure 5.1. Puruándiro library

Figure 5.2. Villachuato's unfinished library

literacy. For instance, what national value does the story of these people's lives have, if the last time that a Mexican archivist wrote about them was 1970? Moreover, what kind of relationship can citizens from Villachuato have to this history if the only means to a library, however modest, includes a half-hour bus ride and the prior knowledge of someone from that other, more established town? Further, what value, indeed, do printed textual materials have in this area, if the five shining computers, barely used, have replaced books in the library budget? All of these are interesting questions—which I will address later in this chapter. However, what struck me most on this particular visit to the library wasn't just my reaction to the resources there, but rather the other patrons' reactions to *me*.

"It's like you just fell out of the sky!" Jorge, a young man in his midtwenties, had just come down to sit with me. The librarian had introduced us, as she knew a little bit about my project, and she knew Jorge, an English teacher at a secondary school in town there in Puruándiro. Jorge was delighted; he could not believe his good luck. After a few minutes asking me questions about the parameters of my study, he told me excitedly that he, too, was about to embark on a research project. Furthermore, he wondered out loud if there might be some way that I could help him. Certainly, I answered, if there was something that he needed—although I remained unclear whether it was research support or English language practice that he was looking for. But it didn't seem to matter. Jorge shook his head excitedly, grabbing up my scribbled email address on a worn post-it note. "Thank you," he said, leaving the library with a grin.

This kind of reaction was not uncommon during my time living and working in rural Michoacán. Each time I entered a new setting—a school, or a new area of town—I was typically met with a range of curiosity, enthusiasm, or flat out disbelief. What was I doing there? people wanted to know. Those

Figure 5.3. Villachuato's middle school

who wanted to learn English were pleasantly surprised. And teachers, particularly those from other parts of Mexico who had been assigned to work in that rural area, were pleased to find another university-educated colleague in their midst. However, what I found most remarkable about these encounters wasn't the reaction to my presence so much as the implications for literacy: for citizens of that geographic area, particularly the smaller ranchos like Villachuato, literacy is something that quite literally comes from someplace *else*. It is an autonomous thing, an entity that travels wholesale into their lives. More importantly, it is something that they are not a part of. It might visit them—for a day, a week, a year—but it is part of a network that exists apart from them, emerging from some other larger, more distant place.

Of equal note, I believe, is that fact that *none* of the teachers who work in the kindergarten, primary school, or secondary school of Villachuato actually live in the town. They come from elsewhere—Puruándiro to the east, or Angamacutiro to the west—and they go back, at the end of each day, to someplace just a little bit more comfortable and civilized. Books, too, exist elsewhere. The only book sales that I encountered during my time there was under a temporary tent composed of three adjoined tables assembled once in awhile in the plaza in Puruándiro. Otherwise, there were no book stores and no books. When the language arts teacher at the #92 school (figure 5.3) asked how many of her seventh graders had ever seen a public library, only four or five of them raised their hands. The lesson of these interactions is that

Figure 5.4. Puruándiro's middle school

literacy in rural areas of Mexico like Villachuato and its "parent" town of Puruándiro exists as an imported entity: a set of information, expectations, and representatives that arrive from the outside world. That is, literacy in this area is *external*.

Earlier in this book, I examined the historical development and implications of increased access to formal education in areas like Villachuato. Now, this chapter focuses on contemporary dynamics of literacy as an imported ideology—one that, I argue, rural citizens, perhaps even more than educators themselves, have learned to manage and exploit for their own uses. As I unpack these tensions, I begin with a consideration of literacy crisis rhetorics as they exist in this context—both on the part of teachers and community members. Thereafter, I demonstrate the ways that contemporary Villachuato citizens both accept and resist the literate values and practices that their schools endorse. By making careful choices about how to strike this balance, I argue, Villachuato citizens take a rhetorical stance toward literacy: enacting those elements that serve them, and resisting the rest. In this way, I likewise present resistance itself as a rhetorical practice, one that is contextual, positional, and strategic.

## "HE KNOWS BEETHOVEN": TEACHER EXPECTATIONS IN VILLACHUATO

The teachers in Villachuato are frustrated. Beyond the considerable personal obstacles that they overcame to become educated themselves, and the work of preparing classes each day, they realize that their students do not seem to appreciate these efforts. The desertion rate in the area is high; and those who continue studying beyond the secondary level are few. "The mentality of many of the young guys," one teacher told me, "is, 'I can't finish school—I'm going to the U.S.' But they think that in the U.S. they're going to have all this work and make a lot of money. And that they're going to have big trucks and things. Because they see what others bring back. Because at a certain time [of year] a lot of people come back, and they bring a lot of things and a lot of money. . . . That's the dream they have. And many of them aren't thinking about focusing on a career—so many are thinking instead about going to the U.S." Indeed, migration (most often illegal) is a huge phenomenon in this area—most especially from smaller towns like Villachuato. Traditionally, the bulk of U.S.-bound migration from Mexico has come from central western Mexico, particularly the states of Michoacán and its neighbors Guanajuato and Jalisco (Cardoso, 1980). And teachers, for their part, recognize students' awareness of a market economy, though they believe that these students' focus within this reward system structure is misguided. "Migration is a really big problem here," the secondary school director told me. "For the kids, more than anyone. It affects us by means of desertion. . . . It makes them lose interest in school. They think that they just want to finish secondary school, and convince their parents, and go to the other side." To that end, migration is often criticized by teachers. Migration represents a false consciousness; it is a temptation that must be extricated. Moreover, migration is perceived to be in direct competition with formal education: the single *right* way to seek self-improvement.

"I really think people lose something when, instead of looking for self-development or professionalization, they just look for more stuff," the Villachuato secondary school director told me:

> They just want more stuff: I have this, so I want that and that. So instead of trying to improve themselves, they just try to increase the things that they have. They don't try to build themselves intellectually, or in terms of knowledge. They should try to learn more, try to improve things. But they just look toward having more and more things. So, they lose the idea of self-improvement, and instead they're left with this idea of going after more money. They want to have everything. And I'm saying that it's the opposite: If you improve yourself and professionalize, the rest just comes as a consequence. If you prepare yourself, money comes as a consequence of being a good, well-prepared person. Somebody who has studied, and worked. Or who has done things well. But we're in the country where, instead of exporting the things that yeah, we *can* produce—instead of that, we're exporting people. This is really what we're exporting—even more than corn or fruits or whatever.

Taken as a composite phenomenon, these assertions about the importance of formal education and of students' misguided priorities constitute a form of *literacy crisis rhetoric*. Such rhetorics are evidence that literacy in rural Mexico is changing. Moreover, these new rhetorics, which focus on the damaging nature of migration, both build on and replace earlier religious rhetorics that advocated self-sacrifice in the interest of educational pursuit. While migration has now become the touchstone to these debates, earlier themes of self-sacrifice and salvation endure. Furthermore, they interact with another important theme: that of temptations to be overcome. On the one hand, migration is conceived of as a threat to education because it influences individuals' life decisions. However, it is likewise considered damaging because of the broader cultural changes that it effects. Continuing on in his conversation with me, the secondary school director explained these dangerous influences:

> The other thing is that migration changes our habits here. For instance, the issue of drugs. They bring back with them drugs, music, clothes . . . and the kids want to imitate them. And they do it. So, this is a new influence. Before,

you didn't hardly see these things. Lifestyles that aren't our own—people are losing their identity. Instead of maintaining affection for their own land, they feel an empty space—and they leave.

This comment in particular harkens back to my earlier arguments about the purpose of public education in Mexico following the Revolution: to unify the country through the realization of a national consciousness. Moreover, this unity and patriotism, as we have seen, depends on the process of producing educated persons who believe in the value of education—and, with it, the specific messages delivered through education. In this way, an influence, like international migration, that draws attention away from nationalist values is indeed a threat: not only to an individual's livelihood, but to the moral character of the broader social fabric.

In contrast, the townspeople for whom teachers and administrators have the most respect are those who find their way, through whatever means, to education—and, by extension, to cultural capital. One teacher explained:

> There's [a] family [here in town]—they have a lot of kids. But they are doctors, dentists, engineers, architects. And almost all of them studied. Because the first one helps the rest. And they're all professional. . . . They have like a family strategy—they wanted all of their kids in school. And they have one in the U.S.—he must send money down to help them. And [the father of this family is] a really cultured man. He knows a lot—he knows about classical music. It's rare that you find a *campesino* like that. He knows Beethoven, Mozart, Chopin, Ravel. And that's how it goes. He knows a lot about music—and other things, too. He's studied. So culturally, he knows a lot. He studies by himself—he learns it all just by reading. He comes and talks with us—and that's how I understood his cultural level. Because he comes around when classes aren't in session. . . . But there aren't many like that.

In this way, many teachers in Villachuato relate most to those few members of the community who have found access to cultural capital. However, as an observer in both the community of Villachuato and language arts classes at the secondary school—many of which are still dominated by canonical readings and liberal arts curriculum—I became aware of the inconsistency between school-based knowledge and the physical and economic realities of Villachuato. Classical music, for instance, is not relevant to a community that survives on small-scale farming. Therefore, the liberal arts curriculum favored by several of the language arts teachers with whom I spoke is not directly useful to their students. Moreover, because the immediate Villachuato vicinity lacks the commercial presence of a labor market, the literacy contract in this area cannot quite deliver on its promise—unless, that is, a young person is willing to permanently relocate to a more urban center. Therefore, although the teachers of Villachuato relate best to families who prize education, these families are losing their children in the same way as do those who send their sons north to work as migrants in the United States.

## "UN CHOQUE DE IDEAS": VILLACHUATO'S OWN LITERACY CRISIS

In my conversations with teachers, however, it seemed to me that they were often losing sight of this irony. During my time in Villachuato, I found few teachers who spoke with intimate knowledge of the lives of their students or of the kinds of sacrifices that an extended education would cause them to make; nor did there appear to be a strong interest to learn about such issues. At parent meetings, directors reported primarily giving out information rather than soliciting parents' questions or feedback. Similarly, teachers held conferences with parents primarily to discuss acute problems, rather than typical daily needs and events. In this way, the majority of school personnel with whom I worked did not seem aware of the disconnect between the schools' curriculum and values and the community's real needs. Indeed, although other researchers have likewise identified a disconnect between school curriculum and community needs (Jiménez, Smith, and Martínez-León, 2003; Teague, Smith, and Jiménez, 2010), Villachuato school officials were not, as some recent educational experts have advocated, seeking information from the community in order to adjust curriculum toward a more meaningful experience for students. As Moll and González (1994) suggest, teachers who actively draw information from the community and bring it into the classroom for discussion are more likely to engage students and keep them motivated to continue on to higher levels of education. In Villachuato, however, I rarely noted instances in which such information was brought into classroom discussions, despite the potential richness of discussing, for instance, the impact of transnational migration on the community.

There were, however, exceptions. In some cases, local teachers did express to me their understanding of the relative literacy crisis in which Villachuato finds itself. One teacher at the primary school, for instance, shared with me her understanding of the general conditions in the town:

> Well, I see that there's a high level of alcoholism. In the majority, this is a normal situation for them: that men of age should be alcoholic. Because he's a man. It's machismo [laughs] It's really strong. And the role of the mother is just to stay at home. Not to have any opinions. That her husband should

decide everything. Women don't have hardly any say in things at all . . . even though—this is really ironic to me—it's the women who come to the meetings. Not the fathers. But it's the men who decide things. Or, for example, I have women who miss appointments, or meetings, because they have to prepare the breakfast for their husbands, and they have to wait to serve him, or else they won't get to eat themselves.

When I asked about the ways in which these patterns affect this teacher's work in her classroom, she responded: "Well, we try to help the kids become more conscientious—well, so that they know that it's an error to think that this is the only alternative. Rather, there are sports, there is school. There are all kinds of possibilities that they can pursue when they are adults—not just become alcoholics." She also explained that, because of the resistance to change that exists in the community, kids often get stuck in the middle. She says it's like a "choque de ideas" (tangle of ideas). The parents don't want change, but the schools are implementing changes, so "kids don't know where to put their loyalties."

Patterns like these constitute an entirely different set of crisis rhetorics in and around Villachuato. Indeed, other comments from community members themselves demonstrate how, even if not intentionally, the schools in Villachuato have driven a wedge between children and their families. "He was really good at hitting us," one seventy-year-old woman described the first teacher in Villachuato. "When he didn't like one of the kids, he hit them a lot. He was really aggressive. It was bad. Because if you don't know something, and they don't tell you, how are you going to learn?" Moreover, she explained, it was typically those children who were poorer who got the brunt of things: "He was really fierce, especially with the kids that he didn't like. He treated them bad. Because there were plenty of kids that he liked—oh, he was really nice to some of them. He didn't do anything to them. But [my siblings and I] had to go out and work the fields, so sometimes we missed class, and I think it was because of that that he didn't like us." In this way, the teachers in Villachuato value and reward a certain kind of knowledge: not that of working the fields, but that of schooled literacy. Those students in Villachuato whose families had the resources to send them to school every day fared well; the others did not. One woman who lived some period of years in a nearby community related her similar experiences:

Over there, we had to walk an hour to get there, so I didn't like it so much. Because it was hard for us to get to school, and then another hour to get back. That's how it was for us. So if school started at eight, we had to leave at seven. And sometimes we got there late, and that's when they would punish us. They hit us with a ruler. That's why I didn't like it so much.

As we can see, corporal punishment in this area tended to be practiced on children who often did not control their learning and life conditions. And because they lacked the financial resources to attend school consistently, and the cultural capital to know and address the appropriate school curriculum, they were punished. A woman now in her late twenties explained to me how this kind of corporal punishment and shaming practices are still being used in Villachuato's schools: "Well, they did, you know, pull your ears, you know, if you got an answer wrong. . . . I only got my ear pulled once. And oh, I got so embarrassed." So, access to school was complicated, and success rates remain low. In the age bracket of parents now in their forties and upward, for instance, the average level of completed schooling is third or fourth grade; those parents who finished primary school speak of it with pride. Moreover, for those who did remain in school, resources were sparse, and learning outcomes were low. "I don't really think we had books," one woman related. "I don't remember. I mostly remember how they made us work on the *tablas* [time tables] to practice math. Nothing else. I don't remember much how they taught us. I learned to read and write a little, but not much. Like adding and multiplying and dividing—I don't know any of that. Well, adding things up, a little bit. But multiplying and dividing, no, not at all."

In light of the town's historical experiences with its schools, it is not surprising that schooled literacy continues to be a contested concept. Throughout the data drawn for this book, patterns of both pain and impossibility characterized many community members' experiences of literacy: It asked too much of them, and it didn't give much in return. Indeed, as I found in my research, the promises that teachers make to their students are often not in line with the students' own priorities (Teague, Smith, and Jiménez, 2010). For instance, the promise of a bright, shining career in Morelia, the state's capital two hours away, is not appealing to a child whose primary desire—as many children reported to me—is to remain in Villachuato and help their mothers, or go to the United States to make money to help their families (Bonfil, 2001). Indeed, this juxtaposition is not unlike what happened earlier in the twentieth century just after the Revolution, when people were given land without any tools to work it. Today education is slowly growing in this area, but there are no jobs. Any employment off the family's *ejido* lands is available only in other towns or cities. The relative unlikelihood that employment will open up in Villachuato is evident in the failure of the single industrial experiment in the town: a fertilizer distribution center that operated and failed in the 1980s. Since then, there has been no growth, other than small-scale family-run businesses out of the home. In this way, although people from the outside (e.g., revolutionary liberators or impassioned teachers) offer the promise of self-promotion and a better life, it has often been the case that these plans were hugely impractical: a bit of land without a plow, a high school education without any jobs to apply for. It is not entirely surprising, then, that Villachuato residents both remain wary of outside advice and continue to choose the same patterns over and over: women work in the home, and men migrate north.

## LITERACY AS SELF-DEFENSE

However, the two central influences on young people in Villachuato—education and migration—both require them to leave Villachuato; for an enterprising young person from Villachuato, the only place to go, is away. Thus it appears that the future of Villachuato lies, in many ways, beyond the borders of the town itself. The question then, for educators, is what kind of outward direction will these children choose? Will they end up in U.S. schools? In Mexican universities? In Midwestern meat-packing plants? While we may not be able to predict the exact shift of populations in the future, it seems likely that both of the now established trends will continue. That is, residents of Villachuato will see the north as their means of self-improvement; and, as migrating adults increasingly take their families with them, more and more students will end up in U.S. schools. We need to consider, then, not only the particular sets of skills and personalities that these students bring, but also the nexus of literacy values that exist in their families and shift along with their migrant lives.

To begin with, it is important to remember the kinds of social traditions from which the town comes. The indigenous groups that originated in the area of Michoacán, the Purépecha, were one of the few groups in Mesoamerica strong enough to withstand Aztec overthrow. And, growing out of this tradition of self-protection, the people of Michoacán have remained ardently independent and strong-willed. For instance, it is claimed that the first planning meetings of the independence movement were held in Morelia,[17] and strong efforts during the Revolution likewise came out of Michoacán. The result is a social fabric rich in traditional values, experienced all the more strongly in the small, largely autonomous *ranchos* of the area (Farr, 2006), of which Villachuato is one. For instance, as one of the primary school teachers explained to me, Villachuato is both a place that is undergoing a lot of change and remains resistant to those changes at the same time (Bonfil, 1996). Remarking on the difference between generations, she noted: "Parents are resistant to change. This used to be a hacienda, and they were exploited. They had to fight for their rights in order to survive. And I think this way of living has been passed down through the generations. The people here don't like change." Moreover, she told me, this dynamic creates problems for children, who are caught between new and old influences. Often, she explained, parents don't want to see change, but the schools implement change. And the result is that "kids don't know where to put their loyalty."

Indeed, as scholars like Guadalupe Valdés (1996) remind us, traditional orientations toward education in Mexico divide responsibilities between families and schools: "What English speakers call *education* is school or book learning. What Spanish speakers call *educación* had a much broader meaning and includes both manners and moral values" (p. 125). That is, whereas *education* refers to academic learning, the Spanish word *educación* refers to the family's role teaching children to be well behaved. As I witnessed in Villachuato, parents in traditional Mexican families respect teachers' roles as the authority figures in the schooling portion of their children's lives. They do not question teachers' decisions but rather defer to their authority on school-related matters. However, because the terrain is divided, parents hold sway over young people's personal development. They are responsible for teaching children how to behave, how to interact socially, what to value, what to expect from this lives, and how to make daily decisions according to this model. This division of responsibilities is consistent with a family market structure (Monroy, 1996), which organizes labor around the home. To that end, it makes sense for families to defer portions of socialization to teachers and to maintain a division: it matches their market realities in Mexico.

In my own work, the best evidence I gathered of these traditional values was the data that I *couldn't* obtain. That is, as has happened to other researchers (Valdés, 1996), there were certain interview questions that simply failed. When I asked participants about important events from childhood, for instance—or even later in life—I received blank stares. "Nothing much happens here," I was told more than once. "My life was *lo normal*. We were just living." During the time between the end of their schooling (usually before sixth grade) and their marriage, most young women had few defining events to report; and my attempt to measure their lives in terms of activities was a woeful failure. They didn't measure their own lives temporally, or in terms of outcomes. Furthermore, when I asked them about their hopes for the future, most responses were bereft of specific goals. More than anything, I was told that they wanted simply to "be together" with their loved ones. In this way, while some of my research questions were, in their way, failures, the fact of these responses suggests something important about the town's value system. That is, because the people of Villachuato, particularly the women, live their lives day-to-day, they aren't highly interested in planning ahead in the way that formal education requires students to do.

Even so, I did find that my participants consider school important, though not for the same reasons that the teachers emphasize. Rather than prizing intellectual growth and increased employment options, Villachuato citizens recognize formal education as an important means of personal and political survival. That is, they consider literacy as an instrument of self-defense rather than a progression toward personal fulfillment. Moreover, despite large historical gaps in learning, Villachuato citizens are well aware of the process of learning, whether or not they have been to school. For instance, the woman cited above who reported low levels of mathematical ability, understands what the next levels of study would be and how they might be applied. More importantly, the participants in this study in general provided anecdotes and opinions that suggest that they understand the broader power systems at play in formal literacy practices. That is, although they may not have much cultural capital of their own, they recognize what such capital is, where it comes from, and the importance of it to their lives.

This broad awareness of *what* official literacy is and *why* it might be useful contributes to a counter-narrative about literacy that stands in marked contrast to the missionary rhetorics described earlier in this volume. That is, rather than characterizing formal education as a practice that leads to personal salvation, the citizens of Villachuato recognize the importance of literacy as a pragmatic tool to be acquired and manipulated. Moreover, as has been noted elsewhere (Seitz, 2004; King, 1994) this tool is particularly important as a means of self-defense. For instance, when I asked middle school students about the purpose of going to school, their answers were both pragmatic and indicative of an understanding of the darker, more exploitative aspects of life. "Why do people go to school?" I asked. "So they can learn, and so that they don't get treated badly," one student answered. Another student, even more astute, told me: "Because when you go to look for a job, so that they don't trick you. You have to be able to read the contract." In this way, students, even at the seventh-grade level, demonstrate an understanding of the pragmatic importance of formal literacy to economic survival. It is important to learn how to read, one student told me:

> Because reading is when . . . like for instance, if you go to a meeting. . . . But sometimes people don't want to, because they don't know how to read and write. And if you can read, you can go and understand things. And writing, well that's the same. Write things that are important. Like if you have to go and sign for official papers, or sign at the bank to get your money. Well, they give you a paper, and you have to sign it. And . . . sometimes people don't know how.

Still others connected these literate skills to job acquisition: "Because, like, for jobs, it's important because they'll tell you, 'Sign here,' or 'Put your name here.'

And if you don't know how to write, you'll lose that job." However, in addition to identifying the pragmatics of reading and writing, students in Villachuato likewise recognize their social significance. It is important to learn to how to read, one student told me, "Because if you go to the secondary school and you don't know how to read, they'll make fun of you. Because you're that old, and you don't know how to read." In this example, the student's awareness of the shamefulness of illiteracy suggests an implicit understanding of the social prestige that literacy carries—that is, its significance as *cultural capital*.

Interestingly, when I asked middle school students what they wanted out of life, many of them responded with specific careers: doctors, teachers, engineers. While I suspect that these particular answers reflected what the students believed that I, as a U.S. researcher, wanted to hear, I was more interested in a related pattern of answers that I received. Several of the students, both past and present, talked about how they wanted to continue pursuing education (often in spite of the fact that, financially, they couldn't) because they wanted to *become somebody*. While none of the participants explicitly explained what they meant by this, their yearning for the prestige that accompanies formal education suggests a sharp understanding that education is the force in life that raises a person's social standing. Moreover, one particular parent's response sent this message home for me. "Sure I want my kids to go to college," he told me. "I want them to be professionalized. So they can get to do what they want, you know? So they can call the shots." Clearly, this parent has made an important realization about the value of formal literacy: While the reality in Villachuato is that education *does not* lead directly to financial opportunities, it does elevate a person's cultural capital, such that they take on more social power. And it is this kind of power that makes the real difference: not the ability to simply apply for a job but to develop enough clout so that one can direct one's own life, rather than be exploited, as so many generations in Villachuato have been. This, then, is the promise of formal education in Villachuato. Parents hope that their children will be able to "call the shots"—a goal that is quite strategic and, therefore, rhetorical in nature.

As per this man's hopes for his children, the strongest motivating factor for continued schooling in Villachuato comes not from teachers' influences or even a pragmatic sense of self-defense, but from familial encouragement. When I asked one young woman in Villachuato—one of the very few teenage girls who is going on for her high school diploma—why she had decided to keep going to school, her answer was very clear: "My father [who works in the United States] told me that I should keep going, that he's going to support me and all of that." Another young woman described her relationship to her father in a different way. "Well, I like . . . being able to read," she explained.

"It's helped me a lot, because my father [who doesn't read and write] . . . for instance, the [government] was giving him some help with our lands [through an agricultural subsidy]. And I was the one who went to gather up the forms and read them and organize them and such." Regardless of the direction in which support moves—whether a family funds their children's education or a child's education helps maintain a family's finances—it is the connection to family that comes first, and the drive toward success in school that comes second. Throughout the stories that my informants shared with me, it was a parent or older family member's concern that inspired a young person to pursue education. "My dad would make us these milk shakes in the morning," one woman who grew up on the U.S. side of the border explained:

> [They had] these crazy like vitamin powders that were absolutely horrible, but were supposed to be really good for your brain. And so, like yeah, so we had these brain power shakes. And we would take these *huge* vitamins, and, you know, and my dad just . . . and he would put two raw eggs in the [milk shakes]. And you know, we were little . . . but I would, um, you know, because school was so important to me, so I thought that this would make a difference. So I drank it no problem.

Discomfort is endured, then, if family members' *consejos* (advice) recommend it. In one last example, another woman who likewise grew up in the United States explains the way in which her older sisters supported her high school and community college education:

> I was the only one who was going to school, because my sisters, they had to work, to pay rent and bills. My oldest sister before me, they were fourteen and seventeen, and they had to work, and they were the ones that kind of pushed me to go to school. . . . And . . . what they used to tell me was: "You know, you really have to go to school, finish up school, so that when you graduate you can have a better job than what we got. You can have a better life than what we have."

### REMITTANCES AND RESISTANCE

A problem of even well-intentioned examinations of minority students can be the propensity to cast them as uninformed victims of larger, powerful institutions. One goal of this book is to highlight the levels of awareness—implicit or explicit—that rural Mexican communities carry with respect to their life conditions and opportunities to obtain resources and to position themselves socially, particularly within or in regard to institutions like schools. In many cases, such positioning and use of resources in these communities have taken the shape of resistance and/or self-preservation in the threat of oppressive conditions. Furthermore, as the narratives in subsequent chapters indicate, members of communities in rural Mexico have historically gained access to such resources—material and symbolic—through social connections (Alba and Nee, 2003; Portes and Zhou, 1993). Moreover, in recent decades, these connections have increasingly extended across the U.S.-Mexico border as family members have migrated north, whether on a temporary or permanent basis. Because ties between Villachuato and its U.S. receiving communities remain close, migrating family members often call regularly, send remittances, or make personal visits to the town. Indeed, in the United States, stores named "Villachuato Supplies" sell Mexican products to Villachuato migrants, reminding them of home and blending their U.S. experience with artifacts from Mexico. In this way, Peggy Levitt's notion of social remittances as the values, expectations, and behaviors that follow immigrants to their new homes and influence the ways in which they interpret their experiences is validated, as is the subsequent pattern of migrants returning their newly adapted values and behaviors back to the home community (1998). Indeed, for members of the extended Villachuato community, social capital continues to be an important and wide-ranging resource.

And what, specifically, do members of the community pass along social lines? How do community members benefit from this additional social capital? First, there is certainly a broader resource base. As migrants send money home, increased financial capital becomes the means by which Villachuato residents can build farms, start small businesses, or send children to school. This pattern of income has remained, even if at a slightly reduced rate for a few years since the global recession of 2008 (Cohen, 2010; Mohapatra and Silwall, 2009), such that families in Villachuato continue to rely on remittances as part of their regular budget. Second, the stories and artifacts that migrants send home expand the community's awareness of the variety of local and global contexts of which it is a member. Third, given these additional material means and expanded awareness of their world, members of the Villachuato community are better able to work strategically to position themselves in the ways that make the most sense for their own needs and desires. Considered together, these outcomes suggest that one effect of the remittances—financial and social—that migrants send home is that they position community members at home to function rhetorically, rather than reactively, to sources of social oppression. As a result, members of the Villachuato community have been able to both seek and resist formal education according to their needs. They have implicitly learned to adopt a rhetorical approach to literacy: one that grants them agency, even if in a limited sense, over the outcome of their lives.

## CONCLUSION

The rhetorical stance that Villachuato community members take toward literacy is important not only to our understanding of educational experiences in Mexico, but likewise in the United States. Thus far, we have seen the ways that competing literacy crises compete for allegiance in rural Mexico. From the perspective of rural teachers, migration poses a significant threat to education, such that teachers begin to fault students for making the *wrong* choices in their lives. Alternately, the community has for decades suffered prejudice and alienation in the school context, such that they are less likely to adopt the principles and life priorities that schools endorse. Rather, they tend to resist sanctioned school priorities by virtue of accepting those aspects of formal schooling that serve them and leaving the rest behind. As this chapter has demonstrated, the community considers literacy skills valuable to the extent that they help them to defend themselves in life; and they participate in school practices only so far as to accomplish this goal. They do *not,* however, accept the school system's broader values, including those that endorse the literacy contract (i.e., delayed gratification), in large part because a contract orientation toward literacy does not mesh with the economic model still present in Villachuato. Moreover, the community is able to be selective in its school participation largely because of the ongoing strength of the community itself—on both sides of the U.S.-Mexico border. As resources—in the shape of both migration dollars and migration experiences—pour into the town, students are granted more physical options, and more agency with which to position themselves rhetorically in terms of school and life choices. As I move forward into the final sections of this book, I will consider the ways that this rhetorical positioning—along with issues of crisis, contract, and resistance— play out in the U.S. context. In particular, the next chapter illustrates the ways in which the stakes of the literacy contract go up for students who migrate to the United States. In this new situation, schools demand more assimilation, but the marketplace also delivers more in terms of professional opportunities and financial reward. As a result, students can feel their loyalties so divided that they often find themselves in a true state of crisis.

## 6. "Like Going from Black and White to Color" / Mexican Students' Experiences in U.S. Schools

It was like going back in time. The classroom had groups of twenty-five, thirty kids in them. They didn't really have books. The teacher taught, you know, from the chalkboard in the front. Many of the rooms had nothing on the walls; it was just very stark. The kids just sat on little benches. And you saw kids of different ages in the same classroom. They said that if a student didn't master all of the content, they stayed in that grade. So there were some kids who maybe had learning disabilities who were three, four years older than the rest of the kids. It was almost like that old one-room school house that you would see from previous times. A lot of the things we saw there in Villachuato we related to a generation ago. You know, people on the farm, a small farm, doing everything. You know, independent. It was very much like our grandparents. And the schools, you know, followed that. . . . It was a generation behind where we are, at least.

Despite good intentions—so clear to me from the passionate tone of her interview—the response of Marshalltown teacher Sharon Kuntz to her trip to Villachuato in 2003 was tempered by a sense of lack. Not what was there so much as what was not: a lack of resources, resulting in outdated pedagogical practices. Similarly, Gaby, another Marshalltown teacher who recently visited schools in Villachuato and surrounding areas[18] reported that, "It was very old-fashioned. There weren't a lot of opportunities for communication and talk. We didn't see a lot of books. What we did see were thin little books where they were just sitting off quiet and working. There wasn't a lot of interaction, or talking." Clearly, these teachers are both concerned about the impact that a low resource base can have on pedagogical practices. Specifically, they noted the teacher-driven nature of the curriculum, as well as the lack of supporting materials like desks, library books, and classroom decorations: "It was a very teacher-centered dynamic. Not a lot of student participation, other than some rote responses and things, but no, you know, little groups, and no centers. It was just a very formal kind of system."

In contrast, these teachers noted a comparatively *informal* style of school management. "I kind of remember a couple of days," Sharon explained, "when they were like, 'Oops, the teacher couldn't come today.' So, the kids were sent back home. The system was just much more informal. You know, no subs. No scrambling to cover. Just, 'Oh, the teacher didn't come today. . . so we don't have school.'" Similarly, Gaby explained that "It didn't seem like there was accountability for their teachers or their students. Because with the host family that we stayed with, the child got up and went to school, but the teacher didn't show up; so, an hour later, he was home. And we were like, 'Ok.' It also seemed to me that if a student didn't feel like going to school that day, that there wasn't anybody to call home, or to say, 'Hey, this child is missing.'"

In both cases, these teachers' critiques center on perceived faults within the system: a lack of material resources leading to outdated pedagogical models and a lack of accountability for both teachers and students. In turn, their implicit assumption is that the system in the United States is better organized and more pedagogically advanced. While Sharon and Gaby noted systemic deficiencies, other instructors in Marshalltown consider cultural differences. While speaking with a teacher at the high school, I was startled to hear her mention a racialized view of differing cultural responses to time:

> You know, you can stand out in the hallways and look to see which kids are late for class, and they're all brown-skinned kids. So part of that is assimilation: it's important. It's priorities. It is knowing what the expectations are and making them a priority. I can walk behind our kids and I'll say, "Hop it up. It's time to go." But the pace doesn't change. You know. I'm not internalizing it as a form of disrespect for me. I am internalizing it as, it's not yet a priority for them. So, it's setting goals and having aspirations to move forward, and we just have a core group of students, and that hasn't happened yet for them.

Whether systemic or cultural, these critiques focus on deficiencies: what isn't yet there. This deficit orientation has two significant effects. First, it communicates to Mexican-origin students that the backgrounds from which they come are less valuable—even flawed—as compared to the U.S. system. This communicated message can drive a wedge between students' new realities (i.e., school in a new country) and their former realities (i.e., home community). Second, it creates "room for improvement": an orientation that assumes that literacy develops linearly and that, therefore, students coming to the United States can achieve upward mobility by virtue of making educational gains. This latter point—a component of the *literacy contract*—is important because the promise of social mobility through education in Mexico has been problematic. Earlier in this volume, I argued that centralized public schooling in Mexico has not always prioritized the interests of rural communities. Rather, as Bradley Levinson (1996) points out, becoming educated in rural Mexico means cutting ties with the home community; and as students in Villachuato remind us, it also means cutting ties geographically. As a result, rural communities like Villachuato have developed coping mechanisms via both relational and covert forms of resistance. In contrast, immigration to the United States promises increased resources: wage labor for parents and consistently accessible and affordable schools for youth. The remaining question, then, is whether or not families' responses to the literacy contract will change in this context. Will a renewed promise of upward mobility-via-education be persuasive enough to compel students forward to higher levels of schooling? Furthermore, in a climate that requires students to culturally assimilate in order to pursue professionalization, does education seem to be worth its price? If not, how is resistance configured in this new context?

In this final chapter before the conclusion, I survey data drawn from Villachuato's principal receiving community, Marshalltown, Iowa. Highlighting the perspectives of the community and its teachers as well as immigrant parents and their children, my aim is to present a multifaceted perspective on migrant literacy. To that end, I begin with an overview of the Marshalltown situation, including ways that the Villachuato immigrant population has impacted the town and vice versa. From there, I highlight schools' sympathies for and frustrations with Mexican students, as well as parents' orientations; and I close with a consideration of students' experiences. The first of these perspectives—teachers and schools—strikes a common chord with teachers' comments in Mexico, as U.S. teachers reinstate beliefs about education's tie to social mobility. This time, parents advocate school participation, though they strive to maintain control of related values about significant life choices. And students, for their part, remain ambivalent about education and its requirements. In the context of migration, the stakes of the literacy contract are raised, as the promises that schools make are higher, but the commitment that they seek—particularly assimilation—is likewise more demanding. Literacy functions *as* assimilation (1) because it is ideological and therefore promotes cultural values, and (2) because schools insert authority, leaving parents uncertain of their role and students uncertain how to respond to school demands and familial patterns.

## MARSHALLTOWN: "YOU ADVERTISED THAT IT WAS FOR *EVERYBODY*"

Marshalltown is a community with a population of approximately twenty-five thousand located forty miles east of Ames, Iowa. The central plaza features a picturesque courthouse (figure 6.1), and the main streets of town are lined with small commercial enterprises. The town itself has a quiet, intimate feel. However, shifting several blocks east toward the outskirts of town, a stale smell clamps down on the air: a thick, animal odor. The neighborhood around the Swift plant, where 10,000 to 16,000 hogs are processed each day, is an undesirable area, populated primarily by the families who work at the plant. Swift itself is monolithic and industrial. Covering the equivalent of three city blocks, it is entirely fenced, and displays almost no identifying information outside. The general public is no longer allowed inside, though anthropologist Mark Grey, who was able to visit the plant during the late 1990s, reported the strong presence of Villachuato workers. Stalls in the men's restrooms, for instance, are graffitied with patriotic notations about hometowns in Mexico and frustrated profanities against the Immigration and Naturalization Service (INS) (Grey and Woodrick, 2002).

Figure 6.1. Marshalltown courthouse

Because of the unpleasant nature of the work, as well as the dangerous working conditions (knives, machinery, slippery floors), meat-packers have long resorted to the lowest-skilled and least-privileged sectors of society. Prior to the union movement in the early twentieth century, many plants were located in urban centers like Chicago, where large populations of African Americans lived. Then, as workers' rights movements grew stronger, the packing houses moved out to more remote areas, where local populations were less likely to organize and strike (Richardson-Bruna and Vann, 2007). For several decades, meatpacking plants found a steady, reliable workforce in the rural heartlands. More recently, however, the farming crisis of the 1980s has resulted in an exodus of native Iowans, and plants are having an increasingly difficult time filling their positions. Despite the wages, which are relatively high compared to other areas of unskilled labor, Iowa's meat-packing plants, including Marshalltown's Swift plant (figure 6.2), are unable to attract the largely Anglo populations of the rural Midwest to work in their plants (Grey and Woodrick, 2002). Instead, they are turning increasingly to (often undocumented) Mexican workers who continue to cross the border in substantial numbers, despite a dampened economy and tightening immigration policies in the United States since 2008 (Cohen, 2010; Consejo Nacional de Población, 2010).

The results are striking. By 2002, Marshalltown's Swift factory, the world's third largest pork processing plant, employed approximately five hundred workers from Villachuato. This number accounted for about one-third of the

Figure 6.2. Swift factory

overall production staff at Swift. The importance of this small Mexican town to the Swift plant, as well as to pork production in the United States overall, is profound. Without the labor force from Villachuato and towns like it, the Swift factory would not operate (Grey and Woodrick, 2002). Furthermore, many of these workers are bringing their families—and the town, and its schools, are taking notice. In 2002, a community news feature, "Positive Exposure: Immersion in Latino Culture Brings Positive Changes," explained to Marshalltown residents the impact of immigrants on their community, visible in part because of new businesses (figure 6.3; Grey and Barker, 2002). More recently, three groups of Iowa educators visited Villachuato as part of an Iowa Administrators and Educators Immersion Experience (IAEIE) funded by the Iowa Department of Education's Director of English Language Learner Education and designed and facilitated by Iowa State University's Assistant Professor Katherine Richardson Bruna as part of her research on the transnationalizing rural Midwest (Richardson Bruna, Forthcoming). On the Mexican side of the border, Marshalltown is spoken of with excitement, almost reverence. When I appeared in Villachuato to conduct my research, it was more than a month before community members finally stopped asking me whether or not I had come from Iowa. For Villachuato, the horizon of economic development and a better life increasingly takes on a single name: Marshalltown.

For Marshalltown itself, the implications are likewise significant. While the newcomers' fundamental economic role in the town has become increasingly difficult to deny (filling factory labor needs, opening new businesses such as the

Figure 6.3. Mexican grocery store in Marshalltown

one pictured, etc.), nonimmigrant residents remain divided in their opinions. While some residents are pragmatic and accepting about the change in the town's demography, others remain unsettled by the change. Indeed, at times residents find themselves in a battle of wills about the situation, as is evident in the following description from the children's librarian at Marshalltown's library:

> One mom yelled that we advertised that this event was for everybody. But, there happened to be a Spanish story teller [who] was alternating between English and Spanish. And it was just so stupid, because her daughter was sitting there in awe, and loved the whole thing. And the mom came over and said, "You advertised that it was for everybody." And I said: it *is*. And she said, "Well, why are they speaking in Spanish?" And I said, "Well, it's because we're celebrating *Día de los Niños*, and it's kind of about Latino culture. And we have an English story, but we're trying to do both." And she was like, "That's what we speak here." And I said, "Well, you know, we have fifty-one weeks of the year when we only speak in English, so I think we can have one day when some of our stories are in Spanish." That's all I'm gonna say.

So, there is a good deal of sympathy and investment—from programming to visits to rural Mexico—on the part of literacy leaders in Marshalltown. However, there are also strong expectations that families will both appreciate these efforts and adopt their corresponding values. Indeed, the stakes of the literacy contract go up in the context of migration, as families are expected to assimilate culturally in order to access what education promises in this new place.

### U.S. EDUCATOR EXPECTATIONS OF IMMIGRANT YOUTH

In many ways, Marshalltown teachers' approaches take into careful consideration the conditions of the families they serve. Particularly those who have visited sites in rural Mexico appreciate the differences that their students encounter, including the visual differences in resources (see the Marshalltown schools in figures 6.4 and 6.5, as compared to Villachuato schools shown earlier in figures 5.3 and 5.4): "In places like Michoacán," the librarian quoted above explained,

> you just really don't have a lot of public libraries. . . . I mean, compared to the books that we have, with the beautiful color . . . It really made me realize when kids came and walked in here . . . how incredible they must feel. I mean, I've seen the reactions. But I didn't really understand it until I saw [what things are like in Mexico]. I mean, it would be like us going from black and white to color! It's so different.

Figure 6.4. Elementary school in Marshalltown

Indeed, the transition to U.S. schools can be nearly immobilizing for some students. Relating her experiences with new arrivals in Marshalltown, Sharon described what it is like to witness young students' processes of acclimatization:

> We could see that sometimes when the kids came in 2nd, 3rd, 4th grades, they just had that look on their face. They were overwhelmed by their visual stimulus, and things that were just like, wow. And we would see that translate into kids who were very quiet, very in some cases nonresponsive. I mean, I've had kids in kindergarten, and the other kids thought they never talked. I remember one kid from a couple of years ago, and maybe about November, the other kids realized, "He talks! We didn't think he talked." And he was, he was just an overwhelmed kid, you know, and he just had to take it all in.

Parents, too, they recognize, are often overtaxed. Explaining the reason that parents don't always get involved in their children's schoolwork, Sharon emphasized that, "Some of these people are so concerned with their day-to-day struggles, whether it's working—you know, dad one shift, mom one shift— they don't carry on conversations with their children. They are busy surviving, and thinking 'How am I gonna get here and there?'"

However, despite these myriad forms of sympathy and understanding, there are limits. Teachers in Marshalltown can find some of these families' needs difficult to work around—particularly those habits that suggest families'

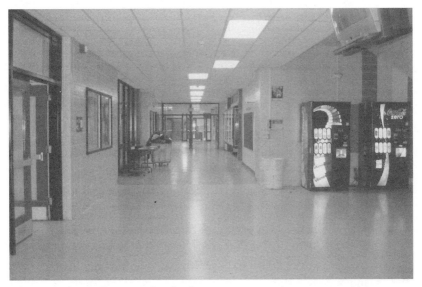

Figure 6.5. Marshalltown High School

insufficient investment in the school process. One such area of contention is Mexican families' tradition of returning home for holidays and town festivals, such as the annual fiesta that takes place around Easter each year. "Often," an elementary school teacher explained, "they want to take their kids out of school to go to Mexico and go visit their families. And then they miss a part of their education. We couldn't mandate that they stay. But we're also being judged on test scores, so the child may get back on Tuesday, and there's a state exam scheduled for Thursday, and they have to take it. So, we had trouble with our school's achievement scores." This teacher's explanation of the situation—similar in tone to parallel discussions that I had with several Marshalltown teachers—was infused both with an awareness of the family's needs and desires, as well as with an urgency about the importance of maintaining educational standards. "Especially around Thanksgiving, they'd start leaving. And Christmas. And then they'd start leaving around the fiesta time [in the spring]. Some of them would go twice. And so that really impacted their education. That's just always a struggle. It's a cultural as well as an educational decision. We understand that we're not going to block your decision, but we want to make you aware. It's difficult. And you know, it's a cultural struggle." In this way, while teachers strive to be understanding and encouraging, they also expect immigrant families to begin shifting their decision making along different lines. That is, they expect them to assimilate to U.S. patterns of priorities and expectations.

Assimilation, however, is a much-debated concept as it relates to the relative success of second generation immigrants. In some circles, scholars identify assimilation and upward mobility as dependent variables, arguing that assimilation is a necessary precursor to upward mobility (Alba and Nee, 2003). However, other scholars argue that assimilation does not always lead to economic improvement, such that some immigrants—particularly second and third generation—become dubious about it. They argue that resisting assimilation is the key to success (Portes and Zhou, 1993). While the outcome of these debates remains undetermined, the education system itself does tend to treat assimilation as a precursor to upward mobility. While this may or may not be the case, the education system often treats it as such. That is, they ask students to forego certain heritage practices, such as returning home for Mexican festivals, in order to be able to participate more fully in education. So, there is sympathy to the extent that we realize that parents don't understand the system and that they are taxed by pragmatic needs on a daily basis. However, the implicit understanding is that these parties agree to the fundamental priorities and perspectives of the formal education system: specifically, the belief that education will lead to desired outcomes.

In this way, the most fundamental request that teachers make—that students complete mandatory levels of education—echoes on both sides of the border. Just as teachers in Villachuato bemoan students' decisions to migrate rather than to complete their schooling in Mexico, so too do Marshalltown teachers voice their concern about students dropping out of high school in order to go work at the Swift plant. "They think: Oh, I just want to go get my check." As migration scholars Alba and Nee argue, this happens in part because students recognize that, regardless of finishing school, they may end up doing just what their parents are doing (Alba & Nee, 2003). Even so, Marshalltown educators would like to see students become more future-oriented: "Start setting goals for yourself. And learn how to do that, and then follow through with the goals that you've set. And allow others to help plan. Because they don't know how to plan. This is all new. And if they're willing to share aspirations—first of all to have aspirations and to set goals—and then to share them, and then allow somebody to help them follow through with it." These suggestions, however, constitute a significant paradigm shift for Villachuato families, as "planning ahead" is a radically different from the "just living" orientation that characterizes life back home in Villachuato. Further, what these teachers hope their students will focus on is college preparation. "We never say 'If you choose to go to college,'" one high school teacher told me. "We say 'when you go to college.'" In this way, the process of cultural assimilation that relates to literacy in the United States involves a shift in both one's vision in life, in addition to the commensurate choices that one makes to pursue that life vision.

But such expectations are not limited to students; teachers also expect parents to become involved in their children's school experience (and, by extension, in the latter's assimilation process), which is a marked difference from the division of expectations of school and parental authority that is common in Mexico (Valdés, 1996). At one recent school meeting, parents were asked, "What are your goals for your child?" One mother responded, "So that he can do better than I can. Or than his brothers did. I want him to be able to get out in the world and be productive and be able to hold a job. And do better than I did, and take care of himself and his family." Not surprisingly, Marshalltown teachers take heart at such responses, because they suggest that parents share their priorities: a conviction that education will lead to that "better life" that they want for their children. Echoing these comments, several teachers told me: "They want what's best for their children. They want their children to do better than they did." In this way, teachers often assume that parents have agreed to the literacy contract: that they share a belief in education as a straight forward means to self-improvement. "Really," one teacher explained, "[it's] this belief that education is going to be what's going to help their child really rise above the socio-economic level that the parents have. You know. That's what I see."

Even so, teachers recognize that parents don't always have the cultural capital to know how best to advise their children toward continued school-ing: "They want to do the right thing, but what is the right thing?" Another teacher elaborated:

Many of the families that are involved in that are low wealth, I think it's just over their heads. Deer in headlights. Cause it's a lot of mandates. It's a *lot* of stuff, and I think it can be very cumbersome for them to navigate and under-stand. So, I always see my role as trying to help them understand their rights, and why we're doing what we're doing. The needs of the child . . . However, perceptions of that are different culturally. So, sometimes you have to have a conversation with a family about a child with hyperactive behavior, and needs medicine for certain things.

Therefore, teachers assume—often correctly—that parents want to be directed toward the ways that they can help facilitate this process: "Parents really want what's best for their kids. You know, they're so grateful to have someone tell them, "These are the goals, you're child's meeting them or not meeting them." And so they do direct them:

We work with them, we really try to show them, by graphs and charts, what we're doing and what the purpose of the meeting is, and we set goals with the kids. If one of the goals is to read [a certain] amount of words per minute, we share that; or if they need to be working on their basic facts, we share that. And how they can help at home with them. And some of the questions then go back, well, how can you help them? And sometimes I get, "Well, hmmm, I don't know." And so then we just have to tell them, Well, you can provide a desk for them, you can make flash cards. If you have a computer at home, you can let them with supervision to look for things that they're supposed to be researching. And most times, once you give them the idea, they're like, oh yeah. But I'm not so sure that they would come up with those on their own.

While there may be a mutual connection in many such cases, and good general outcomes, as well, I suggest that there are some significant implications of this kind of teacher-parent interaction. As scholars like Guadalupe Valdés remind us, traditional orientations toward education in Mexico divide responsibilities between families and schools (1996). However, when these families are introduced to wage labor, their physical paradigm shifts, and with it, the division of responsibility. Parents are invited—and indeed expected—to take part in school conversations. While this may seem like an expansion of their parenting, I view it as a de facto curbing of their authority because they are being asked to adopt the school's values and to help schools orient students accordingly. I am not critiquing the relative right or wrongfulness of this dynamic, though I do wish to highlight its impact. As schools' agendas seep into the home, parents have less agency. This is a profound means of assimilation, and one that I don't believe all parents are signing on to. Rather, I believe that many teachers are mistaking parental concern about schooling for full-fledged complicit agreement to the terms of the new "contract" that they are being offered.

This is indeed one of the principal points that I wish to make in this chapter: The complexity of the terms of the literacy contract is heightened—most particularly because the contract itself becomes more difficult to detect. In a wage market, the contract culture makes more sense: *You do this for me, and I will reward you accordingly.* Indeed, Marshalltown teachers promise—and deliver—on several items: concrete programming, as well as general moral support. For instance, the Marshalltown school community is establishing college readiness programs. "I'm working right now with a group called 'Latinas al Éxito,'" Gaby told me. "And we mentor 8th grade girls to try to encourage them to finish first high school, and then encourage them toward the pathway of college or university studies." Moreover, several of the teachers I spoke with mentioned working with their students to help them recognize their own value: "And we keep telling them, too: you are bilingual. Look at how many monolingual people there are, that you would take a job before us, because of your abilities. So we really try to nurture that bilingualism, but we also try to tell them that being bilingual isn't going to help you as much as being biliterate. And to encourage them to keep up with their native language, reading and writing. . . . I tell them: People will pay for what you know. So, what do you know, and what can you learn to do?" Such teachers have high hopes for their students, and they exhibit a fair amount of cultural sensitivity. Even so, they maintain a set conviction that education is the right means for their students to be successful and happy, and they argue against following in their parents' footsteps: "They see their parents coming home crippled or hurt or in pain, and they're like, 'I don't want that.' And we would say: 'You need to be smarter in using your brain than using your back.' And a lot of them after watching their parents go through the pain and the suffering from working in the cold all day, they start to see that that's not what they want. They want a better life for themselves. And that includes postsecondary [education]." In this vein, teachers are both correct about many of their students' motivating factors, and they are taking steps to be positively supportive. At the same time, this conviction leaves teachers blind to some subtle ways that parents continue to resist full conversion to the U.S. paradigm and students continue to struggle between old and new influences.

## PARENTS' PERSPECTIVES ON SCHOOL IN THE UNITED STATES

In many cases, teachers are correct about parents' and students' desire for something other than the kind of work that migration—rather than educational training—can afford. "It's hard, working there all day," one woman said of the demands of Swift factory work. "We tell our kids that—it's very hard work there, where we go. All day with the knife. All day. And you just think: how much longer?" This woman told me that she wants to see her sons complete their high school education because she hopes they can find work somewhere other than Swift. Even so, despite the hardship of factory work, families recognize the improved quality of life that they experience in Marshalltown. Isabel, the mother of three young boys, explained, "Here, when you get your paycheck on Friday, if the kids want to go eat a hamburger, we can go get hamburgers. It's another life here. It's not equal to that other one down there. Here, every three months, when the kids want new shoes, we go get them. We get what our children need. So, how could we go back down there? There's nothing. Nothing at the schools. No place to work. Nothing." Indeed, Isabel, who has been in the United States for nine years, cannot now imagine returning to her former life. When her children ask her about it, she explains:

They don't suffer now like we did in the past. . . . And I tell my kids how it was, but they just say, "Oh Mom, enough with your stories." And they just ask for things and ask for things, and when I was little, I didn't have *anything*. So I say to them: Ok fine, we'll go to Mexico. We'll eat nothing but beans and nopales. No pizza, no hamburgers—nothing. Because where would we get money down there? How would we pay for things? And they say: "No, we don't like beans." Nothing but beans and nopales we're eating down there. Because down there, that's all there is. Nothing for work. Nothing.

In some cases, this sense of want trails into perceptions of schooling as well, and several parents in Marshalltown remember the hardships of school in Villachuato. "We used to have . . . how many subjects?" a woman named Guermina remembers. "Math, social studies, science, Español, and whatever else. And all those books to carry. And I remember, my mother didn't have enough money to get us even a bag to carry them." Indeed, in accord with other stories from Villachuato residents, adults who have migrated to Iowa remember the sense of alienation that they felt at school. "Sometimes, the teachers would take you by the ear," a man named Jorge told me:

I remember that the teacher I had when I was six years old, we had a really strict teacher. My family told me I had to find a way to put up with it, but oh no, she would just hit us. . . . I didn't want to go over there, if all they were going to do was keep hitting us. . . . And my parents didn't believe it, but I explained to that them that yeah, they would hit us, or call us names—you burro!—they'd punish us. And even if it was our fault, why did they have to go on like that?

In contrast, these parents thought that schools in Marshalltown offer more: "Down there, the teachers miss a lot of school," Guermina told me:

There's a group of kids that don't have teachers. I know, because I talk to my sister on the phone, and she tells me she's stopped sending Ricardo to school because it's been close to a month, and there hasn't been any teacher. So the kids just come and stay a second, and they go back home. The school sends them. But here, if our kids get sick and miss school, the school calls right away to see what happened. They're worried about them. So, the schools are very different. Here, the school is really good. But there, no. Here, they're more concerned for the kids than down there. Down there, if a child misses a week of school, they just hold them back—that's it. But here they call to see what's happening. And if the kid is sick, they say to take them to the doctor.

And there, no. . . . The schools here are very good, so I tell my kids to take advantage of it. . . . Here, they give you breakfast and lunch at the school, and down there, no.

As other studies have identified (Monroy, 1999), these parents see schools as being of better quality in the United States. In particular, a resounding note in my conversations with Marshalltown families was the sense that the schools care about their students. They were, therefore, more inclined to trust the schools and teachers. And because many of these parents do not want to see their children end up at the Swift factory, they encourage their children to continue on in school. Noting a qualitative difference in resource base, they do begin to feel convinced that formal education will lead to increased financial possibilities. At the same time, however, their approval of school continued to focus on school's ability to protect their children: to teach them the tools necessary to keep them away from dangerous work like meat-packing, and to give them tools like English that will help them survive socially.

However, it should not be assumed that recognizing the value of schooling is equivalent to complete assimilation. As in Mexico, these parents still draw an implicit distinction between learning and behavior, suggesting that they still wish to maintain agency in their children's development via *educación*. Referring to parent-teacher conferences, one parent said,

Mostly they tell us that our children are doing well. Not fighting with other children at school or anything. And that they smile, and they're good children. . . . I always tell my children that it's important that they respect others. They have to respect other people. . . . One time, my son told me that one of the students said a bad word in the class, and the teacher got mad and sent him to the office. So there are kids who say bad things, but the teacher knows about it. I tell them they've got to behave themselves.

Teachers, too, recognize the ways that parents draw this distinction. "When I talk to parents," one teacher explained, "many times, the focus goes to behavior. 'Are they behaving very well?'" Another teacher told me that nearly all of her parent-teacher conferences at the kindergarten level are similarly structured: "The first thing that parents ask is 'How is he behaving?' They don't care about if he knows the numbers or [other academic things]. They want to know, how is he doing? How is he behaving? That's far more important to them. You know, I'm showing them: here's how he's been doing his alphabet letters. . . . But they're just like: How is he behaving? And I feel like, he's a sweet kid, but he doesn't know his letters!" Indeed, Villachuato parents living in Marshalltown continue to draw a distinction between *education* and *educación*: the school's responsibility (academics) as opposed to the family's responsibility (behavior). The division between behavior and academic work represents a distinction that continues to exist, and one that does bar a full conversion to U.S. approaches to learning. This distinction is rarely discussed, despite its importance. Truly, it marks a distinction between U.S. assumptions (i.e., behavior is tied to learning) and rural Mexican community assumptions (i.e., learning is separate from behavior). The disconnection between behavior and literacy is, indeed, the ideological basis of the reasons why this community doesn't accept the literacy contract.

I believe that this contrast is more than just a cultural distinction. It is about power: specifically, who yields the power to shape immigrant and generation 1.5 students' values, priorities, and life plans? This power is particularly related to issues of assimilation and resistance to the literacy contract itself. Moreover, parents' continued reliance on this distinction suggests to me that families from Villachuato want to maintain power over their children's lives and futures. They do not wish to conflate family identities and cultural foundations with the process of schooling. Furthermore, it is indeed problematic to conflate these two, as combining behavior with learning allows behavior, as well, to be evaluated in the school context (e.g. the perception that students do not "care" sufficiently for school). And, as such, inappropriate behavior (i.e. behavior that does not align ideally with the learning process and, therefore, with the literacy contract) can be considered another form of cultural deficit. So, whereas Marshalltown teachers have made strides connecting with Villachuato families over the past several years, they continue to miss a fundamental disconnect. They assume that these families agree with them about priorities. They mistake the orientation toward school—and a partial belief in the ability of school to produce more life options—for complicit adoption of the complete set of values that underlie public education. In truth, these parents, whether they are aware of it or not, are still drawing divisions in their minds between the role of school (protect my child from difficult life conditions) and the role of family: behavior and identity. In short, even if they encourage their children to attend school, they do not prepare them to let go of one identity in order to take on another one. And the fact that schools still implicitly apply this pressure makes for difficult tensions in students' experiences—even for those students who go on in school and who broadly experience school in a positive light. That is, because the tension between teachers and parents is nearly invisible, students' confusion has not only to do with pressures of assimilation, but also the lack of clarity surrounding the assimilation dynamic.

In the robust literature that exists on second-generation students, scholars on both sides of the border have identified the centrality and importance of migrants' preexisting social networks to both their survival and their potential access to upward mobility (Alba and Nee, 2003; Cohen, 2010; Levitt, 1998; McKenzie and Rapoport, 2010; Pereyra, 2001). A major component of the assimilation debates has to do with the assertion that social contacts are perhaps the most important resource that migrants have. Indeed, we have seen that, in Mexico, literacy as a socially shared practice led to its usage for self-defense, as well as other forms of resistance that allowed people to defend themselves against oppressive manifestations of schooling. Similarly, when literacy is experienced positively in the United States, it is most often in social contexts. For instance, students living in Marshalltown reported on the process of learning English through peer groups: a process that felt like gaining membership into a new community:

> I remember, like, in kindergarten, [I tried to play with my sister and friends] but when I tried communicating with them I didn't really know what they were talking about. [laughs] I remember that after that, they took me in to, like, like to learn English, and I picked that up really really quick, so that the next time I approached them, we got along a lot better and I just remember that that was a really really happy day for me because. . . . the other days, nobody wanted to play with me, and I'd just be there [alone]. And then that day, everything was just like . . . it was like every day was sunny.

This dynamic between language and social participation is echoed in another common pattern of generation 1.5 students: helping family members with literacy and language brokering. Many young people translate for their parents, a practice that has been widely debated, but which new research identifies as potentially positive (Orellana, 2009). Furthermore, students are often able to apply other literacy lessons to help their families. For instance, once Margarita learned English and related literacy skills, she was able to contribute to her family in ways that made her feel valuable. During her high school years, she helped her father navigate the process of buying a house. Even though he speaks some English, he found it difficult to navigate the computer system: "I always had to help him because like, he's not very good with computers, and I would like look up different realtor websites, and it's funny 'cause like the house that we live in now I actually like, I found it, but it was out of our price range." In these examples, literacy is experienced as something connective and, therefore, purposeful. Indeed, several students expressed the importance of their families' attitudes toward their own motivation in school. One student said, with regard to her life plans:

Well, definitely, education beyond high school. My dad always talks to us about that. That like he wants us to have . . . like we have so much opportunities more than they have when they were our age. So, he's always telling us that he doesn't like care if it's something simple, like nursing, or something that takes just like a year, or two years. But something that I'll at least like. . . . Like my mom, she worked at like Swift and it's very like, it's a very labor-intensive job. And she said that like they just don't want us to have that lifestyle. If we have like so many different opportunities, they just like want something different for us.

In a similar vein, Lupe, a young woman at Marshalltown High School, explained that her family is a crucial motivation for her continued work in school: "They're supportive, and that's like a lot of my motivation. Like, I want to do all this stuff 'cause I know that, like, I'm pretty, I think I'm capable of doing it. And, like, you have to have the mindset. And I do. Yeah, I'm really like doing it for them."

In contrast, when families do not demonstrate an expectation that their children will pursue higher levels of education, even otherwise inclined students, like high schooler Victoria, begin to lose momentum:

I've noticed that like my parents, when I talk to them, they don't really encourage me to go to school, and I think it's just kind of like subconsciously I think that they think it's kind of odd that I haven't you know, like gone with my boyfriend.[19] I think it's just kind of like an expectation in a way, like they kind of expect it, not that they want it. When I talk to them about like school and things, like I've had my mom sometimes. . . . Like I'm going to go on to MCC this year, like I've had her tell me sometimes that I shouldn't start something that I'm not going to finish. . . Well, I declared my major as political science and a minor in economics. But I've . . . I'm starting to get kind of unmotivated . . . I don't really see myself as really becoming something big in the political world. So um . . . I'm a little confused right now.

As Victoria reports, these difficulties began particularly at the high school level: the point in school at which she was asked to begin making decisions toward a professional life. "Like when I was in elementary school, I just went because I was like . . . that's what you did. But, like, as you go to high school, it's more like you're doing things for yourself. Like I always like try to get into hard classes and like try to do my best in school 'cause I knew that that was going to help me for college. So like I think the motivation changes as you get older." Further, as motivation shifts from family to individual, students can begin to encounter difficulties. For instance, Victoria is implicitly aware that, as in Bradley Levinson's model of becoming an educated person (1996), she is being asked to relinquish one identity for another. Moreover, she feels quite conflicted about this dynamic: "Well, yeah . . . yeah, I guess it's kind of going against my culture."

Therefore, not unlike the dynamics in Villachuato, the principal factors that impact students' experiences with schooling in Marshalltown have to do with social connections. In addition, pragmatism plays a significant role, particularly as students become implicitly aware that their material conditions have shifted in Iowa. Living now in the context of a functioning labor market, students are aware both that the promised rewards of the literacy contract are more available, and that domestic and familial work alone will not be sufficient for their future survival. These nuances effect a change in social organization. Whereas women in Villachuato typically do not work outside the home, the young women with whom I spoke in Marshalltown believe that they will: "Like, you know that you don't make a living off of washing your dishes. You're not going to pay yourself from washing dishes. You're going to make a living doing something else." Now that her family has entered a wage market, she understands that the family economic model doesn't work anymore. This realization highlights the utility of schooled literacy in a new way, and broadens into a new form of motivation for students, as they begin to believe in the promise of the literacy contract to grant them a better life. Explaining her thoughts about the purpose of school, student María explained: "So that when you grow up you can get a good job. Something nice. And you don't end up working somewhere that you don't like it." Indeed, as students transition into a new way of thinking—one that is more aligned with the literacy contract—they began to recognize a variety of rewards and attractions to the school environment. One student admitted that she now felt more comfortable at school than at home:

ADELA: I guess I just liked it better. I feel like I actually get rewarded for what I do. That's one way to put it.

MEYERS: So, at home, it was just kind of an expectation, like you help out. It's just kind of what you do to be in a family.

ADELA: Yeah.

MEYERS: But at school there were just kind of these ways to be motivated and to be recognized and things like that.

ADELA: Yeah. I think I liked being at school more than I liked being at home. I think I really looked forward to learning, I guess you could say. Learning all that. . . . all those things that I didn't get here at home. Um. . . . I always really liked school.

This note of surprise in several students' stories is one last pattern that I would like to highlight, particularly as it relates to their relative process of maintaining family ties and acclimating to a new environment. Similar to Victoria's slightly baffled confession that she prefers the school context to her home dynamic, other students similarly expressed notes of surprise. "I'm not really sure where I got my way of thinking," Celeste, another teenage girl explained:

Like for example, at my old school, other girls, they started having boyfriends and things like that and I still thought that was gross and things like that. Like I said, I think middle school's really hard for people. . . . . I never really looked at myself. . . . Like I'm sure you know it's very common [in Villach-uato] for fifteen-, sixteen-year-old girls to run off with their boyfriend, and have kids and things like that. But I never. . . . I don't think it ever crossed my mind to ever do that.

This anecdote suggests that Celeste found that she had, unbeknownst to herself, assimilated to the goals of U.S. high school education, rather than to more traditional patterns in her home community. In this way, she seems to feel that she has "accidentally" assimilated into her new context. This "accident" of cultural shift, though, can go both ways. For instance, in Nicole's story below, she explains how, as a young student, she converted away from school success, almost without her own awareness or intention:

I remember being just a super motivated little kid. And then, like, junior high came, and I started caring less. I mean, I started doing things that, you know, an average student [would do]. But, like, in elementary school, I only got As and Bs. You know, really rare any Bs. But in junior high, they were like Cs and Ds. You know, I just did enough to get by. And I think—one of the things that I think about now that I think I really hate about myself is that I learned um just enough to get by. . . . As junior high student, I never hung out with like the wrong crowd or anything like that. I never cared much about that. Like, it was never an interest of mine to be cool, or be with the cool kids, or smoke, or drink, or do drugs. I was like, you know, whatever. Like that was fine. But you know, I just remember my classes, just doing enough to get by. 'Cause I would see, well I can do, god, one-tenth of what I had been doing. You know, especially in the L.A. school district, you know like, I could do one-tenth, and still get Cs. So, that was fine with me. That's all, you know, that's all I really cared about. And I'm thinking you know like, what was I doing with all my spare time? You know, because obviously I wasn't freaking out about my homework being all lined up, you know. Again, you know, it wasn't anything bad. Like, I wasn't, you know, smoking or drinking or anything like that. I was just at home watching TV and not doing anything. And I transferred schools once because I would go to Mexico a lot. So one time they were like: You missed too much time. You're out.

This near damning story of Nicole's suggests that the complexity of the shifting sands of assimilation—a process that can feel both invisible and out of control—bears powerfully on young students whose families have newly emigrated from Mexico. Moreover, because this process seems so accidental, students can feel that they are losing agency. So, even if they *do* participate in schools—as Nicole had, and Victoria and Celeste continue to try to do—they may or may not ultimately be successful. Indeed, in the examples above, such students internalize self-hatred, both for assimilating and for failing to assimilate: a dynamic that can both confuse and distract from a concentration on school and future goals. In this way, such students find themselves in a crisis: uncertain of how to make choices about their lives—given the influence of old and new contexts—and equally uncertain of how much of that same decision-making process they actually control. Whereas in rural Mexico, communities like Villachuato often share a collective consciousness that allows students to position themselves rhetorically with respect to the demands of formal schools, the emphasis on individual learning and professionalization in the United States draws students' attention away from shared, interactive contexts and leaves them uncertain of how to position themselves. At the same time, although they have been promised, in this new context, that social mobility is now a real possibility for them, in many cases, they have yet to see the results. Uncertain of how to position themselves, whether via acceptance or resistance of schooled values and processes, and likewise uncertain of the promised result, students like Nicole, Victoria, María, and others become profoundly ambivalent about literacy—especially as to its role in cultural assimilation.

## CONCLUSION

A key issue in this final chapter is that fact that, for immigrant students in the U.S. context, the stakes of the literacy contract go up at the same time that the parameters of the contract become more blurred—and therefore more difficult to question or resist. There is more promised now, and also more delivered. By virtue of migrating (whether to a Mexican urban center or to the United States), rural Mexican families enter a wage economy, where students may indeed train for a profession and obtain a job. Thus, as the contract orientation comes to make more sense, it is more difficult to resist. At the same time, though, the U.S. context requires students to assimilate culturally, and it asks parents (though not necessarily successfully) to relinquish their hold on the value formation of young people. Furthermore, because teachers and parents in many ways believe that they are in agreement about their hopes for the next generation, the demands of the literacy contract become much more difficult to identify, such that students find themselves "accidentally" assimilating or resisting assimilation. Moreover, they find themselves profoundly ambivalent about fulfilling school demands and the literacy contract itself.

The results presented in this chapter build both on the findings in previous chapters, as well as on scholarly debates about the relationship between cultural assimilation and academic success. Like educators in rural Mexico, Marshalltown teachers view formal schooling as the best means to upward mobility, and they therefore encourage assimilation at both the parental and student levels. Indeed, many of the comments and programmatic plans conveyed in this chapter reveal a strong sense of support and sympathy on the part of Marshalltown educators. However, at the same time, these educators do not seem to be aware of the assumptions they make (e.g., U.S. school opportunities are superior to those in Mexico, parents should relinquish behavioral control of their children, etc). As result, parents continue to resist certain aspects of school demands, and students find themselves quite confused.

For students, literacy is experienced positively in the United States when it is social—a finding that suggests that social capital is indeed one of the most important aspects to migrants' school success. However, in the new context, which includes both a functioning labor market and an emphasis on the privacy of literacy, these social connections break down. Students find themselves pitting one context (home) against another (school). Students realize this change, so they are once again thinking carefully about their context. However, the lines are blurring now, and positioning gets more difficult, leading to a kind of crisis for students.

# Conclusion /

## "CALLING THE SHOTS": LITERACY VALUED DIFFERENTLY, NOT LESS

This study opened with a consideration of the experiences of students who migrate from Mexico to the United States—and sometimes back again. In a context that is becoming not just binational but *transnational* (Waldinger, 2011), these young people experience literacy in ways that merit attention both because such experiences influence students' life outcomes and because they demonstrate how literacy itself is changing in an increasingly transnational world. In the context of this analysis, one of my principal concerns has been how communities with lower levels of cultural capital cope with and respond to dominant institutions and ideologies. Given the imbalance of power between community members and educational institutions in places like Villachuato, I have characterized this relationship as a kind of contract that requires individuals to invest and comply with institutional expectations; in return, those institutions promise to provide individuals with the means toward economic mobility.

However, as we have seen throughout the ethnographic portraits in this book, the literacy contract does not always deliver on its promise. Moreover, the ways in which individuals from Villachuato have either survived or improved their lives has often had to do with social—rather than institutional—resources. As such, they have often found ways of accepting those aspects of formal education that they find useful and leaving the rest. In this way, their approach to literacy is rhetorical: Drawing on the available means at their disposal, they assess the contexts of their lives and make strategic choices about how to position themselves as literacy practitioners. My findings suggest that this balancing act functions nominally for students in Mexico, though it may weaken and prove more problematic when students immigrate and enroll in U.S. schools. Whether because they resist assimilation or because they fail to meet standards—that is, whether they fail the literacy contract or it fails them—such students are perceived to lack investment in their learning. This, indeed, was one of my opening questions: Do students in migration communities "care" about education? Moreover, does the choice to migrate impede their ability to become educated? That is, how is literacy *valued*, and how is it *valuable*?

While educators on both sides of the border voice continued concerns about migrant students' choices and values, I don't believe that literacy and migration are mutually exclusive options, or that the latter devalues the former. Rather, as immigrant families from Villachuato demonstrate, they value literacy not less but differently than the parameters of the literacy contract require. For instance, Jiro Ramírez, a member of the family who originally connected me to Villachuato, wants all of his three children to go to college. Having been born and raised in Los Angeles, Jiro works with his family business. Four decades after his parents immigrated to California, the family bus company is doing well—so well, in fact, that it is possible that Jiro's children won't earn a commensurate salary in a private career. But Jiro doesn't care. "I want them to do something that they like," he says. "So they can go to work each day and enjoy it. Like their aunt [Nicole]. She likes what she does, you know? She's a lawyer. She's professionalized." With respect to his own work, Jiro speaks enthusiastically about growing the family business, and he takes pride in the material goods that he has procured for his family: a nice home in a predominantly white neighborhood of Los Angeles and private schooling for his children. By most middle-class standards, Jiro is successful and happy. But for his children, he wants something even more: not just economic stability, but the social prestige that comes with education and professionalization. He wants them, he says, to be more able to "call the shots" in life.

Like other members of the extended Villachuato community identified in this book, Jiro identifies literacy as a means of self-defense. Even more so, however, he understands that, while basic levels of literacy may increase an individual's survival skills, more advanced levels of formal schooling increase his or her *cultural capital*. By becoming formally educated, Jiro's children will gain increased autonomy commensurate with their social standing as educated individuals. Ironically, given the success of the family business, they may not earn as much financially, but Jiro believes that the intangibles of social prestige are worth the sacrifice. In this way, his desires for his children demonstrate the fact that, despite educators' promises on both sides of the border, formal education is *not* the Villachuato community's primary means to economic growth. Quite the contrary, formal education is often the *result* of a family's financial success.

## "WORKING IN THE SHADE": EDUCATION AS AN END, RATHER THAN A MEANS

Without question, families in and from Villachuato value literacy—although their attitudes toward literacy vary in ways commensurate with their experiences. As one secondary student in Villachuato told me, the purpose of going to school is to "be able to work in the shade, and not in the sun, like our parents." On both a literal and metaphorical level, this student describes the situation in which Villachauto now finds itself. Life in this area has not been easy; people have worked, literally, *in the sun* for most of the town's history. Beyond the reality of physical labor, the townspeople have likewise experienced strong histories of oppression throughout the town's centuries as a hacienda and later on under the complicated and negative influences of NAFTA policies. This child's response, then, reveals a high level of awareness of the role of formal education: Not only is it a means toward job qualifications, but it is also important to accruing the kind of prestige and power that Jiro identifies above.

However, the formal literacy offerings in Villachuato don't meet the community's needs (Bonfil, 2001). While Villachuato teachers emphasize the importance of school as a means of economic self-advancement, the many community members' testimonies demonstrate the fact that formal education is *not* this community's primary means to economic growth. Quite the contrary, as the case of Nicole Ramírez illustrates. The youngest of ten children, she was the only member of her family to attend college because, after three decades building a business, her immigrant parents finally had enough money to pay college tuition. For Nicole, formal education was the *result* of a family's financial success, not its source. Indeed, during my subsequent conversations with Nicole after the completion of formal data collection, she confirmed this conclusion. "Of course," she told me:

> The people there [in Villachuato] know that the way you get ahead in life isn't through school—it's through your connections to other people. But they still want their kids to become educated. Because once you have money and can move north or to another city in Mexico or something, then their kids need to get educated so that they can become part of that bigger community. It helps them have more independence, so they can decide things in their own lives.

So, the community of Villachuato understands literacy primarily as a form of *cultural capital,* or social standing; and in many ways, they are actually much more critically aware of the ideologies and power structures embedded in schools than are educators themselves. Similarly, in terms of their long-range goals (meaning, those goals that stretch throughout various generations of a single family), formal education is important to them. However, literacy and education as such do not have much direct bearing on their lives in their home community, primarily because the skills and values taught in public schools aren't relevant to their survival as farmers and migrants; these complex roles require much different sets of literacies. Finally, the skills acquired via the migration experience can actually feed back into the process of formal schooling. In this way, members of the extended Villachuato community demonstrate an awareness of the profound connections between education and migration: connections that many educators themselves often fail to recognize.

## MIGRATION AS A SPONSOR OF LITERACY

By now, it should be clear that the connection between migration and education is a strong one. This book has shown that the process of becoming educated requires rural Mexican students to leave their home communities—often permanently. In this way, education necessitates migration. On the flip side, we have also seen that migration facilitates more access to education through migrating family members' financial sponsorship of younger family members so that they can afford a high school or college education. So, just as education necessitates migration, so too does migration facilitate education. The two phenomena are intimately connected and, as I will argue in this section, this connection extends beyond social dynamics into the territory of ideological impact.

First, however, I would like to briefly remind us of the ways in which migration has historically been faulted for sullying educative endeavors in both the United States and Mexico. On the one hand, recent literacy crisis rhetorics in the United States treat minority students as a problem that must be remedied; they are not integrated into the school system the way that mainstream domestic students are, and, as such, they threaten to dilute the quality of U.S. education. In contrast, my research has identified related crisis rhetorics in Mexico, the most recent of which fault migration, both as a form of misplaced priorities and as brain-drain. As one teacher explained, outbound migration is causing Mexico to lose one of its most important resources: its young people. In both cases, then, orientations in both the United States and Mexico fault migration for problems that each country is experiencing in education. These rhetorics maintain a crisis pitch that supports existing institutions, but they likewise mask the important cyclical, causal connections between migration and education. Furthermore, the fact that migration is downplayed in this way is, I believe, another means of maintaining social control—in both countries. It should not surprise us, therefore, that students from relatively less privilege would remain resistant or dubious about their relationship to an education system that neither recognizes nor endorses the material conditions, including migration, that most directly impact their lives and families.

Throughout all of the narratives presented in this book, the impact of social connections on students' literacy experiences has remained high. While the significance of friendships and family support is not, in and of itself, a surprising outcome, I would like to suggest that the impact of these relationships may be more profound than we think. Rather than simply facilitating or discouraging scholastic achievement, these social ties and experiences facilitate a new ideology of literacy—or, in Deborah Brandt's terms, a new form of literacy sponsorship. Certainly, as in the cases of Jackie and Nicole in this book, migrating families financially sponsor schooling for younger family members. However, financial means alone are not enough. In addition, the narratives presented in this book suggest that they must be accompanied by social remittances: those beliefs, values, and practices that migrants carry with them to the receiving community, which then impact the ways that they make sense of their experiences in a new place (Levitt, 1998). In the same vein, as migrants adjust their beliefs and behaviors based on these experiences, they then channel these new "remittances" back to the home community via letters, phone calls, and visits, such that members of the home community likewise become affected by migration experiences. In this way, the lessons that migrants draw in their new context are channeled back to influence their home communities. The dynamic is additive in the sense that as migrants learn new perspectives, they offer them back to their home communities. Therefore, migrants represent new forms of social capital for those in the home community—social capital that, in some cases, has very real effects. Therefore, social capital in the Villachuato community often serves to undo the negative impact that cultural capital—or, more rightly, a lack of cultural capital—can have on students who are tracked for low achievement.

Whereas the cultural beliefs that tend to dominate school's values on both sides of the U.S.-Mexico border tend to support the flawed "literacy myth" that suggests that education correlates directly with economic development, new social capital in Villachuato is otherwise oriented. First, as suggested in the preceding section, community members tend to see education as a reward (an end in itself) for sacrifices made, rather than a means to an end. Second, members of the Villachuato community are pragmatically oriented, as they find strategies to combat negative experiences and influences. In Esperanza's case in Chapter 4, she drew on social capital in order to protect herself physically from an unwanted marriage; and in Myra's case in that same chapter, she drew on social capital in order to find an alternative means to literacy. Furthermore, because this approach is so different from a blind acceptance of education-as-a-path-to-development, I argue that it represents a new ideology—and, as such, a new form of sponsorship. As Brandt (2001) argues, sponsorship represents the material forces that contribute to new ideological orientations toward literacy. Certainly, transnational migration represents a significant contemporary economic condition, and it is logical that it will have an impact on beliefs and practices related to education.

In this way, I argue that migration actually sponsors literacy—in the sense that it facilitates literacy and offers a new ideological orientation—rather than threatens or limits it. Indeed, the social influences on migrant communities, and therefore on migrant experiences of literacy, are more complex and ultimately more transformative than financial remittances. As such, these patterns suggest once again that literacy's tie to personal and collective development does not function in a straightforward, predetermined way. Rather, the role that literacy plays in migrant community's long-term shift into higher levels of economic gain and social standing is complex, recursive, and socially impacted.

## LITERACY IN CRISIS IN A TRANSNATIONAL WORLD

So, where does this leave us? Transnational migration represents a significant economic pattern (Waldinger, 2011), and, as Brandt and others have identified, during periods of economic change like the transnational pattern that we are experiencing now, the material conditions that impact literacy tend to shift, thereby introducing new ideological patterns, or sponsorship. At the same time, these changes can lead to the emergence of new crisis rhetorics, as formerly dominant institutions strive to hold onto their power (Trimbur, 1991). Currently, one of the most pronounced areas of crisis rhetorics in the United States focuses on minority students, particularly Latinos, falling behind our nation's educational standards (Gándara and Contreras, 2009). Indeed, the literature to date has focused ample energy on the experience of Mexican-origin students' experiences in U.S. schools (Orellana, 2009; Valdés, 1996; Valencia, 2002; Valenzuela, 1999; Vázquez et al., 2000; Villenas and Deyhle, 1999), and more recent studies have begun to examine the transnational context, though with a focus on language use (Farr, 2006) or writing technologies (Vieira, 2013). On the Mexican side of the border, scholars have attended to histories (Gonzalbo Aizpuru, 2000; Greaves Laine, 2001), practical uses (Peredo, 2005), and case studies (Hernandez-Zamora, 2010) of literacy, though this work attends primarily to the Mexican context. My project has expanded these conversations by examining the phenomenon of literacy in the transnational U.S.-Mexican context—a perspective that has allowed me to interpret not only literacy and migration but likewise their intersections.

Above, I argue that migration itself serves as one form of literacy sponsorship: one that is distributed via social remittances and impacts migrating students and students living in migration communities in a variety of significant ways. It is curious, then, that migration itself is so negatively cast with respect to education. As presented in this book, Mexican educators tend to identify migration as a significant threat to literacy, despite the fact that in many ways it contributes to literacy development. On the U.S. side of the border, migration is literally criminalized; and, in the progressive circle of educators presented here, it is essentially made invisible, as educators focus their energies on helping students assimilate. Migration, then, is demonized, criminalized, and patently ignored, despite its huge influence on the lives and literacy outcomes of a vast number of young people who are or have been students in our classrooms. Why have we been so apt to ignore this factor of the equation, and why have rhetorics that depict rural Mexican families as "not caring" about education continued to hold such sway on both sides of the border?

Part of the reason, I believe, is that we have entered into another phase of literacy crisis. However, while most of the debate about the generation 1.5 achievement gap focuses on the how's and why's of students' low performance, I would like to suggest that the real "crisis" here is one of profound ideological change—change that could significantly alter that way that we have constructed, legislated, and delivered public education since the post–World War II period. Again, as transnational economics change (e.g., free trade, leading to the movement of labor across the U.S.-Mexico border), so too does literacy. Thus, literacy is shifting in our country as our demographics shift: an influx of labor from Mexico, driven north by the complex trade relations between the two countries. As a result, we are experiencing growing pains, as we have at many other points in the history of U.S. mass education (Brandt, 2001; Connors, 1994; Gee, 1990; Trimbur, 1991). The problem is that we're blaming the people who represent part of the change, rather than considering how we ourselves are going through larger changes. The focus perhaps shouldn't be so much on how to get these students access and how to make them successful (though of course these human rights aspects are important) as it should be on the question, "How is literacy changing?" Or, perhaps more significantly, "How is our understanding of literacy changing?"

A particular aspect of this change relates back to the specifics of this demographic cohort. Whereas other groups of immigrants may arrive across more distance and come with educational degrees, the largest groups from Mexico emerge from rural areas—the same areas that NAFTA has essentially drained of economic viability. So, this part of the demographic pool is coming without advanced educational preparation. (Indeed, I have at times been surprised to hear some of my more progressive colleagues inadvertently cast Latino students as "lazy" or "disengaged.") And this pattern is particularly significant because Mexican migration increased most strongly after World War II: a time when higher education was just becoming part of the U.S. middleclass experience. Following the war, the U.S. government launched programs to help working-class citizens access college training, and thereby gain admission to the middle class. At the same time, we likewise imported Mexican workers, who in many ways became the next working class. Since then, we have been trying to figure out how to legislate them: legal to not, educated or not, professional or not.

What I believe is actually happening is that we are beginning to be asked to reconsider the beliefs about literacy that emerged during this time—specifically, a conceptualization of literacy as a contract. The juxtaposition between members of communities with radically lower resource bases has thrown into relief the assumptions that we make: education leads to economic development—education is a *means to an end*. However, as the findings in this book identify, this pattern isn't true for immigrants from rural Mexico who first make sacrifices and investments in migration and later in education. So, are we being asked to see it as symbolic (i.e., an end, not a means)? This is a profound shift for us to consider. An ideology that shifts us away from thinking of education as a means to an end is profound, both because it necessitates a new orientation and because it negates the contract culture that has dominated our approach to education for decades. Indeed, the contract is crumbling. Increased overlapping contexts create more awareness of the complexity of literacy and of its rhetorical nature. The repercussions are, of course, intense, and they have not surprisingly led to a number of tensions among literacy players. However, this shift is a necessary component of life in a transnational world, where contexts are expanding, markets are getting more and more complex, and literacy is becoming increasingly rhetorical.

Moreover, within this context of movement and change, migration, as I have argued above, is intimately tied to literacy development. It has become a *sponsor* of literacy, whether in the sending or receiving community. Migration expands both financial and social capital (i.e., an individual's available means and awareness of context), and it likewise shifts related ideology. These shifts are both powerfully good and profoundly taxing. When we ask, then, what is at the root of our "problem" of Latino students in education in the United States, I believe that the answer lies in the necessary discomfort in this ideological change to our constructions and experiences of literacy that are occurring as part of the economic pattern of transnational trade and labor movement between Mexico and the United States Indeed, as these social, political, and economic patterns continue to develop over the next several years, further research will need to consider specific angles of literacy as a transnational phenomenon. For instance, while my study attends to a gap in the literature regarding the backgrounds of immigrant students from Mexico, further studies should consider the impact of reverse migration on students' development because many young Mexicans find themselves enrolled in several different U.S. and Mexican schools throughout the course of their developmental years. As the migratory ties between the two nations grow deeper and more complex (Consejo Nacional de Población, 2010; González Gutiérrez, 1999), the impact—personal, educational, and political—of reverse migration is likely to become an increasingly significant part of the landscape of migration and education studies.

## CODA: EVERYBODY WRITES HERE

Like so many other field researchers I, too, am haunted by these tensions and changes (Gordon, 2008). The experience of living in Villachuato hasn't left me. I am continually startled by the connections that still brush past me: people who have grown up in Marshalltown, or who have visited rural Michoacán. Recently, I met a man in Portland, Oregon, who had emigrated from Morelia, the capital city of the state of Michoacán. I met with him for coffee to hear about his experiences. He described his work as an independent scholar, and I probed him with questions about how he had been able to produce and publish his books without institutional support. In Mexico, he told me, publishing and marketing a book by oneself is fairly easy. But here, he said, it is different. "Here," he told me, "everybody writes." Everybody is trying to get heard. The United States, it seemed to him, is a cacophony of voices—a market run amuck with texts to buy and sell. The implication is that formal written literacy is so much of an expectation that it almost loses its meaning. What does it mean to be a reader or a writer in the United States? In Mexico? According to Martín, whose books are self-published rather than edited or peer reviewed, he felt more successful as an author in Mexico because he was able to produce and sell his written work. Here in the United States, he told me, literacy is different. It is constructed differently, accessed differently, and experienced in radically different ways. In one sense, the question ceases to be one of success—either what it is or how to achieve it—or caring. The essence of Martín's message is that literacy does manifest in radically different, and often quite subtle ways, across geographic and cultural contexts. It does behoove us, therefore, to consider contrastive analyses of literacy and literacy acquisition—particularly as contexts continue to blur in a transnational world.

While this book was able to trace out only a fraction of those contrasts and tensions, the findings here do suggest a variety of implications for our broader understandings of literacy. As indicated in my earlier discussions of key theories related to critical analyses of literacy, literacy has been characterized as interactive, layered, and ideological. In addition, I have likewise characterized literacy as profoundly rhetorical: bent on context, audience, and choice. When we consider the trends that influence or sponsor literacy, we need to consider not only the larger patterns, but also the rhetorical choices that local communities make. Rather than subscribing to state-sponsored meritocratic ideals, or U.S. schools' promise of financial fulfillment, Mexican students are motivated to continue with formal education when it is part of a larger familial project. As educators, then, when we consider working with students from these backgrounds, we need to keep in mind the rhetorical nature of their experience, the importance of context, of how much of their experience with literacy in school is impacted by a backdrop of centralized education values in Mexico coming out of the colonial period, of family initiatives to migrate, and of ongoing dynamics between loyalties and concrete life possibilities.

Finally, I began this text with questions about the complexities of immigration, education, and language policy in the United States. I continue to believe that we cannot make good policy—whether conservative or liberally inclined—without understanding more about key demographics of people for whom these policies are created. If, for instance, literacy is primarily tied to family, then an English-only policy is likely to have the effect of lowering student motivation to continue in education. This is not a policy that seeks to create opportunity for immigrant children. On the other hand, the push for legislation that will allow high school graduates to further their studies in the United States may not be sufficient in and of itself. A brief answer to why students don't "care" sufficiently for school is that the structures that we present them with don't match their own material conditions—or, truly, those of our own. We are no longer living in the same material context that once facilitated a literacy contract, and this model has indeed begun to crumble. In a transnational world, we live constantly with overlapping economies, people from different material conditions overlapping, their lived realities throwing back into question our assumptions about literacy, education, power, knowledge, etc. A rhetorical perspective of literacy is empowering, but it is also complex. Rhetoric, by definition, entails choice and possibility, as well as restraints and parameters. A rhetorical perspective, like that of transnationalism, is dynamic and constantly moving. It cannot be contained or managed. And this, I argue, is our ultimate crisis. We live now in a world of movement and change: a world that will continually challenge our assumptions about what it is to know, to learn, to participate, and to succeed.

**Appendix / Notes / References / Index**

# Appendix / Interview Questions

## I. QUESTIONS FOR SCHOOL ADMINISTRATORS

1. Demographics:
   - What is the size of your birth family? What places did you live in when you were young?
   - What are your parents' occupations and educational levels?
   - What is your own educational background?
   - What has been your career trajectory?

2. What was your teacher training like? How would you characterize this training (logistics and philosophy)? What was the main philosophic approach that you were taught? Did you agree/disagree with it?

3. What are some major theories/theorists that continue to influence you? How would you describe your general philosophical approach to education?

4. What kind of professional development activities do you continue to engage in?

5. What are the main components that take up your time?

6. Describe your contact with teachers. How do you observe/mentor/evaluate them? What is "good teaching" to you?

7. Describe your contact with parents. What do you know of the backgrounds of the students at this school?

8. Do you know where your students end up after school?

9. What are the most important needs/challenges of this school? What is your vision for this school for the next 5 years?

10. Questions related to the 2006 curriculum reform:
   - What has impacted this school's decision to adopt/not adopt it?
   - What is likely to happen?
   - What are the components of the reform? How would it change things if it were adopted?

11. Migration: How does U.S.-bound migration impact your school? Do you have any idea of how many students are impacted? Are there any noticeable trends from those who come back?

## II. QUESTIONS FOR TEACHERS

1. Demographics:
   - What is the size of your birth family? What places did you live in when you were young?
   - What are your parents' occupations and educational levels?
   - What is your own educational background?
   - What has been your career trajectory? How many years have you been teaching, and where are the schools located?

2. What was your teacher training like? How would you characterize this training (logistics and philosophy)? What was the main philosophic approach that you were taught? Did you agree/disagree with it?

3. What are some of the major educational ideas/theories that continue to influence you? How would you describe your overall teaching philosophy?

4. What is your approach to the teaching of writing? What things do you think are important? How do you teach them?

5. Writing Assignments:
   - How often do you assign writing? And how often do students turn in these assignments?
   - How long are these assignments?
   - How are paper topics selected in your class?
   - Do students revise their writing? If so, how do they revise? And how often?
   - What kinds of writing do students do in your classes? What is/are the purpose(s) of these genres?

6. What is "good writing"? How do you explain/demonstrate/teach this?

7. How do you evaluate writing? (Do you have samples?)

8. What place do exams have in your class, if any? How are exams integrated into the students' final grades?

9. What kind of writing do you expect that your students will have to do once they leave school? How do you think that your class prepares them for this kind of writing?

10. What kind of contact do you have with parents? What sense do you have of your students' home lives?

11. What are some recent professional development activities that you have been involved in?

### III. QUESTIONS FOR STUDENTS

*Part I. Interview questions for students who have not migrated*

1. Demographics (Name, Age, and Grade)

2. Where do you live? Who do you live with?

3. What kind of work do your parents do? Do you know if your parents went to school?

4. What other places have you lived in (if any)?

5. What is your favorite thing about school? Least favorite?

6. What school subjects do you like? Not like?

7. When did you learn to read? Who were you with? How did you learn?

8. What is your favorite book? What is it about?

9. Do you like to write? What kinds of things do you write (in and out of school)?

10. Do you think that it is important to be able to read and write? Why?

11. Why do you think people go to school?

12. How long would you like to go to school?

13. Outside of school, what other things do you like to do?

14. What do you want to do when you grow up? What things are important to you?

*Part II. Interview questions for students who have migrated to the United States and returned to Mexico*

1. Demographics (Name, Age, and Grade)

2. Where do you live now, and who do you live with?

3. When you were in the United States, where did you live, and with whom? How long were you there? Are there any other places that you have lived?

4. What kind of work do your parents do? Do you know if your parents went to school?

5. What are some of your first memories/impressions of U.S. schools? How did you feel early on?

6. How did you learn English? What was it like? How did you feel?

7. What kinds of reading and writing projects did you do in the United States? What do you remember about them? Did you like/dislike them? Were they easy/difficult? Why?

8. In general, what were the easiest things about U.S. school? The most difficult thing? Why?

9. How did you happen to come back to Mexico? Do you know how long you will stay? Now that you are back, what do you notice about the schools here?

10. What kinds of reading and writing projects do you do here in Mexico? How are they different from those in the United States?

11. What do your like best/worst about school in each place?

12. What are your plans? What do you want to do in life? How do you think that you came to decide this?

13. Besides a career, what other things do you think are important in life?

14. What do you think that U.S. teachers should know about students who are coming from Mexico? How can teachers help these students?

### IV. QUESTIONS FOR MEMBERS OF THE VILLACHUATO COMMUNITY

1. Family background (mother, father, siblings, place(s) lived and years)

2. Personal data (birth year and place, place(s) lived and years)

3. Early life: What was your home like when you were young? Who did you live with? Where did you live, and what was the place like?

4. Important memories: What are some of your earliest memories? Some important events of your early life? What people were involved in these events? How did these things make you feel?

5. Early learning experiences: What is the first thing that you remember learning how to do (e.g., getting dressed, fixing food, etc.)? How did you feel about doing this/these things?

6. Habitual activities in childhood and adolescence: As a child, what did you do on a daily basis? Did you do these things alone or with other people? How did you learn to do these things? How did these things make you feel?

7. Reading and writing memories: What is the first time that you remember reading a book? Where were you? Who were you with? Who was reading—you or another person? Did you like/dislike the book? Do you have any early memories of writing things down on paper? If so, what?

8. School: What years were you in school? What are your general memories of school? What things did you likes/dislike? What did you see as the *purpose* of going to school?

9. Youth Values: When you were young, what did you expect/hope would happen in your life? What things did you think were important? How do you think you determined that these things were important?

10. Life Events: What happened to you in the years after childhood/schooling? Marriage? Children? Jobs? Moves? What major events have occurred?

11. Using school literacy: What lessons from your school years do you remember best? What things have been most useful? What things do you read on a regular basis? What things do you write?

12. Adult Values: Now, as an adult, have your opinions about things changed? Did you get/do the things that you'd expected/hoped? Do these things still feel important? What things are important to you now in your daily life?

13. Hopes for the future: What are the things that you want/hope for your children? What things do you do in order to help this happen?

14. A vision of Villachuato: How has this place changed, that you can see? What is your opinion of migration to the United States? How is it impacting Villachuato, and do you see this impact as positive or negative?

# Notes /

**INTRODUCTION: "SO YOU CAN BUY A TACO OVER THE INTERNET"**

1. These economic figures are estimates drawn from my field research in a rural, migrant-sending area of Mexico in 2007–8. More details about economic conditions in my research site are available in chapter 2.

2. Self-described as "The Turk," a food vendor in Portland, Oregon, advertises kebab sales through descriptive tweets about the allure of his food as he cooks meat and prepares food each evening. In order to purchase a kebab, clients must tweet back with their order. Thereafter, a delivery service brings the food to each client's home. The Turk has no storefront or publicly available menu. All transactions are conducted over the internet via Twitter accounts. See M. Korfhage (2011), "Pre-midnight express," *Willamette Weekly*, April 20–27, p. 23.

3. Recent studies have characterized school-based, work-based, and community-based skills as important forms of "literacy" (Cushman, 1998; Grabill, 2001; Prendergast, 2003).

**1. CRISIS AND CONTRACT: A RHETORICAL APPROACH TO TRANSNATIONAL LITERACIES**

4. The DREAM (Development, Relief, and Education for Alien Minors) Act is a legislative proposal that would provide undocumented youth with the means of pursuing college-level education, legal work options, and pathways

to citizenship. Stymied for more than a decade, a version of the bill was first introduced in 2001. A recent, though incomplete, version was passed at the federal level in 2010, and several states have adopted their own versions of DREAM Act legislation. Proponents of the bill continue to press its passage at the federal level, and a new version passed through the Senate in May 2013, although the outcome in the House of Representatives remains uncertain (Nevarez, 2013).

5. The relative rights of immigrants have been debated over time. For instance, the equal protection clause under the 14th Amendment has been considered the right of everyone on U.S. soil. However, the right to education has been questioned, and at times threatened, as in the state of California (Bosniak, 1994).

6. Current estimates assert that between 11 and 13 million people living in the United States are undocumented (Motomura, 2010).

7. In 1994, California passed Proposition 187 (the "Save Our State" initiative), which restricted the access to public services, including schools, by anyone without legal documentation. Later on, Proposition 227, which was billed as the "English for the Children" initiative, banned bilingual programming throughout the state (Lu, 1998). That latter initiative passed in 1998.

8. GEAR UP (Gaining Early Awareness and Readiness for Undergraduate Programs) is a program offered by the U.S. Department of Education. The program offers six-year grants for institutions, such as universities that partner with local schools, to help prepare middle and high school students at low-income schools for success in postsecondary education. In 2006, the Office of Early Academic Outreach at the University of Arizona was awarded a grant. The Tucson GEAR UP Project served five impoverished high schools in the greater Tucson area.

9. In rural areas like Villachuato, the first schools typically emerged following the Mexican Revolution. According to local reports, Villachuato gained its first elementary school in approximately 1930. Thereafter, a middle school (i.e., grades 7–9) was established in the late 1980s, followed by a preschool in the mid-1990s. At present, the only available high school, located in neighboring Puruándiro, requires a thirty-minute public bus ride. Therefore, while access to public education has increased over time, resources remain limited.

10. Several scholars have debunked this theory in one of two ways: using data that demonstrate that achievement levels in fact are *not* declining, and by means of the argument that, rather than achievement declining, the literacy bar itself is going up (Brandt, 2001).

11. Mexico has three models of middle school education (i.e., grades 7–9). Urban centers offer a traditional academic curriculum at standard *secundarias*.

Semi-rural areas and low-income urban areas train students in professional tracks, assuming that many of these students will not continue their education beyond ninth grade. These institutions are known as *secundarias técnicas*, and they focus on agriculture, fishing, or office work. In more remote areas, *telesecundarias* amass students from all three grade levels into a single classroom with a single teacher who facilitates curriculum that is delivered via television programming.

12. A notable example, highlighted in chapters 3 and 4 in this volume, as well as in the work of Katherine Richardson-Bruna and Mark Grey, is that of Villachuato's annual town festival, known as *la fiesta*. Held during Easter week of each year, *la fiesta* draws large crowds of return migrants who make the journey home to celebrate with their families. Those who are not able to make the trip in a given year are remembered by name at large public gatherings like rodeos and the Catholic mass.

## 2. "AREN'T YOU SCARED?": THE CHANGING FACE OF OPPRESSION IN RURAL, MIGRANT-SENDING MEXICO

13. The Bracero Program (1942–64) originated as a means of covering the U.S. labor shortage during World War II. Following the war, agricultural leaders were successful in petitioning an extension, although the program was eventually discontinued as part of broad efforts to cut down on undocumented immigration from Mexico.

## 3. "THEY MAKE A LOT OF SACRIFICES": FOUNDATIONAL RHETORICS OF THE MEXICAN EDUCATION SYSTEM

14. The Secretaría de Educación Pública, or SEP, produces its own textbooks for preschool through 6th grade. Books for 7th through 9th grade, of which the example discussed is one, are produced by independent publishers under contract with the SEP, which must endorse the books. Schools are then able to choose from among a half dozen options.

15. Interviews for this study were conducted with school administrators and teachers at the kindergarten, primary, secondary, high school, and college levels.

16. CONALITEG (Comisíon Nacional de los Libros de Textos Gratuitos, or National Comission of Free Textbooks) is the Mexico City office of the nation's Secretary of Education that oversees the production and distribution of the nation's textbooks. Every child in Mexico is issued his/her own set of new textbooks each year. These textbooks represent a significant investment on the part of the Mexican government. For instance, according to SEP's website, some 827,203 books were distributed during the 2006–7 academic

year. Furthermore, these books are particularly significant in rural areas, as they may be the only books that a child ever owns.

### 5. "SO YOU DON'T GET TRICKED": COUNTERNARRATIVES OF LITERACY IN A MEXICAN TOWN

17. Historical information located at the central visitors office in Morelia, Michoacán, indicates that Morelia was the site of the first planning meetings for the independence movement.

### 6. "LIKE GOING FROM BLACK AND WHITE TO COLOR": MEXICAN STUDENTS' EXPERIENCES IN U.S. SCHOOLS

18. According to Dr. Katherine Richardson Bruna, who brought three groups of Iowa educators to visit Villachuato schools during 2007–8, Iowa's Department of Education has been forthcoming with funds for teacher visits and exchanges because the state is aware of its dependence on labor forces from Mexico. In addition to the trips led by Richardson Bruna, additional educators and civic leaders from Marshalltown have visited Mexican schools on at least three other occasions since the late 1990s.

19. In communities like Villachuato, a girl who "goes with her boyfriend" leaves her family home, and often her studies at school, in order to move in with her boyfriend and his family. The couple marries, and the arrangement is permanent. Quite often, these transitions are very abrupt, such that a girl "goes with her boyfriend" without advance notice to friends or family. See Chapter 4 for more examples.

# References /

Alarcón, R., R. Cruz, A. Díaz-Bautista, G. González-König, A. Izquierdo, G. Yrizar, and R. Zenteno. (2009). La crisis financiera en Estados Unidos y su impacto en la migración mexicana. *Migraciones Internacionales*, 5(1), 193–210.

Alba, R., and V. Nee. (2003). *Remaking the American mainstream: Assimilation and contemporary immigration.* Cambridge, MA: Harvard University Press.

Alexander, R. J. (2000). *Culture and pedagogy: International comparisons in primary education.* Oxford: Blackwell.

———. (2001). Border crossings: Towards a comparative pedagogy. *Comparative Education*, 37(4), 507–523.

Althusser, L. (2001). *Lenin and philosophy and other essays* (B. Brewster, Trans.). New York: Monthly Review.

Ángeles Cruz, H., and M. L. Rojas Wiesner (2000). Migración feminina internacional en la frontera sur de México. *Papeles de Población*, 6(23), 127–150.

Anzaldúa, G. (1999). *Towards a new consciousness.* San Francisco: Aunt Lute Books.

Arnaut, A. (1998). *La federalización educativa en México.* Distrito Federal: SEP, Biblioteca del Normalista.

Arnot, M., and S. Fennell. (2008). Gendered education and national development: Critical perspectives and new research. *Compare*, 38(5), 515–523.

Bayona Escat, E. (2012). La migración en Pamatácuaro: La participación e inversión de los 'hijos ausentes.' *Gazeta de Antropología, 27*(2). Retrieved from http://www.ugr.es/~pwlac/G27_34Eugenia_Bayona_Escat.pdf.

Berliner, D. C., and B. J. Biddle. (1995). *The manufactured crisis.* Cambridge, MA: Perseus Books.

Bernardino, M. G. (1978). *Educación no formal en el medio rural de México.* Mexico City: Central Nacional de Productividad de México.

Bizzell, P. (1998). Arguing about literacy. *College English, 50,* 141–53.

Bonfil, P. (2001). ¿Estudiar para qué? Mercados de trabajo y opciones de bienestar para las jóvenes del medio rural: La educación como desventaja acumulada. In E. Pieck (Ed.), *Los jóvenes y el trabajo: La educación frente a la exclusión social* (pp. 527–550). Mexico City: Universidad Iberoamericana.

Bonfil Batalla, G. (1996). *México profundo: Reclaiming a civilization* (P. A. Dennis, Trans.) Austin: University of Texas Press.

Bosniak, L. (1994). Membership, equality, and the difference that alienage makes. *New York University Law Review, 69*(6), 1047–1149.

Bourdieu, P. (1998). *Practical reason: On the theory of action.* Oxford: Polity.

Bracho, T., et al. (2006). El debate por la RIES. *Observatoria Ciudadano de la Educación: Debate Educativo.* Retrieved from http://www.observatorio .org/comunicados/ debate012.html.

Brandt, D. (2001). *Literacy in American lives.* Cambridge: Cambridge University Press.

Brandt, D., and K. Clinton. (2002). Limits of the local: Expanding perspectives on literacy as a social practice. *Journal of Literacy Research, 34*(3), 337–356.

Brannon, L. (1995). The problem of national standards. *CCC, 46*(3), 438–445.

Brooke, R. (2011). Voices of young citizens: Rural citizenship, schools, and public policy. In K. Donehower, C. Hogg, and E. E. Schell (Eds.), *Reclaiming the rural: Essays on literacy, rhetoric, and pedagogy* (pp. 252–270). Carbondale: Southern Illinois University Press.

Butts, R. F., and L. A. Cremin. (1953). *A history of education in American culture.* New York: Holt, Rinehart, and Winston.

Cardiel Reyes, R. and R. Bolaños Martínez. (1981). *Historia de la educación pública en México.* Distrito Federal: SEP.

Cardoso, L. A. (1980). *Mexican emigration to the United States 1897–1931: Socioeconomic patterns.* Tucson: University of Arizona Press.

Carter, S. (2006). Redefining literacy as a social practice. *Journal of Basic Writing, 25*(1), 94–125.

Cerrutti, M., and D. S. Massey. (2004). Trends in Mexican migration to the United States, 1965 to 1995. In J. Durand and D. S. Massey (Eds.), *Crossing the Border: Research from the Mexican Migration Project* (pp. 17–44). New York: Russell Sage Foundation.

Churchill, C. J., and G. E. Levy. (2012). *The enigmatic academy: Class, bureaucracy, and religion in American education.* Philadelphia: Temple University Press.

Cintron, R. (1997). *Angle's town: Chero ways, gang life, and rhetorics of the everyday.* Boston: Beacon.

Citrin, J., B. Reingold, E. Walter, and D. P. Green. (1990). The "Official English" movement and the symbolic politics of language in the United States. *Western Political Quarterly, 43*(3), 535–559.

Clifford, J. (1988). *The predicament of culture: Twentieth century ethnography, literature, and art.* Cambridge, MA: Harvard University Press.

Cohen, J. H. (2010). Oaxacan migration and remittances as they relate to Mexican migration patterns. *Journal of Ethnic and Migration Studies, 36*(1), 149–161.

Connors, R. (1994). Crisis and panacea in composition studies: A history. In W. R. Winterowd and V. Gillespie (Eds.), *Composition in Context: Essays in honor of Donald C. Stewart* (pp. 86–105). Carbondale: Southern Illinois University Press.

Consejo Nacional de Población. (2010). *Índices de intensidad migratoria México-Estados Unidos 2010.* Retrieved from http://www.conapo. gob.mx/swb/CONAPO/Indices_de_intensidad_migratoria_Mexico -Estados_Unidos_2010.

Cortina, R. (1989). La vida profesional del maestro mexicano y su sindicato. *Estudio sociológicos, 7*(19), 79–103.

Crable, B. (2006). Rhetoric, anxiety, and character armor: Burke's interactional rhetoric of identity. *Western Journal of Communication, 70*(1), 1–22.

Cremin, L. A. (1980). *American education: The national experience 1783–1876.* New York: Harper & Row.

Crowther, J., M. Hamilton, and L. Tett (Eds.). (2001). *Powerful literacies.* Leicester: NIACE.

Cushman, E. (1998). *The struggle and the tools: Oral and literate strategies in an inner city community.* New York: State University of New York Press.

Dewey, J. (1926). Mexico's educational renaissance. *New Republic, 48*, 116–118.

Durand, J., and D. Massey (Eds.). (2004). *Crossing the border: Research from the Mexican Migration Project.* New York: Russell Sage Foundation.

Fairbanks, C. M., and M. Ariail. (2006). The role of social and cultural resources in literacy and schooling: Three contrasting cases. *Research in the Teaching of English, 40*(3), 310–54.

Farr, M. (2006). *Rancheros in Chicagoacán: Language and identity in a transnational community.* Austin: University of Texas Press.

Federal Security Agency. (1945). *Report on the cultural missions of Mexico.* Washington D.C.: U.S. Office of Education.

Fennell, S., and M. Arnot (Eds.). (2008). *Gender education and equality in a global context: Conceptual frameworks and policy perspectives.* London: Routledge.

Flores, J. R. (Ed.). (1966). *Estudios históricos* (2nd ed.). Mexico City: B. Costa-Amic.

Flores-Crespo, P. (2004). Conocimiento y política educativa en México: Condiciones políticas y organizativas. *Perfiles Educativos, 26*(105), 36–65.

Fox, T. (1999). *Defending access: A critique of standards in higher education.* Portsmouth, NH: Boynton/Cook.

Fraser, J. W. (2007). *Preparing America's teachers: A history.* New York: Teachers College Press.

Fulton, M. L. (2007). Transnational literacies: Immigration, language learning, and identity. *Linguistics and Education, 18*(3), 201–214.

Furlong Zacaula, A. (2010). Migración y pobreza en las cuentas nacionales: Puebla, México. *Observatorio Laboral Revista Venezolana, 3*(6), 133–154.

Gándara, P., and F. Contreras. (2009). *The Latino education crisis: The consequences of failed social policies.* Cambridge, MA: Harvard University Press.

Gee, J. P. (1990). *Social linguistics and literacies: Ideology in discourse.* London: Falmer.

Ghandnoosh, N., and R. Waldinger. (2006). Strangeness at the gate: The peculiar politics of American immigration. *International Migration Review, 40*(3), 719–734.

Glenn, C. J. (2012). *The American model of state and school: A historical inquiry.* New York: Continuum.

Gómez Calderón, H. A., B. Martínez Corona, and M. Da Gloria Marroni. (2007). Relaciones de género en procesos migratorios periurbanos en Puebla. *Ra Ximhai, 3*(3), 621–648.

Gonzalbo Aizpuru, P. (2000). La educación colonial: Una mirada reflexiva. *Historia de la Educación Latinoamerica, 2,* 178–186.

González Gutiérrez, C. (1999). Fostering identities: Mexico's relations with its diaspora. *Journal of American History, 86*(2), 545–567.

Gordon, A. F. (2008). *Ghostly matters: Haunting and the sociological imagi-nation*. Minneapolis: University of Minnesota Press.

Grabill, J. T. (2001). *Community literacy programs and the politics of change*. New York: State University of New York Press.

Graff, H. J. (1987). *The legacies of literacy*. Bloomington: Indiana University Press.

Greaves Laine, C. (2001). Política educative y libros de texto gratuitos: Una polémica entorno al control por la educación. *Revista Mexicana de Investigación Educativa*, 6(12), 205–221.

Grey, M. A., and P. L. Barker. (2002). Positive exposure: Immersion in Latino culture brings positive changes. *Cityscape*, 8–9.

Grey, M. A., and A. C. Woodrick. (2002). Unofficial sister cities: Meatpacking labor migration between Villachuato, Mexico, and Marshalltown, Iowa. *Human Organization*, 61(4), 364–76.

Gross, A. G. (1994). The roles of rhetoric in the public understanding of science. *Public Understanding of Science*, 3(1), 3–23.

Guerra, J. C. (2004). Emerging representations, situated literacies, and the practice of transcultural repositioning. In M. H. Kells, V. Balester and V. Villanueva (Eds.), *Latino/a discourses: On language, identity, and literacy education* (pp. 7–23). Portsmouth, NH: Boynton/Cook.

Hall, A. (2006). Keeping *La Llorona* alive in the shadow of Cortés: What an examination of literacy in two Mexican schools can teach U.S. edu-cators. *Bilingual Research Journal*, 30(2), 385–406.

Hamann, E. T., V. Zúñiga, and J. Sánchez García. (2008). From Nuevo León to the USA and back again: Transnational students in Mexico. Faculty Pub-lications: Department of Teaching, Learning and Teacher Education. No. 79. Retrieved from http://digitalcommons.unl.edu/teachlearnfacpub/79.

Hawhee, D. (2006). Performing ancient rhetorics: A symposium. *Rhetoric Society Quarterly*, 36(2), 135–142.

Hernandez-Zamora, G. (2010). *Decolonizing literacy: Mexican lives in the era of global capitalism*. Bristol: Multilingual Matters.

Hughes, L. H. (1950). *The Cultural Mission Programme*. Paris: UNESCO.

Humanitarian volunteers discover, help recover human remains in desert. (2010, October 18). *No More Deaths*. Retrieved from http://www .nomoredeaths.org/Press-Releases/humanitarian-volunteers -discover-help-recover-human-remains-in-desert.html.

Jiménez, R. T., and P. H. Smith. (2008). Mesoamerican literacies: Indigenous writing systems and contemporary possibilities. *Reading Research Quarterly*, 43(1), 28–46.

Jiménez, R. T., P, H. Smith, and N. Martínez-León. (2003). Freedom and form: The language and literacy practices of two Mexican schools. *Reading Research Quarterly, 38*(4), 488–508.

Jiménez Alarcón, C. (1975). *Historia de la Escuela Nacional de Maestros (1887–1940).* Distrito Federal: SEP.

Johnson, D., and G. Kress. (2003). Globalization, literacy, and society: Redesigning pedagogy and assessment. *Assessment in Education, 10*(1), 5–14.

Kalman, J. (1999). *Writing on the plaza: Mediated literacy practices among scribes and clients in Mexico City.* Cresskill, NJ: Hampton.

Kandel, W., and E. A. Parrado. (2005). Restructuring of the U.S. meat processing industry and new Hispanic migration destinations. *Population and Development Review, 31*(3), 447–471.

Kenney, K. (2002). Building visual communication theory by borrowing from rhetoric. *Journal of Visual Literacy, 22*(1), 53–80.

King, L. (1994). *Roots of identity: Language and literacy in Mexico.* Stanford, CA: Stanford University Press.

Kobayashi, J. M. K. (1999). La conquista educativa de los hijos de Asís. In J. Z. Vásquez (Ed.), *La educación en la historia de México* (pp. 1–28). Mexico City: El Colegio de México.

Labov, W. (1972). Academic ignorance and black intelligence. *Atlantic Monthly, 229*(6), 59–67.

Levinson, B. (1996). Social difference and schooled identity at a Mexican *secundaria.* In B. Levinson and D. Holland (Eds.), *The cultural production of the educated person: Critical ethnographies of schooling and local practice* (pp. 211–238). New York: State University of New York Press.

———. (2001). *We are all equal: Student culture and identity at a Mexican secondary school, 1988–1998.* Durham, NC: Duke University Press.

Levitt, P. (1998). Social remittances: Migration-driven local forms of cultural diffusion. *International Migration Review, 32*(4), 926–948.

Lu, M. (1998). English-Only Movement: Its consequences on the education of language minority children. *ERIC Clearinghouse on Reading English and Communication Bloomington IN.* Retrieved from http://www.ericdigests.org/1999-4/english.htm.

Lugones, M. (1992). On borderlands/la frontera. *Hypatia, 7*(4), 31–7.

Marsiske, R. (2000). Movimientos estudiantiles en América Latina: Historiografía y fuentes. *Historia de la Educación Latinoamerica, 2,* 189–197.

Martin, C. (1993). The "shadow" economy of local school management in contemporary West Mexico. *Bulletin of Latin American Research, 12*(2), 171–188.

Martínez, R. B. (1981). Orígenes de la educación pública en México. In F. Solana, R. C. Reyes, and R. B. Martinez (Eds.), *Historia de la Educación Pública en México* (pp. 11–40). Mexico City: Secretaría de Educación Pública Fondo de Cultura Económica.

Martínez González, B. G., and A. Valle Baeza. (2008). Oaxaca 2006–2008, rebelión ejemplar. *Laberinto, 26–27*(1–2), 93–101.

Martínez Jiménez, A. (1996). *La educación primaria en la formación social mexican (1875–1965).* Distrito Federal: Universidad Autónoma Metropolitana-Xochimilco.

McAslan, E. Social development. (2002). In V. Desai and R. B. Potter (Eds.), *The companion to development studies* (pp. 139–142). London: Hodder Arnold.

McKenzie, D., and H. Rapoport. (2010). Self-selection patterns in Mexico-U.S. migration: The role of migration networks. *Review of Economics and Statistics, 92*(4), 811–821.

Méndez, M. E. C. (1981). La educación normal. In F. Solana, R. C. Reyes, and R. B. Martínez (Eds.), *Historia de la Educación Pública en México* (pp. 426–462). Mexico City: Secretaría de Educación Pública Fondo de Cultura Económica.

Meneses Morales, E. (1983). *Tendencia educativas oficiales en México.* Distrito Federal: Editorial Porrúa.

Meyers, S. V. (2009). Pura vida: What my life in Costa Rica taught me about teaching ESL." *Writing Lab Newsletter, 33*(9), 11–13.

Mohanty, C. T. (1991). *Third world women and the politics of feminism.* Bloomington: Indiana University Press.

Moll, L. C., and N. González. (1994). Lessons from research with language-minority children. *Journal of Reading Behavior, 26*(4), 439–56.

Monroy, D. (1999). *Rebirth: Mexican Los Angeles from the great migration to the Great Depression.* Berkeley: University of California Press.

Montañez, C. M. (2007). *Los libros de texto de historia de México: Génesis y trayectoria 1959–1994.* Zacatecas: Universidad Autónoma de Zacatecas.

Moreno Fernández, X. L. (1985). *La constitución del magisterio nacional (1920–1933): La normativización de la práctica docente, la formación magisterial, y el mejoramiento profesional.* Distrito Federal: Centro de Investigaciones y de Estudios Avanzados del Instituto Politécnico Nacional.

Motomura, H. (2006). *Americans in waiting: The lost story of immigration and citizenship in the United States.* Oxford: Oxford University Press.

———. (2010). What Is "Comprehensive Immigration Reform"? Taking the long view. *Arkansas Law Review, 63*, 225–241.

Naples, N. A. (2003). *Feminism and method: Ethnography, discourse analysis, and activist research*. New York: Routledge.

Nevarez, G. (2013). Dreamers get best version of DREAM Act in state senate immigration bill. *Huffington Post: Latino Politics*. Retrieved from http://www.huffingtonpost.com/2013/05/24/dream-act-senate-immigration-bill_n_3332872.html.

Ogren, C. A. (2005). *The American state normal school*. New York: Palgrave Macmillan.

Orellana, M. F. (2009). *Translating childhoods: Immigrant youth, language, and culture*. New Brunswick, NJ: Rutgers University Press.

Pagán, J. A., and S. M. Sánchez. (2001). Gender issues in workforce participation and self-employment in rural Mexico. In E. G. Katz and M. C. Correia (Eds.), *The economics of gender in Mexico: Work, family, state, and market* (204–226). Washington, DC: World Bank.

Panagariya, A. (1997). *An empirical estimate of static welfare losses to Mexico from NAFTA*. College Park, MD: Center for International Economics.

Peredo Merlo, M. A. (2003). The importance of context in reading on the job. (Trena Brown, Trans.). *Mexican Journal of Educational Research, 8*, 13–35.

———. (2005). *Lectura y vida cotidiana: Por qué y para qué leen los adultos*. Paidós: México. *Revista Mexicana de Investigación Educativa*.

Pereya, I. (2001). Género, educación y economía popular: Los emprendimientos productivos liderados por mujeres de sectores populares (la integración intergeneracional): Aportes para la agenda. In E. Pieck (Ed.), *Los jóvenes y el trabajo: La educación frente a la exclusión social* (pp. 551–562). Mexico City: Universidad Iberoamericana.

Poinsett, J. (2002). The Mexican character. In G. M. Joseph and T. J. Henderson (Eds.), *The Mexico reader: History, culture, and politics* (pp. 11–14). Durham, NC: Duke University Press.

Portes, A., and R. G. Rumbaut. (2006). *Immigrant America: A portrait*. Berkeley: University of California Press.

Portes, A., and M. Zhou. (1993). The new second generation: Segmented assimilation and its variants. *Annals of the American Academy of Political and Social Science, 530*, 74–96.

Pratt, M. L. (1992). *Imperial eyes: Travel writing and transculturation*. London: Routledge.

Prendergast, C. (2003). *Literacy and racial justice*. Carbondale: Southern Illinois University Press.

Pugach, M. C. (1998). *On the border of opportunity: Education, community, and language at the U.S.-Mexico line*. Mahwah, NJ: Erlbaum.

Ramírez, R. (1982). *La escuela rural Mexicana*. Mexico City: Secretaría de Educación Pública.

Ratha, D., S. Mohapatra, and A. Silwall. (2009). Migration and remittance trends 2009: A better-than-expected outcome so far, but significant risks ahead. *World Bank Migration and Development Brief.* Retrieved from https://openknowledge.worldbank.org/bitstream/handle/10986 /10958/521710BRI0Migr10Box345553B01PUBLIC1.txt?sequence=2.

Reagan, T. (2000). *Non-Western educational traditions: Alternative approaches to educational thought and practice*. Mahwah, NJ: Erlbaum.

Reyes, M., and J. J. Halcón (Eds.). (2001). *The best for our children: Critical perspectives on literacy for Latino students*. New York: Teachers College Press.

Richardson Bruna, K. (Forthcoming). Transcultural sensitivity, transnationalization, and the global soul. In Hamann, Harklau, and Murillo (Eds.), *Revisiting Education in the New Latino Diaspora*.

Richardson Bruna, K., and R. Vann. (2007). On pigs and packers: Radically contextualizing a practice of science with Mexican students. *Cultural Science Education, 2*, 19–59.

Riquer, F., and A. M. Tepichín. (2001). Mujeres jóvenes en México: De la casa a la escuela del trabajo a los quehaceres del hogar. In E. Pieck (Ed.), *Los jóvenes y el trabajo: La educación frente a la exclusión social* (pp. 493–526). Mexico City: Universidad Iberoamericana.

Robertson, R. (1995). Glocalization: Time-space and homogeneity. In M. Featherstone, S. Lash, and R. Robertson (Eds.), *Global Modernities* (pp. 25–44). London: Sage.

Rockhill, K. (1987). Gender, language and the politics of literacy. *British Journal of Sociology of Education, 8*(2), 153–167.

Rockwell, E. (1996). Keys to Appropriation: Rural Schooling in Mexico. In B Levinson and D. Holland (Eds.), *The cultural production of the educated person: Critical ethnographies of schooling and local practice* (pp. 301–324). New York: State University of New York Press.

Rodríguez Gómez, R. (1999). Género y políticas de educación superior en México. *La Ventana, 10*, 124–159.

Rogers, A. (2001). Problematising literacy and development. In B. V. Street (Ed.), *Literacy and development: Ethnographic perspectives* (pp. 205–222). London: Routledge.

Romero, M. M. (2002). *Ex-hacienda de Villachuato: Antecedentes historicos*. Puruándiro: Ayuntamiento de Puruándiro, Michoacán.

Rong, X. L., and J. Preissle. (2009). *Educating immigrant students in the 21st century*. Thousand Oaks, CA: Corwin.

Salas, S., P. Portes, M. D'Amico, and C. Rios-Aguilar. (2011). Generación 1.5: A cultural-historical agenda for research at the 2-year college. *Community College Review, 39*(2), 121–135.

Santiago Sierra, A. (1973). *Las misiones culturales (1923–1973)*. Distrito Federal: SEP Setentas.

Sarroub, L. (2008). Living "Glocally" with literacy success in the Midwest. *Theory into Practice, 47*, 59–66.

Seitz, D. (2004). *Who can afford critical consciousness?: Practicing a pedagogy of humility*. Cresskill, NJ: Hampton.

Smith, P. H., R. T. Jiménez, and N. Martínez-León. (2003). Other countries' literacies: What U.S. educators can learn from Mexican schools. *Reading Teacher, 56*(8), 772–781.

State of Arizona. (2010). House Bill 2281. Phoenix, AZ. Retrieved from http://www.azleg.gov/legtext/49leg/2r/bills/hb2281s.pdf.

Street, B. (Ed). (2001). *Literacy and development: Ethnographic perspectives*. New York: Routledge.

———. (2003). What's "new" in New Literacy Studies? Critical approaches to literacy in theory and practice. *Current Issues in Comparative Education, 5*(2), 77–89.

Tanck de Estrada, D. (1989). Castellanización, política, y escuelas de indios en el arzobispado de México a medidos del siglo XVIII. *HMex, 38*(4), 701–741.

Teague, B. L., P. H. Smith, and R. T. Jiménez. (2010). Learning to write in a Mexican school. *Journal of Language and Literacy Education, 6*(1), 1–19.

Trimbur, J. (1991). Literacy and the discourse of crisis. In R. Bullock and J. Trimbur (Eds.), *The politics of writing instruction: Postsecondary* (pp. 277–295). Portsmouth, NH: Boynton/Cook.

UNESCO. (2008). Literacy Portal. Retrieved from http://portal.unesco.org /education/en/ev.php-URL_ID=54369&URL_DO=DO_TOPIC&URL _SECTION=201.html.

Valdés, G. (1996). *Con respeto: Bridging the distances between culturally diverse families and schools: An ethnographic portrait*. New York: Teachers College Press.

Valencia, R. R., and M. S. Black. (2002). "Mexican-Americans don't value education!"—On the basis of the myth, mythmaking, and debunking." *Journal of Latinos and Education, 1*(2), 81–103.

Valenzuela, A. (1999). *Subtractive schooling: U.S.-Mexican youth and the politics of caring*. Albany: State University of New York Press.

Vaughan, M. K. (1977). Women, class, and education in Mexico, 1880–1928. *Latin American Perspectives, 4*(1), 135–142.

Vázquez, H. A., C. García, S. Erkut, O. Alarcón, and L. R. Tropp. (2000). Family values of Latino adolescents. *Making invisible Latino adolescents visible: A critical approach to Latino diversity.* New York: Palmer.

Vela, A. (1975). *Escuela superior de Michoacán.* Mexico City: Organización y Funcionamiento de las Escuelas Normales Superiores.

Vieira, K. (2013). On the social consequences of literacy. *Literacy in Composition Studies, 1*(1), 26–32.

Villagomez, A. (2008). Michoacán's rural education: Making an impact through recognizing the importance. *Mexico Connect.* Retrieved from http://www.mexconnect.com/mex_/travel/avillagomez/avruraledu.html.

Villegas, D. C., et al. (1995). *A compact history of Mexico.* (M. M. Urquidi, Trans.) Mexico City: El Colegio de México.

Villenas, S., and D. Deyhle. (1999). Critical race theory and ethnographies challenging the stereotypes: Latino families, schooling, resilience, and resistance. *Curriculum Inquiry, 29*(4), 413–45.

Waldinger, R. (2011). Immigrant transnationalism. *Sociopedia.isa,* 1–13.

Young, V. A. (2007). *Your average nigga: Performing race, literacy, and masculinity.* Detroit, MI: Wayne State University Press.

Yúnez-Naude, A., and F. B. Paredes. (2006). The reshaping of agricultural policy in Mexico. In L. Randall (Ed.), *Changing Structure of Mexico: Political, Social, and Economic Prospects* (2nd ed.), (pp. 213–235). Armonk, NY: Sharpe.

# Index /

Immigration and Naturalization Act (1965), 27
Immigration and Naturalization Service (INS), 132
indigenous peoples of Mexico, 30, 46–47
INS (Immigration and Naturalization Service), 132
intersectionality, 10, 12
interview questions: failed, 123; for members of the Villachuato community, 168–69; for school administrators, 165–66; for students, 167–68; for teachers, 166–67
Iowa Administrators and Educators Immersion Experience (IAEIE), 134
Iowa Department of Education, 134, 174n18
IQ tests, immigrants and, 26–27
Isabel (research participant), 141–42

Jacqueline (research participant), 1–3
Jesuits, 66
Jiménez, Robert, 31–32
Jorge (research participant), 114
Juárez, Benito, 67–68

Kalman, J., 22
King, Linda, 23–24, 30
Kuntz, Sharon, 129–30, 136

Laine, Cecelia Greaves, 81
land redistribution following Mexican Revolution, 49–50
Latinos, comparisons to "model minorities," 28
Levinson, Bradley, 77–78, 131
Levitt, Peggy, 38–39, 127
liberal arts curriculum and, 118–19
libraries, 112–14, 113, 135
literacy: alternate means to, 102–4; assumptions about effects on economic development, 22–25; denial of, 98–101; as enacted practice, 38; as form of cultural capital, 154; function in assimilation, 132; historic political struggles over, in Mexico,

29–30; and immigration in U.S. historical context, 25–29; immigration policy and, 26; as imported entity, 115–16; institutionalized, as oppressive force, 104; as means of self-defense, 96–98, 152; migration and, 19–22, 24–25, 92–93; national campaign, 80; NLS's characterization of, 10–11; official models of, 11–12; pragmatic aspects of, 82, 124–25; as resource in contemporary capitalist market structure, 34–35; rhetorical perspective of, 37, 161; rhetorical stance of rural Mexican communities toward, 36–37; as self-defense, 122–26; shift in, along with demographic shifts, 157–58; and social capital, 125, 145–49; and social control, 32–33, 39; as tool to subdue and control, 29; as topic of international concern, 22; transnational character of, 6, 159, 160; UNESCO's definition and measurement of, 23–24; uses of, in Mexico, 32; value of, to families in and from Villachuato, 152–54; as vehicle for oppression, 110. *See also* education, formal
literacy campaigns in Mexico, 30–31
literacy contract: breach of, in rural Mexican communities, 35–36, 39–40, 119, 128, 151; in context of functioning wage labor market, 21–22, 140, 147; in context of migration, 131–32, 135, 149–50; as framework, 33; incongruence with values and life choices in Villachuato, 79–80; national curriculum and, 69; orientation toward, 16–17; rhetorical positioning as alternative to, 36–39; roots of, 63–64; rural communities' resistance to, 83, 87, 131, 144; as threat to rural life, 83
literacy crisis: emergence in Mexico and U.S., 65–66, 69; immigration crisis and, 21, 28–29; literacy contract and, 33–36; new phase of, 157; rhetorics of, 26, 32–34, 117, 154–55;

migration-education connections: centralized formal education and, 71–72, 87; migration as catalyst to increased literacy, 18; remittances and educational access, 4–5, 154–55

migration vs. education rhetoric, 5, 105, 107, 117–18, 128

missionary schools, 66

missioners (supervising teachers), 73

Myra (research participant), 92, 102–4, 156

NAFTA agreement (1994), 51–53

narrative case studies, 17, 110–11

National Coming Out of the Shadows Week demonstrations, 19

National Commission of Free Textbooks (CONALITEG), 173–74n16

nationalism, public schools and, 70

nationalization movement following Mexican Revolution, 70–71

national literacy campaign, 80

New Literacy Studies (NLS), 10–11, 25

nondiscrimination principle regarding immigration, 27

normal schools, 74–76

oppression: gendered, 98; literacy as vehicle for, 110; resistance to, 95–96, 109, 127; in Villachuato, 17, 46–51

Paredes, F. B., 49

parental-school authority division in Mexico, 139–40

parents of students from Mexico: behavioral concerns, 143–44; meetings with teachers, 119; perceptions of U.S. schools, 141–44; U.S. educators' perceptions of, 136–37, 139–40; views on role of school vs. role of family, 144

participant observation in ethnographic field research, 14–16, 42–46, 114–15

Patricia (research participant), 96–98, 110

persona construction by author, 15

plague, 50

Poinsett, Joel, 4

Purépecha indigenous communities, 47, 122–23

Puruándiro, Michoacán: adult education classes, 103–4; distance from Villachuato, 55; library in, 112–14, 113; middle school, 115; Villachuato hacienda as food supplier for, 46

racialization of immigrants, 26

Ramírez, Jiro, 53, 152–53

Ramírez, Librorio, 49–50

Ramírez, Nicole: assimilation and cultural shift, 148–49; in case studies, 92; on family's financial success and educational access, 153–54; motivating factor for continuing education, 108–10; research site suggested by, 13, 41–42

Ramírez, Rafael, 74

rancho farming communities, 46–47

rape, 91, 94, 96, 98

reflexive critical ethnography, 12–16

religion, as literacy sponsor, 24. See also Catholic Church

religious holidays/feast days, 84–85, 137

religious rhetorics of morality in education, 66–67, 78–79

remittances, 4–5, 38–39, 58, 126–28

research participants, 12. See also names of individual participants

reverse migration, 159

Reyes, Francisco, 74

Reyes, M., 26–27

rhetoric, common understanding defined, 37

rhetorical aspects of literacy, 37

Richardson-Bruna, Katherine, 134, 173n12, 174n18

rural communities in Mexico: awareness with respect to life conditions and opportunities, 126–27; coping mechanisms and resistance in, 131; division between home and school literacies, 31–32; meaning of becoming educated, 131; Mexico's literacy campaign, 30–31. See also

farmland outside of, *52*; fear of physical danger in, 42–46; governance, 48–49; home, adobe-style, *56*; home, constructed of manufactured materials, *57*; inconsistency between realities of, and school-based knowledge, 118–19; "just living" orientation, 138; leadership figure in, 84; legacy of fear, 59; legacy of Mexican Revolution in, 48–49; literacy crisis in, 119–22; main street (*bajada principal*), *55*; oppression in, 17, 46–51; as quintessential site of Mexico-U.S. migration, 13; religious events/social gatherings, 84–85, 89–90; rhetorical approach to literacy by citizens of, 151–52; selection as research site, 13, 41–42; social fabric of, 14–15; social management processes, 32–33, 39, 45–46; social traditions, origins of, 122–23; unfinished library, *113*; "waking up the baby Jesus" custom, 84–85. *See also* schools in Villachuato

Villachuato hacienda, 46–47, *47*

wage labor markets: education developed for, 75; education level of Mexican immigrants and, 4; family labor model in context of, 140, 147–48; literacy contract in context of, 21–22, 140, 147
"waking up the baby Jesus" custom, 84–85
Waldinger, Roger, 33–34
wife abuse, 98
women, education and employment opportunities for, 90
women's rosary groups, 84
work ethic emphasis in U.S. education system, 67
world dynamics, contemporary, 7–8
writing practices in Mexican primary and secondary schools, 31–32
written literacy in U.S. compared to Mexico, 159–60

Yúnez-Naude, A., 49

**SUSAN V. MEYERS** is an assistant professor at Seattle University, where she teaches composition and creative writing. Her essays have appeared in *Gender and Education*, *Power and Education*, and the *Community Literacy Journal*. She has been the recipient of grants from the Fulbright Foundation, the National Endowment for the Humanities, and the American Association of University Women.